CW00551206

M
P

The Sons of Adam

A Memoir of Egypt

Alan Mackie

The Sons of Adam

Published by The Muswell Press Ltd

ISBN 978-0-9572136-2-3

A CIP record of this book is available from the British Library.

Design by Barney Beech
Maps by Lyn Homan
Photographs by Alan Mackie
Printed and Bound by Short Run Press Ltd.

Muswell Press Ltd
www.muswell-press.co.uk

For my late beloved wife Jean and her children,
Lindsay, Alistair and Emma.

Acknowledgements

The events in this story happened so long ago that it seems invidious to single out the help of individuals. However I would like to pay tribute to my two 'gurus': Hassan Fahmi who provided the lateral dimension to my understanding of Egypt and Fares Sarofim, who as a Copt provided the vertical dimension,' l'Egypte profonde'. And I am indebted to Jean and Pattie Kahil for lending me their villa in Agami in the spring of 1974 where all these experiences were distilled.

A number of people have given me much appreciated support along the way. I am particularly indebted to J.D.F. and Dalu Jones for encouraging me to put my experiences down on paper back in 1974. I am also obliged to Janie and Michael Phillips for persuading me over three decades later that the memoir still merited publication.

The Arab Spring has resurrected its topicality and I am indebted to Pamela Ann Smith for mentoring me through the implications of the Tahrir Square Revolution, which has transformed Egypt's prospects and thrown a spotlight on its fractured relations with the West. And I would like to thank Liz and Essam Awni for generously putting me up in Maadi in mid June 2012, so enabling me to keep abreast of political developments at a crucial time. Finally I would like to thank Ruth Boswell, my publisher, for steering the project to fruition with such understanding and consummate ease.

Foreword

The Sons of Adam

From the Arabic saying Kullina beni Adam... We are all Sons of Adam

On December 17 2010 a fruit seller in the central Tunisian town of Sidi Bouzid set fire to himself in protest at police corruption and harassment, thereby triggering a chain reaction of uprisings throughout the Middle East that came to be known as the Arab Spring. Egypt's precursor was a 28-year old computer programmer called Khaled Mohammed Sa'eed who some six months earlier had been hauled from an internet café in Alexandria by the police in plain daylight and beaten to death in a nearby alley. Images posted on Facebook and the internet of the brutal beating and of his mutilated corpse hardened public opinion against the regime so that it only needed the quick and clinical dispatch into exile of Tunisian president Zineddin ben Ali to persuade Egypt's nascent protest movement that the same could be done to Hosni Mubarak.

The democracy movement had prepared assiduously for this moment, studying the political psychology of non-violent protest – even contacting peace activists in Serbia to find out how they ousted Slobodan Milosevic – and the role of the new technologies in engaging world opinion.

The Revolution when it came was breathtaking in its speed and efficacy, surprising and delighting those like myself with a deep affection for Egypt who had despaired that Egyptians could ever slough the yoke of a primitive 'pharaonic' rule and disprove western stereotypes of Arab societies as congenitally incapable of finding a middle way between the sterile dichotomy of autocracy and Islamic extremism.

I was travelling through central India when the protests started on January 25, 2011. It was surreal and frustrating to be watching events in real time unfold in Tahrir Square as if from another planet, so insulated is India.

However, if my innate optimism about Egypt built over two decades working in and covering the country as a journalist and consultant had waned in recent years the manner of the Revolution when it came did not surprise me. I had witnessed the temper of the people living in Shobra, a populous suburb of northern Cairo during the October 1973 War. That war came out of the blue just like the Arab Spring.

Eighteen months on and the Revolution is still some way from achieving its two principal goals: removing the army completely from politics and business and installing an accountable, civilian government; and putting an end to western meddling in the region's internal affairs. None of the issues that sparked it: the rampant corruption of the business elite and the excesses of an out-of-control security apparat have been properly addressed. No one has been charged for any of the deaths of over nine hundred protestors, or for hundreds of documented cases of torture. The military remains firmly in control of its vast fiefdom of tourist development projects and toll roads, armament manufacturing and industrial ventures – effectively a parallel economy outside civilian purview amounting to as much as 15 per cent of the country's gross domestic product (GDP).

Far from being dislodged the generals appeared for a time to have consolidated their hold on power, helped by the failure of politicians of all persuasions to exploit the opportunities created by the November 2011 parliamentary elections to consolidate civilian rule. Political uncertainty, concerns over the stagnating economy and fears over deteriorating law and order persuaded a significant minority of Egyptians to vote for the candidate of the *filoul* (the remnants of the ancien régime) in the first round of the presidential elections in May 2012. Ahmed Shafiq, a retired air marshal as well as having been Mubarak's last prime minster, went on to run the Moslem Brotherhood candidate, Mohammed Morsi, a close second in the runoff in mid June.

However the confirmation, after nail biting delays, of Morsi as Egypt's first civilian president may mark a decisive turning point in the Revolution, signifying the end of the beginning of the democratic march rather than the beginning of the end of the whole experiment, which it would have been had he not been confirmed. For the precedent of free and fair elections and the legitimacy this bestows is now established.

It was an extremely close run thing. The fear was that the Supreme Council for the Armed Services (Scaf), which had governed the country after the Revolution, would find a pretext to shoe in Shafiq. Morsi assumed the presidency shorn of any real power, however, as the Scaf had dissolved the Brotherhood dominated People's Assembly on the eve of the election and arrogated to itself control of security and its funding, foreign policy, the national budget and the right to draw up the Constitution.

Yet Morsi's confirmation offered Egypt's fledgling democracy a second chance, one the Brotherhood which had been mainly responsible for its failure first time round seemed keen to seize. Morsi resigned from all political affiliations as he had pledged, and formed a bipartisan administration.

His biggest challenge is the economy which is in freefall. Tourism has been badly hit, at least in the Nile Valley, throwing a large swathe of the urban workforce out of work. The government has been forced to draw down reserves at an accelerating pace to keep people fed. His most pressing priority is to formulate a credible plan to create jobs, tackle corruption, staunch the haemorrhage of reserves and rebuild business confidence. In the crucial matter of economic competence - arguably the greatest threat to the viability of the transition - the Brotherhood has a solid record. Morsi, himself, is said to advocate 'productive' as opposed to 'corporate' capitalism and to want to build a market economy for the poor.

That aside, the stage is set for a possibly protracted power struggle between a fledgling political authority and the military. In mid August 2012 Morsi unexpectedly turned the tables on the military and reignited the power struggle by 'retiring' the Defence Minister and head of the Scaf, Mohammed Tantawi, sacking the top military command and annulling the law that had given the military broad powers.

The political and constititional issue is thus the manner in which the transition is undertaken: whether Egypt repeats Turkey's experience in the 1980s, suffering a decades long and ultimately destabilizing power struggle between the military (as guardians of the secular tradition) and civilian rule, or whether this phase can be bypassed.

Democracy may be a fragile seedling, but the soil in which it is planted has been considerably enriched by the Revolution. The main change is within Egyptians themselves. In facing down Mubarak's intimidating security machine Egyptians overcame their fear as they had done in the October War when they challenged Israel's vaunted invincibility and stormed the Bar Lev line. Just as in 1973 they experienced for a few exhilarating days what it was like to control their destiny. The reliving of that experience is why Sadat, the *batal al-ubour* (Hero of the Crossing), has undergone a belated rehabilitation.

The main difference between 2011 and 1973, however, is generational. The Tahrir Square generation is travelled and better educated than its forbears and above all plugged into a global culture. Of course, not all young people supported the Revolution, and by no means did all their parents support the regime. But this younger generation is less likely to take at face value what its elders say – and this break in the hierarchical link goes for the Brotherhood and elements in the Army as well.

The transition has been messy because the political elite signally failed to create a united front to the military. The chief culprit was the Moslem Brotherhood's Freedom and Justice Party which interpreted a landslide in the legislative elections – it gained 37.5 per cent of the votes cast and the Salafists who call for the strict imposition of Sharia law picked up a further 27.8 per cent – as a green light to steamroller an Islamist programme through parliament at the expense of other political stakeholders such as the secular New Wafd Party and the Nasserists.

This naked power grab confirmed a widely held suspicion that the Brotherhood was incapable of putting the national interest before its own. And it was punished at the polls. So disenchanted was the electorate with the ineffectualness of the Brotherhood in office that Morsi garnered a mere 24.8 per cent of the vote in the first round of the presidential elections on a turnout of less than 50 per cent, compared with 23.7 per cent for Shafiq. This may have had something to do with the fact that Morsi was not the Brotherhood's first choice and was little known – voting for a president is as much about personalities as it is about policies, in contrast to voting for a constituency candidate. Nevertheless it represented a disturbing drop in support for the Brotherhood that left it vulnerable to the military countercoup. It also left Egyptians polarized. Morsi's narrow victory over Shafiq in the runoff – by less than a million votes – begged the fact that more than half the electorate had voted for neither of them in the first round and felt cheated in the choice it had to make in the second. He therefore faces an uphill struggle to build a consensus with such limited authority.

However, it is the flux at the grass roots of conventional affiliations that gives the Revolution its energy and Morsi, using the prestige of the presidency, everything to play for.

The revolutionary experience has brought Egyptians together across traditional alliances, turning established structures on their head and pitting friend and foe of the ancien régime against new forces that occupy the middle ground. It has thrown together some strange bedfellows: Brotherhood disciplinarians allying with the military and the business elite; open-minded Salafists siding with progressives.

It has energized political debate at all levels of society. The Revolution may have been sparked by the Tahrir Square activists communicating on Facebook and Twitter but it gained momentum and heft by news spreading by word of mouth in the popular quarters of Cairo and Alexandria and in provincial cities where processions formed, processions that in Cairo converged on Tahrir Square. Labour and professional syndicates also played their part in activating mass support, as did feminist groups.

As the demonstrations became more established, neighbourhoods set up community centres and organized their own social and security networks just as they had done in the October War, which accounted for the extraordinary self discipline with which the demonstrations were orchestrated. Shops adjacent to Tahrir Square and the adjoining streets escaped without a pane of glass being broken, while the flat dwellers above came down to the streets, as they did in the slums, offering demonstrators food and drink, and took them in for a change of clothes and a wash and brush-up.

Religion has not escaped this intellectual ferment. Egyptians have shown a healthy scepticism to the whole idea of formal or politicized religion – as the Brotherhood discovered to its cost. The political movement can no longer take the backing of members of its social networks for granted. The foundations of conventional authority are being challenged; women in particular are clamouring for a better deal. All this has ramifications for both the Brotherhood and the Salafists who may well have to abandon outdated orthodoxy if they are to shore up their support base.

Tahrir Square proved a particularly formative experience for

Islamist militants. Writing in the *New York Times Magazine* in May 2011 the journalist Robert Worth illustrated just how formative in interviews with members of the radical Islamist group, the Gamaat Islamaya. These hardened activists, many with blood on their hands, referred to Tahrir Square as 'a holy scene, not a human scene' and admitted the success of nonviolent protest reaffirmed their conviction that their use of violence in the 1990s had been wrong not just, wrote Worth, 'as a matter of principle but also because violence failed to achieve any of their goals.' Asked if they were bitter about the persecution they endured under Mubarak, the spokesman said: 'When you see a thing like this [Tahrir Square], you forget everything you suffered.'

Their avowal of peaceful democratic change was an unexpected upshot of the Tahrir Square uprising and suggests Islam in Egypt is not necessarily set on the arid, sterile course of Wahhabi extremism but, given half a chance and building on the sacrifices of the Revolution's martyrs, a regenerated and reformed Islam may emerge, one that draws on gentler, more tolerant observances and in particular the syncretic traditions of the Sufis who travelled the trade routes in the ninth and tenth centuries spreading Islam through the exchange of ideas, so helping to create the greatest civilization of the time.

The children of the Revolution need no reminding that there are powerful forces at work abroad as well as at home with no interest whatsoever in seeing it succeed, which brings us to the activists' second objective: an end to western meddling in the region's affairs.

Egypt's relations with the West have always been fraught. Infitah, the West's most recent engagement has been a mixed blessing, seen by many as an invitation to crony capitalism and an open door to exploitation.

However, there is a neo-colonialist dimension to relations that harks back several generations to the 'veiled' protectorate and the politics of oil, and of course Israel, more particularly to the West's unequivocal support for the Jewish state and by default – through its failure to rein them in – its territorial ambitions. These neo-colonial interests have a particular concern to ensure Egypt remains 'locked down', not out of any designs on the country itself but because a 'progressive' Egypt, as the most influential and populous Arab state, could indirectly threaten and undermine their stakes in the region.

The nationalization of the region's oil resources in the 1970s forced the US to recalibrate its game. Having lost physical control over the oil the US sought to protect supplies by underpinning the region's conservative rulers who by then had no interest in playing politics with oil as Saudi Arabia's King Feisal had done in the October War – the 1973 oil embargo was in this respect an aberration; the Saudi establishment is now so vested in Wall Street it would never rock the boat – and maintaining a military and naval presence in the Gulf. No less important in this recalibration have been the longstanding security arrangements dating back to the colonial era the UK and the US maintain with Oman, Bahrain, Saudi Arabia and more recently Qatar which give them informal 'advisory' access to their rulers.

Israel is an altogether more complex issue, tied in as it is profoundly with ideas of national and pan-Arab identity. Egyptians, in line with most Arabs, are outraged that Britain in 1917 should have unilaterally purloined their patrimony to bestow a national homeland in Palestine upon the Jews. The contemporary argument had it that Britain was quite within its rights to do so; it had acquired the Palestine Mandate as part of the post World War I imperial settlement. Moreover the Bible associates the Holy Land uniquely with the Jews and granting them a homeland in their ancestral lands atoned conveniently for centuries of western anti-Semitism. It was a gesture given terrible poignancy by the Nazi Holocaust a quarter of a century later.

Meanwhile America's overwhelming economic and military power, which underpins the Jewish state, has come to be accepted as a basic fact of Egyptian life, especially since the demise of the Soviet Union. However, it has not made Americans or for that matter the British any more loved or respected. America backed two military dictators simply to keep the Peace Treaty with Israel intact. It is not coincidental that the US and UK embassies in Cairo's Garden City occupy a cordoned off 'Green Zone', encircled by barricades, armoured personnel carriers and paratroopers.

For Egyptians Pax Britannica gave way to Pax Americana – an eighteen year flirtation with non-alignment proved a damp squib – there merely being a change of imperial dispensation answering to the US Congress in place of the Palace of Westminster. And Congress has pretty much done Israel's bidding when it comes to Middle East matters over the past two decades.

The Lex Imperium is primarily about control, keeping order and projecting its interests; it has little to do with justice. It may be benign to those in its ideological camp – western allies, emerging markets playing by International Monetary

Fund (IMF) rules and of course the Arabian Peninsula oil states with plenty of money to splash around – although allies better beware not to step out of line, especially post 9/11. The Americans can be as ruthless with their allies as they are with their enemies, threatening to cut them out of the intelligence loop – a fate tantamount to being cast into outer darkness – if they fail to back policy objectives deemed vital to US security interests. And these include protecting Israel from UN censure, especially in the Security Council. Further, membership of Pax Americana does not come cheap; the US still runs a huge network of sovereign bases around the globe, maintained to a large degree at the host countries' expense.

However with Israel the exploitation has worked the other way thanks to a shared sense of 'manifest destiny', the Zionist lobby's deep roots in the American political system and 9/11, which has enabled the Jewish state to clone its own security interests onto those of America's in the 'War on Terror'. Thus perhaps uniquely in imperial annals a small foreign power has come to dictate policy in an area of vital interest to the imperium.

For those on the wrong side of the American imperium it is not the force for good its allies and fellow travellers would have us believe. Stripped of its bonhomie and undoubted generosity to some friends it can be every bit as baneful as other empires. The peoples of Latin America, living for nearly two centuries under the aegis of the Monroe Doctrine, have a very different perspective of US power, as do those Arab states who have tried to steer an independent path – and, of course, the Palestinians.

Egyptian (and indeed most Arabs) identify with the Palestinians' tragedy, because it is part of their story, their struggle for a national identity and self respect. There was a time in the late 1960s when Egyptians, embroiled in costly adventures in Yemen and elsewhere, turned against Nasser's attempts to force-feed them his brand of Arab nationalism. Sadat won popular support in 1971 when he scrapped the United Arab Republic and restored 'Egypt' to the country's name. But the history of the subsequent four decades has made Egyptians realize they are part of the Arab world and their destiny is to be at the centre of it. And Palestine has come to epitomize that struggle and all that is wrong with the Arab world's relations with the West.

The first prejudice relates to a neo-colonial attitude to territory. The West, or rather its body politic, primarily the US political, military, business and media establishments and those western liberal democracies (including the EU although not necessarily individual members) that are locked into defence alliances with the US fail to grasp why the Arabs, and especially the Palestinians, get so emotional about land. Yet established states are inordinately sensitive about territory. Imagine anyone breaching the territorial integrity of either the US or the UK Consider too how exercised is Spain at the UK continuing to occupy Gibraltar (though this sense of injustice does not extend to Moroccan claims to the Spanish enclaves of Ceuta and Melilla) or Argentinean claims (backed by the Organization of American States) to Las Malvinas.

Colonized lands are different; fair game, uninhabited. They don't belong to anybody, or so the colonialists would have us believe, and the indigenous people who live on these lands either by undertaking pastoral activities or arable farming do not 'inhabit' them as civilized peoples do and therefore cannot claim the same rights to them. Winston Churchill vividly illustrated this mindset when in 1937 he described Arab opposition to Jewish immigration into Palestine thus:

'I do not agree,' he wrote to the Peel Commission which was investigating the setting up of a Jewish Homeland in Palestine, 'that the dog in a manger has the final right to the manger even though he may have lain there for a very long time. I do not admit that right. I do not admit for instance, that a great wrong has been done to the Red Indians of America or the black people of Australia. I do not admit that a wrong has been done to these people by the fact that a stronger race, a higher-grade race, a more worldly wise race to put it that way, has come in and taken their place.'

The key difference between Palestine and the 'terra nuova' described above by Churchill as a land ripe for exploitation by a more deserving race – an idea that gave rise to the Zionist myth of 'a people without a land, a land without a people' – is that Palestine was long settled. Some Palestinians possess house deeds dating back generations if not centuries.

There has throughout been an assumption in the West that Israelis' right to a state is of a higher order than that of Palestinians despite the fact that the competing claims are between a people established on the land over several generations if not centuries, and another based on a two millennia old ancestral title. True, the waters were muddied by the Palestinians in the late 1940s having no clear political identity and Jordan laying claim to the territory as well. But there was a world of difference for the Palestinians in being subsumed into a Jordanian political entity rather than into an utterly alien Israeli one.

Thus in 1948, thanks mainly to the West's intercession, Israel got the UN chair when the music stopped. And with the chair, came the incomparable advantage of legitimacy and international recognition while the Palestinians were left in the cold, disenfranchised, on 'common land' to which the Israelis, ensconced in their new 'territorial integrity' continued to lay claim although they were not entitled under international law.

And did they lay claim! Israel has implacably exploited this dynamic by building settlements on this 'common' land.

Now the international community, including the US, is unanimously agreed that settlement building is not only illegal but an obstruction – indeed not just an obstruction but a comprehensive roadblock – to resolving the conflict. However, Israel has somehow been able to buck the international will on settlements and one has to ask how they have been able to get away with it.

The conspiracy theorists would say – and there are plenty in the Middle East – it is down to Israel's control over America's Middle East policy.

American democracy works through the separation of powers between an executive president and a legislative Congress. Liberals complain that the executive has been steadily accruing power at the expense of the legislative branch since the Vietnam War. However, with issues on which Congress is bipartisan, such as Israel, the executive defers; it may propose but it is ultimately Congress that disposes. Only twice has the executive challenged Israel. The first time was in 1956 when President Eisenhower called a halt to the tripartite invasion of the Suez Canal by Britain, France and Israel and ordered Israel to withdraw its troops from Sinai – which it did in double quick time.

The second was in 1991 when President George Bush Senior, flush from ousting Saddam Hussein from Kuwait and keen to exploit the opportunity to build a new, more stable world order, threatened to withdraw US loan guarantees if Israel didn't stop its settlement building. It came to a standoff with Congress. The administration blinked and Bush went on to lose the ensuing presidential election to Bill Clinton. Commenting on Bush's defeat, which was attributed amongst other things to the defection of the Jewish vote, Israeli Premier Yitzhak Shamir declared it was ill-advised of any US president to cross Israel on its vital interests. The lesson was well learnt; those vital interests it was tacitly conceded included settlement building.

With US resolve broken, the dye was cast. However, rather than admitting they were compromised and recusing themselves, successive administrations set about covering up their impotence by assuming the role of 'honest broker' in the conflict and playing true dog in a manger by excluding anyone else from the peacemaking. Then, to cap it all President Clinton in mid 1993 appointed Dennis Ross, a founding member of the American Israel Public Affairs Committee, as his special Middle East envoy. Aipac is the most powerful Israeli lobby in Washington. Ross has played a pivotal role in formulating the Middle East policy of successive Democratic administrations over the past two decades.

Having conceded the principle of settlement building (or rather failed to impose sanctions that would have stopped it) the Clinton Administration then engineered the massive fudge that was the Oslo Peace Process. Oslo left the question of final borders open while allowing Israel, on an 'agree to disagree' basis, to continue settling Palestinian lands. It was the best possible outcome for the Jewish state, providing it with seven years of relative tranquillity in which to double the number of settlers implanted in the Occupied Territories, before it all disastrously unravelled with the outbreak of the second *intifada*.

No one should have been surprised that the Occupied Territories erupted in September 2000, least of all the Americans. For no matter how the cat was skinned, the endgame of Oslo as far as the Palestinians were concerned, was a state in the lands east of the 1967 demarcation lines (with small modifications to iron out anomalies as intended by UN Security Council Resolution 242) in return for a comprehensive peace. For Israeli premier Ehud Barak therefore to declare that Israel bent over backwards to accommodate the Palestinians by offering to return '97 per cent' of the Occupied Territories (a figure that is disputed) simply begged the point. It was the sovereignty of that 'common land' that counted which Resolution 242 apportioned to the Palestinians to build their state. After the denouement President Clinton confessed – a trifle disingenuously – he hadn't realized land was so important to the Palestinians!

Oslo set the framework for the charade of the current peace process that goes through pointless motions to keep a certain number of international bureaucrats employed and the fiction alive that the West is doing something.

The second major hang-up relates to the way the US uses security as a means of control just as Israel does to further its territorial ambitions.

Israel exploits America's settler instinct – hardwired into its DNA as deeply after 9/11 as it is into Israel's – to view threats existentially. The concept of mutual security is alien to Americans at the best of times as it is to Israelis. They exploit fear to arrogate to themselves the sovereign right to impose their defence requirements on others, no matter how unreasonable, burdensome or an infringement of the other's sovereignty these may be.

How else to explain why their security concerns differ qualitatively from anyone else's? Thus America feels free to ring China and Russia with nuclear bases but objects to the same being done to itself on the self righteous premise that America is working for freedom and democracy and all right thinking people should understand that. Israel cites its own beleaguered birth in a hostile neighbourhood and the Holocaust as justification for requiring a defence capability several times greater than all its neighbours put together. It is a nuclear power, though not publicly admitting to it, declaring it will not be the first to 'introduce' nuclear weapons into the region, (whatever that means) but considers it a casus belli for any of its neighbours to seek to become one too.

As the confrontation with Iran illustrates nuclear capability is not ultimately about security, it is about control. Israeli Premier Benyamin Netanyahu has admitted Israel does not fear physical annihilation from Iran. How could it with an arsenal of several hundred nuclear warheads and the fourth most powerful military in the world? Rather, Iran having a nuclear capability would spell the end of Israel's (and by extension America's) hegemony over the region. Here lies the real threat from Iran and why Iran enjoys such popularity on the Arab street, despite its appalling human rights record, as the only power in the region prepared to stand up to the US and Israel.

Israel has taken this notion of security into its negotiations with the Arabs, never dealing with them as equals and instead taking to heart Churchill's dictum: only make concessions to people you have beaten. In the immediate aftermath of the June 1967 War Israel offered to make a complete withdrawal to its June 5 borders, and made much of the 'The Three No's' this offer elicited from the Arab League in Khartoum four months later as evidence the Arabs were not interested in peace.

Yet behind the scenes moderate Arabs were already putting out feelers for a peace settlement based on Resolution 242 which to them represented an historic compromise: a bargain between equals, not the victor's diktat.

We will never know if the Arab world would have swung behind Sadat's trip to Jerusalem in 1977 if Israel had responded to his peace initiative in the spirit in which it was made. Certainly the Arab League and the Islamic Conference Organization have come round to endorse unanimously the 2002 Saudi Peace Plan based on Resolution 242. But by then Israel had moved on and the West had bought the line the Arabs did not want peace, or at least the peace Israel was prepared to offer them (whatever that is; it has never been defined).

With a seat at the table and thus legitimacy Israel has been able to exploit the West's predisposition to side with democracies. For instance, settlement building has never been taken as seriously as the resistance (or terrorism in settler parlance) it provokes. So a Palestinian rocket fired from Gaza (invariably in response to an Israeli raid or targeted killing) is considered qualitatively more heinous than the systematic clearance of

Palestinians from their homes and lands which is the original cause of the conflict. Dennis Ross drew attention to this telling distinction when in mid 2010 he took exception to the Obama Administration 'condemning' Israel for announcing the construction of new East Jerusalem settlements on the eve of Vice President Joe Biden's arrival in Israel to resurrect peace talks, which was language he complained usually reserved for terrorism.

Nothing more eloquently illustrates the West's colonialist mindset (and its hypocrisy) than the complaisance with which it turns a blind eye to Israel's recourse to 'legality', the meretricious and selective use of laws and administrative orders, some dating back to the British Mandate, to evict Palestinians from homes they may have occupied for generations while branding resistance to these evictions as 'terror'. If the Palestinians were given the protection of the law the West so piously advocates they would never have needed to resort to terrorism.

The West has also been scandalously, shamefully blind to Israel's liberal resort to excessive force as an instrument of policy. It was the case in the first *intifada* in 1987 where stones were met with bullets and the resistance eventually segued into the desperate and tragic blind alley of suicide bombings. But it reached grotesque heights in Operation Cast Lead, Israel's 2009 invasion of Gaza. The lengths Israel's western friends went to neuter the highly critical conclusions of the Goldstone Commission set up by the UN to investigate allegations of war crimes said much for Israeli sensitivities to perceptions of its moral standing. But these criticisms were conveniently overshadowed by the Arab Spring and the righteous (and justified) furore over the barbaric response of certain autocracies to it.

However, nothing in the Arab Spring, not even the well aired brutality of the Assad regime in Syria, quite matched Israel's overwhelming and merciless onslaught on the Palestinians of Gaza in January 2009. In the space of three weeks the Israeli Defence Forces (IDF) killed more than one thousand three hundred Palestinians for the loss of thirteen Israelis. In a statistic beloved of Israelis to show how small, vulnerable and beset by powerful and vengeful neighbours they are, this kill rate represents close to 0.1 per cent of the entire population of the Strip. It was the most spectacular turkey shoot since Churchill witnessed the dervishes being mown down by Maxim machine guns at Omdurman in 1898. The way western governments (as opposed to popular opinion) 'bought' into the invasion as an unfortunate but necessary measure to put an end to rocket attacks that had been 'terrorizing' the inhabitants of southern Israel enraged Arab opinion.*

In its efforts to bring the Palestinians to heel the West has been happy to do Israel's dirty work by attempting to finesse Hamas, which is affiliated to the Moslem Brotherhood, out of the political equation. It connived with Israel to subvert the result of the Occupied Territories' first ever legislative elections in

*In the twenty-one months from September 2005 when Israel withdrew from the Gaza Strip through to May 2007, just before Hamas seized power (a period of intense shelling), Palestinian armed groups fired almost two thousand rockets into Israel and killed four Israelis according to the UN Office for the Coordination of Humanitarian Affairs. In the same period, the IDF fired over fourteen thousand six hundred shells into Gaza, or more than seven times the number of rockets and missiles fired out, and killed at least fifty-nine Palestinians. In fact, during this twenty-one month period the IDF launched more than one and a half times the number of shells and mortars into Gaza as were fired by the Palestinian resistance into Israel in the eight years from the start of the second intifada to the Gaza invasion in late December 2008. Given Gaza is the size of a pocket handkerchief, the intensity of the shelling and the disproportionate losses on the Palestinian side, it is rich indeed for Israelis to claim they were the 'terrorized' party.

January 2006. Unhappy Hamas won the election – one of the freest and fairest ever held in the Arab world – the West sought to sideline the group by imposing sanctions on the Occupied Territories and helping the Palestine Authority (PA) to cling to power. The PA had been rejected at the polls because it was endemically corrupt and deeply compromised by its links with the Israeli forces. The internal divisions stirred by this meddling led sixteen months later to Hamas seizing control of Gaza and to Israel imposing a blockade – and eventually to Operation Cast Lead.

With the Rafah Crossing to Egypt, open since May 2011, some of the pressure on Gaza has been relieved. But the economic and financial limbo imposed on the Strip and also the West Bank by the withholding of funds by Israel, the West and its financial institutions and Arab oil states essentially inimical to the Arab Spring continues to create enormous hardship and resentment.

Popular anger at the way the Palestinians have been treated, and the West's collusion in their oppression, colours the political discourse in the new Egypt. In the face of realpolitik the transition government had to rein in its initial open embrace of the Palestinian resistance – as it did approaches to Iran – and Morsi has declared Egypt will honour existing agreements. However, future relations with the Jewish state will be on a different footing. There has even been talk of a referendum on the Peace Treaty at some point to give the authorities diplomatic cover for a tougher policy.

As it runs down its foreign exchange reserves to dangerous levels, Egypt also faces a financial squeeze, principally from the drying up of the Gulf and Saudi funding which had sustained the pre crash boom.

These states have indicated their financial backing is contingent on an IMF seal of approval; Egypt has balked at some conditions the IMF has put on its lending, but in late 2012 was negotiating a $4.8 billion loan with the fund. Their support has consequently (and predictably) been parsimonious. As Egypt's potential paymasters the oil sheikhs are distinctly uncomfortable with the populism inherent in the Revolution for the future not only of their investments in Egypt – although some big investors have renegotiated the terms of their deals – but for the challenge it represents to the neoliberal policies that underpin their own power base and indeed their very legitimacy. For the logic of the Revolution raises the discomfiting question who really owns the Middle East's oil: a handful of ruling families or the *umma*, the common weal?

We can expect the pro business Brotherhood to avoid creating waves and to be pragmatic in its dealings with the Saudi and Gulf leaderships. However, it is the private sector in these countries, carrying less baggage than its political masters that may offer the best hope for an Egyptian economic recovery, for all things being equal, Egypt is more familiar terrain to Gulf investors than competing markets in Africa, South America, South Asia and the Far East. And the Brotherhood, with its long and successful experience running medical clinics and social welfare networks, not to mention commercial enterprises large and small, is well attuned to understand what is needed to attract them.

I have written at length about Israel and Palestine. It is necessary to do so because Palestine defines the Arab world's relations with Israel and Israel defines the West's relations with the Arab world. US attitudes to its Gulf States proxies are determined by Israel's interests as are its attitudes to Egypt. This is the political landscape Egypt's new leaders will have to navigate.

Israel is umbilically linked to the Anglo-Saxon colonial tradition by ties that predate the Geneva Conventions and the UN Charter and go back to a time when imperiums assumed the right to occupy other people's lands. Israel is thus as much a product of the British colonialist tradition as is the US itself and the Dominions.

But Israel was a colonial enterprise a century too late. Unlike its liberal democratic cousins who were able to establish themselves and subjugate their indigenous populations without much ado, Israel has yet to find its place in the sun. It survives by force of arms, unable to find the internal and external equilibrium that will ensure its long term viability. As the Belgian photographer I was to meet during the October War observed, coming from a small country himself he could not understand how holding land in depth could guarantee security; the only way to do that was to make peace with your neighbours.

The peace feelers the Arabs have put out to Israel have been systematically rebuffed, rebuffed one can only conclude because Israel's leaders believe the deal offered by Resolution 242, the cornerstone UN Security Council resolution generally regarded as the basis of a settlement which gives the Jewish state 78 per cent of historic Palestine, was insufficient. Putting the kindest interpretation on their expansionist policies, their aim has been to get their hands on as much of the remaining territory as they can and then swap the choicest expropriated real estate for less desirable property, trading Old Kent Road for Mayfair as it were, and corralling the politically emasculated Palestinians into Bantustans. Or they may feel locked in a zero sum game where simply to admit the Palestinians have rights undermines their own legitimacy.

But occupation has ineluctable and unpalatable consequences: it brutalizes and dehumanizes the colonizer and it breeds racism. Israel's politicians and religious leaders make racist comments about Palestinians and Arabs which, if reiterated by an Arab counterpart against Jew, would immediately provoke furious charges of anti-Semitism. Worse still is an apartheid mentality that values a Jewish life above a Palestinian one. How else to explain defence minister Ehud Barak during the Gaza invasion extolling the 'bravery' of young Israeli airmen about to embark on a mission to bomb the living daylights out of utterly defenceless Palestinians, or indeed the obscene disparity in casualties in the campaign?

Despite their wholesale annexation of large swathes of the West Bank, Israelis are no nearer achieving the peace, security and global acceptance they purportedly crave as they were when Sadat addressed the Knesset in 1977 and warned them there would be no peace in the Middle East that was not a comprehensive one. Indeed, they have lost ground; for western governments are finding it increasingly difficult to shield Israel from the consequences of its occupation and to resist calls to brand it an apartheid state.

Though still brainwashed by Zionist propaganda, American opinion is fracturing too.* Public confidence in Congress, the main bulwark of Zionist support, is at an all time low; confidence in Wall Street, the other main bulwark, is even lower. Populist dissent at the way the political and business establishments have run the country has never been greater. And interestingly, the most salient manifestation of this ferment, the Occupy Wall Street and the other Occupy movements that have sprung up throughout the country, draw their inspiration directly from Tahrir Square.

There is nevertheless, a newfound introspection about America's role in the world after the foreign misadventures of the past decade, an uncomfortable awareness that it ill behoves the US to cast the first stone on the question of human rights abuses when it has Guantanamo, Iraq and Afghanistan and Israel's treatment of the Palestinians to answer for.

Secretary of State Hillary Clinton's reticence over the three hundred and twenty Palestinian children killed by the IDF in Gaza contrasts eloquently with her rush to judgement on the Syrian regime's 'slaughter' of twenty-three children in Houla in May 2012. And what does it say about America's moral compass that the House of Representatives should vote three hundred and ninety to five in favour of a resolution supporting the Gaza invasion, an invasion that killed in all some seven hundred and fifty Palestinian non-combatants for the loss of three Israeli civilian lives, an invasion moreover that was invoked to put an end to rocket attacks that had killed fourteen Israelis in some

*The conflicting objectives set by Congress lead to a collective schizophrenia in Washington over US Middle East policy. Consequently different arms of government pursue objectives that often work at cross purposes with each other. This was vividly illustrated at a prestigious conference the author attended in Washington in October 2010. The annual US Arab Policymakers' Conference brings together the US diplomatic and military elites with those of their Middle East allies. The military sessions were mostly given over to the prosecution of the 'War on Terror' and protecting America's interests in the region: namely maintaining the security of these autocratic regimes. On the other hand, the diplomatic sessions and those of NGOs and aid agencies, being mainly given over to promoting American values, were preoccupied with damage control: mitigating the political and material fallout from these military interventions and Israel's occupation of the West Bank and East Jerusalem and its blockade of Gaza.

three years – a death toll which would barely merit comment on the other side of the ledger, being considered minor collateral damage in Israel's illegal occupation of Palestinian lands?

The administration has tried to work round the massive roadblock of Congress. Its rearguard attempt at damage limitation could bear fruit should Barack Obama be re-elected in November. But whatever the election outcome, America still has a huge goodwill deficit to make up in the Arab world. Redressing that deficit will only begin in earnest when it stops treating Israel as the fifty-first state of the Union and starts dealing with it as a foreign power whose interests may, and often do, conflict with those of most Americans.

At the heart of America's dilemma is a divorce between its interests and its principles. The US claims to stand for freedom and democracy. Yet it tacitly accepts Israel's illegal occupation thereby denying Palestinians their human rights. And to sustain the unstable equlibrium this creates it has to underpin neighbouring autocracies. Continuing a policy of blind support for Zionist expansionism will simply condemn the US and by extension its western allies to fraught relations with any truly independent Arab state that may emerge from the Arab spring. It will be a stumbling block in relations with a democratic Egypt.

The conundrum for the West is whether these societies will be able to reach consensus, with all that implies in terms of political institution building, or whether they will fall apart, with all that implies for regional secrurity. I would argue the process of consensus building in Egypt is in hand but will need goodwill and practical help and above all space to bring to term in the face of the gathering storm in the Fertile Crescent and the Arabian Peninsula. As the biggest country in the region, a successful Egyptian transition will have a profound impact on the future of the Arab Spring.

When the great Arab explorer Ibn Battuta traversed the globe in the fourteenth century he would have relied on a ganglion of medieval trading connections and on interpreters to pave his way. And nothing else came between him and the experience. He would have taken with him the cultural values of the *umma* and for much of the time been amongst coreligionists. But the reach of even the greatest empires in those days were finite and he would have soon rubbed up against alien customs and beliefs and had to accommodate them. Travel being so slow, he would hardly have been conscious of change, adjusting organically to geography, climate and cuisine. His experiences therefore had an authenticity it is very difficult to replicate today. For the combination of fast travel and the overarching pervasiveness of American power make it very difficult for the western traveller to step out of the bubble of his culture.

The West has tended to engage with other cultures through its own stereotypes: alien cultures demonized if considered hostile or 'anthropomorphized' if thought merely quaint. A small group, which is quaint but refuses to be stereotyped presents a quandary like Churchill's famed bacillus which may be interesting to observe in the laboratory but poses a potential threat if allowed to exist in a natural state. Into this category fit Egypt and Palestine.

Resisting America's view of reality has been one of the most daunting challenges Egyptians and other Arabs have had to face, so overbearing and ruthless is the juggernaut of military and economic power deployed to impose it and unnerving the faith Americans place in their democracy to 'do right'.

But resistance to it, or more accurately, the instability that attends resistance, there has always been, exacerbated by US support for Middle Eastern autocracies and an expansionist Israel. The wars America has fought to avenge 9/11 have exposed the limitations of its military might, which in turn has affected its ability to project soft power and is now affecting its ability to control the narrative.

The new media have something to do with this. The cell phone has become a potent and ubiquitous propaganda tool making it difficult for security forces to manage the reporting of their nefarious activities; the media blackout Israel successfully imposed on its Gaza invasion was probably the last of its kind, certainly in the western world.

Then there is the emergence of foreign English language news channels like Al Jazeera and Russia Today that provide a perspective on events often at odds with the western media. They plug a certain agenda, we know, but in so doing show up the western media for doing the same.

And then there is Tahrir Square which has presented western audiences with a whole new perspective on the Arab world and on Islam, young Egyptians talking to camera in excellent English about their dreams and aspirations, calling for honest, competent and above all accountable government – aspirations that find considerable resonance with western audiences. Their breathtaking courage in facing down and unmanning the Mubarak security machine, often with little more than their bare hands, and the way they have since conserved the energy of the Revolution through their wit, humour and self-discipline, despite several attempts to derail it, have transformed western perceptions of Egypt and Egyptians.

As regards the broader Arab Spring, it was always unrealistic to imagine that the kind of autocratic power structures to be found in most other Middle Eastern countries, interlaced as they are with tribal and sometimes sectarian rivalries, could be neatly dismantled; or that the full scale reformation of Islam which must follow if the revolution is to succeed would be easy. Islam does not have a copyright on extremism even if it is entirely legitimate to be concerned at extremist elements in Islam. However, these same elements have been and continue to be provided with oxygen by the West's antipathy and prejudice towards and ignorance of Islam - as the region wide protests sparked by the release in the US in September 2012 of a sacrilegious film of the Prophet attest - and its tendency to meddle in the region's affairs.

Soon after coming back from Egypt in 1974 I wrote an unpublished memoir: part portrait of a city, part personal journey, part journal. I came away then with the sense that the West, and by that I meant the loose association of vested interests that has at its core the US establishment – Congress, the administration, the military, Wall Street and the media – which since the Second World War has orchestrated the liberal democracies (and much of the rest of humanity besides) in a Manichean struggle to save the world from totalitarianism and other malign forces, isn't very good at 'listening'. Rather, it tends to talk down to other cultures, assuming a natural projection of its values a universal good. Neither does it 'do' introspection – apart from a kind of narcissistic self-analysis that leaves little space for other ways of seeing and doing things. This has created enormous problems with the Arab and Muslim worlds whose cultural dye has proved extraordinarily impervious to western cultural imperialism.

All this changed shockingly with 9/11 when the West woke up to the fact that a large part of the world, if not actively 'hating us' as a flummoxed George W. Bush was challenged at a press conference to explain, at least wanted to be taken into consideration and heard. Since then a profound shift in economic power eastwards is forcing the West to adapt to different ways of seeing things, whether it likes it or not.

The Austrian philosopher Ludwig Wittgenstein famously averred that if a lion could speak we wouldn't be able to understand what it said as there would be no context in which the words it uttered could have any correspondence of meaning with human beings. Philosophers since have explored this paradox to gain a better understanding of how language is rooted in cultural constructs. Although bewitched by Wittgenstein at university I didn't realize at the time the extent to which he conditioned my own understanding of how we see the world through a cultural lens and that only by total immersion in Cairo and coming up from within it to find a commonality of experience could I make sense of my Egyptian adventure.

Prologue

This book is the product of a dream, the universal dream for home.

It begins in Beirut in 1965. It was never, I should immediately say, my intention to go to Beirut or to the Middle East for that matter. But in the manner sometimes of events, it happened that way. That summer vacation hitching to Greece my luck ran out in the southern Austrian town of Graz. I caught a student train which I imagined was bound for Athens; but somewhere in Yugoslavia it turned left, and went instead to Istanbul. Once there it seemed best to head east and, by way of Antioch, Aleppo and Damascus, I eventually landed up in Beirut.

It was August and Beirut was submerged under a pea soup haze which kept the temperature rock steady at eighty-four degrees and the humidity around 90 per cent. The city was deserted, anyone with the time and the money having disappeared to the hills. The place was creepy and I had no desire to stay. However, it proved more difficult to get out of Beirut than it had been to get in. I could find no boat leaving with deck class accommodation. I was stuck and running out of money. Linda saved me.

Linda Kanelous was American and then about twenty-eight. She had been at various times she told me a New York model, a secretary to a Senator and girlfriend to a baseball star. One day she had received an invitation to a girlfriend's wedding in Baghdad. Bored with life she packed her bags and went. That was 1963. Linda's first encounter with the Arabs made a deep impression on all concerned. She arrived at Baghdad Airport in a minidress, an experience she likened to stepping out at Idlewilde in her birthday suit. Thereafter, sensation was to follow her like a comet's tail.

She had ended up in Beirut where she had met Farid, a small time mobster. He wooed her persistently and extravagantly. Linda succumbed. Before she knew it he had sent her home to collect the remainder of her wardrobe and set her up with a flat and a chauffeur driven car.

Linda thought she had met her Mr. Right, an unusual helpmeet you might have thought for an all American girl. But she soon found he didn't just want to pay her bills but to tell her what clothes to buy and how to wear them. This was an attack on her liberty which brought out all her instincts for self-preservation. She had been well cast in the dye, a credit to her education. She defended herself as she would no doubt the Constitution, ruthlessly and vindictively. Farid was not only shown the door but booted out.

I caught her on the rebound. We met spasmodically in a number of cafés and at the swimming club of the St. Georges Hotel. It was there during one of my breathless monologues on the true nature of travel that I made the breakthrough. She was lying regally in a deck chair sipping a lemonade it had cost me my supper to buy when she suddenly raised her grey green eyes, cut me in mid sentence and pronounced: 'We were travellers scattered around the world living our separate lives unaware that all paths led us back to the city.. It's the *Quartet*, you know.' I didn't. '*Justine*, I think.'

The significance of the remark was other than its veracity or even its relevance to what I was saying. She was interested. And when Linda showed interest the earth moved. I was accepted. We resolved to leave Beirut together. I explained the difficulties.

'You leave it to me,' she said.

Next afternoon she phoned. 'There's a Syrian boat leaving tomorrow. I've managed to get deck class tickets. I'm afraid they're $45 each; it was the best I could do.'

We set sail for Alexandria and Athens in high spirits. However, it soon became evident I was not to have her undivided attention. Her visceral dislike of Arab men engendered by her unfortunate entanglement with Farid, coupled with her aloofness, seemed only to excite them further. In the limited confines of the ship this caused problems and for me frustrations. The First Officer, a spruce, chunky Egyptian took an especial interest in us. The second night out he threw a party. It was a mixed success. Linda was the only girl amongst a dozen males; there were language problems. When the party broke up the First Officer suggested I might like to go up to the bridge to observe Orion and the Milky Way. Alone with Linda the First Officer proposed. It was a bad omen; by the time we arrived in Alexandria Linda was simmering.

Our reception in port didn't help matters. No sooner off the boat than we were seized and borne like relics in a saint's day procession. A horde of fix-it men fought fiercely for possession of us while a collective hand edged us towards a taxi and dumped us in. My introduction to the city of the *Alexandria*

Quartet was a surreal drive to the station in a 1930 Austin Seven with no floor and random steering.

We reached Cairo about ten in the evening. Linda by then was beyond words and ready to explode. However, she had earlier intimated a desire to see the Sphinx. So we caught the last bus out to the pyramids. We found the Sphinx and a bewitching tranquillity which could not have been further removed from the hurly-burly of Alexandria and Cairo. The floodlights had been turned off, the stars glimmered and the desert seemed to float under a curtain of veils, infinitely mysterious, ethereal. From a nearby nightclub wafting over the still night air came laughter and snatches of the Beatles song 'I want to hold your hand'.

Linda was briefly mollified. But even the Sphinx could not mend things between us. For the remainder of the trip we squabbled and at Athens we parted. I never saw nor heard of her again.

Linda was not to know how prophetic her enigmatic remark at the St. Georges would be or what part she played in shaping events; indeed, it would have been a matter of supreme indifference to her. However, something happened in that thirty-six hour shore leave in Alexandria that was to change my life.

I was born in the East and used to return there infrequently from boarding school in England as a child. These trips by air had the quality of being transported on a magic carpet to another world. In Egypt there were the unmistakable whiffs of the East: the smell of slaked dust, donkey carts, water buffaloes, palms and mangoes. It was only a suggestion, but the more powerful for that. The effect of that brief visit was to leave me with the impression of having touched an atavistic nerve. I knew in an odd way that I had arrived, that this overland trip through Asia Minor to the shores of the Sahara had covered the dead ground between these two worlds and united them.

The nostalgia lived with me through six years working as a journalist in London and when circumstances conspired to allow me to go back to live in Egypt I seized the day.

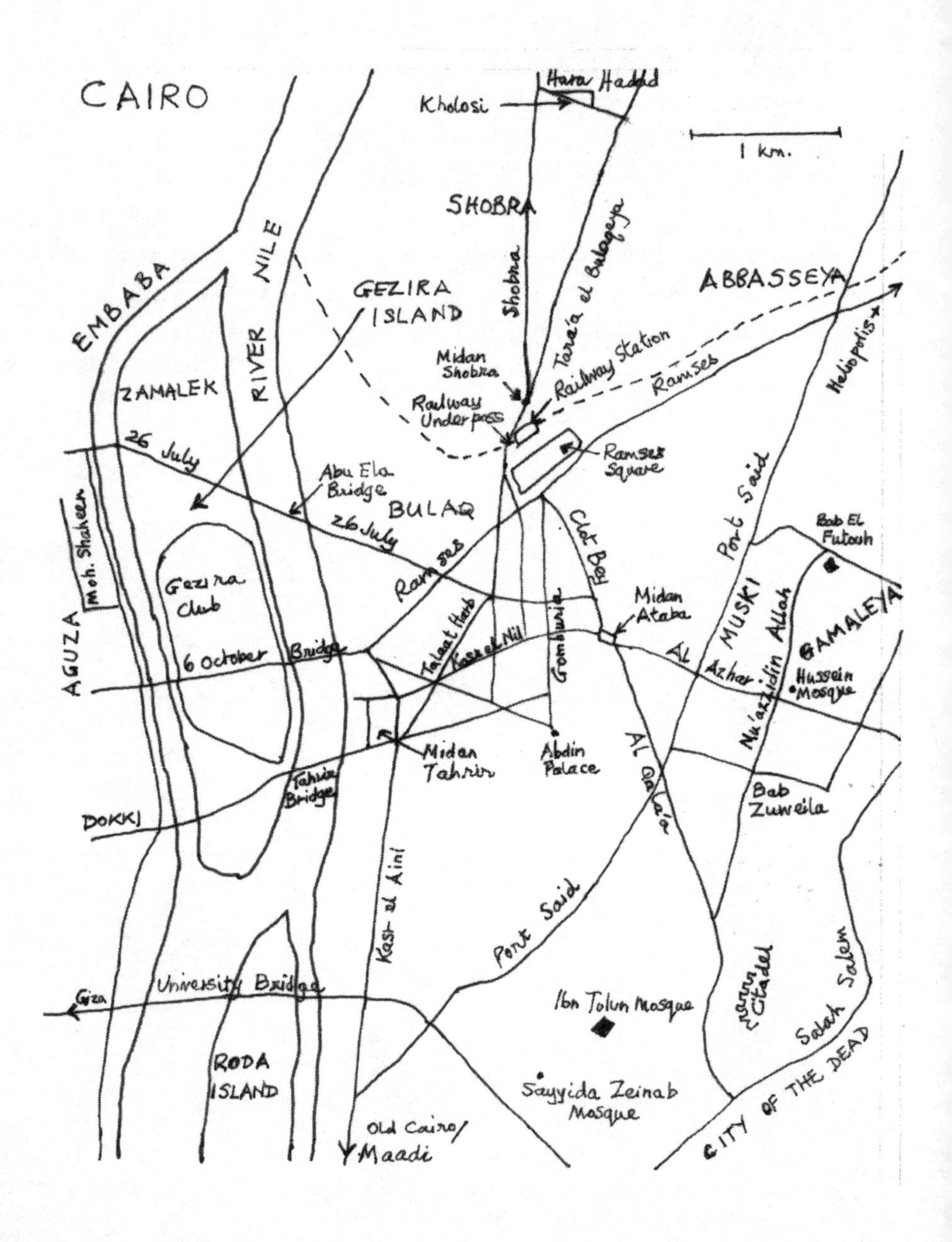

CAIRO
Hara Haddad
Kholosi
1 km.
SHOBRA
Shobra
Tara'a el Bulaqeya
ABBASSEYA
EMBABA
RIVER NILE
GEZIRA ISLAND
Midan Shobra
Railway Station
Ramses
Heliopolis
ZAMALEK
Railway Underpass
Ramses Square
26 July
Abu Ela Bridge
BULAQ
26 July
Clot Bey
Port Said
Bab El Futouh
Moh. Shaheen
Gezira Club
Ramses
Talaat Harb
Kasr el Nil
Gomhuria
Midan Ataba
MUSKI
Mu'azzidin Allah
GAMALEYA
AGUZA
6 October Bridge
AL Azhar
Hussein Mosque
Midan Tahrir
Abdin Palace
Al Qala'a
Tahrir Bridge
Bab Zuweila
DOKKI
Kasr el Aini
Port Said
Salah Salem
Giza
University Bridge
Ibn Tulun Mosque
Citadel
RODA ISLAND
Sayyida Zeinab Mosque
CITY OF THE DEAD
Old Cairo/ Maadi

Chapter One

'You know why Cairo is so good for medicine?' The Lebanese medical student seated next to me on the short hop from Beirut to Cairo on the last leg of my flight out from London peered earnestly.

'No,' I replied.

'It's the practical experience students get in diagnosis. Some diseases are common in Egypt but quite rare in the West now. Students here have a much better working knowledge of them. It's why Cairo medical students do so well in Europe as physicians.'

It jolted me more than the rather bumpy landing. My own doctor had pooh poohed a natural desire to be pumped with whatever inoculations were on offer. 'Healthiest climate in the world,' he'd said. 'You'll have a wonderful time.'

So there I found myself disgorged on the tarmac apron, last strip of neutral ground between me and for all I knew the dreaded plague. And blissfully unaware of what lay in store. Of that I was about to be disabused most rudely crossing an invisible line at the entrance to the airport building.

Nothing in a year of desultory tutoring in Arabic or previous experiences of arriving at Cairo, or even arriving at Alexandria with Linda, prepared me for the maelstrom of health and immigration controls. All that imperfectly assimilated vocabulary garnered at evening classes to assist the traveller with the doctor, the dentist, visiting the police station, checking into the hotel, passing through customs, evaporated. Instead a dozen hands grappled to help, offer advice and be my friend. I had forgotten how good it was to feel so wanted. Young men in tight trousers and nylon shirts asked for bottles of gin, whisky, brandy, vermouth: 'Just one please,' from the duty free shop.

I joined what I took to be a queue and waited. It didn't diminish; it got larger, fed by ancillary ducts. I edged forward, angling myself into a strategic position, and stood there. A few of the more intrepid tried to go round; they tried to go under. I wouldn't let them. They looked at me in astonishment. 'What's this?' they demanded. I shrugged my shoulders, raised eyes and hands and blurted out: '*ana asif*'. It was well received; they glowed with comprehension. 'He's sorry,' they said and smiled as if glad to know I was sorry. All, that is, but the half dozen or so who wanted to go round and under. They stood their ground and regarded me with beady eyes.

'About what?' The Arabic for 'queue' had deserted me. I knew where to find it, as it were. It was in 'At the Post Office' jumbled with counters, booking clerks, first and second class mail, stamps, forms and posting times. But I couldn't tell them that. So I waved my hand in a vague gesture of a queue and said: '*nass*'. Now whether it was the presence of the British in Egypt for many years or an innate yearning for order I had unconsciously tapped, or simply an extraordinarily quick grasp of associations I don't know. But to my amazement they understood; not only understood but wanted to play the game. In no time there was a proper queue and everyone was enjoying themselves hugely, beaming and nodding as if to say: 'What a splendid idea.' This unexpected success did wonders for my self-confidence; I sailed through customs like a seasoned pro and into a waiting taxi.

The ride into Cairo after the cold grime of Europe in mid winter is one of the experiences of life. The diesel powered Mercedes purrs as it gathers speed. You lie back and relax, as certain as night follows day – for every Cairo cabbie coddles his brakes and conserves his fuel – that neither traffic lights, corners, nor other cars will disturb the inertial rhythm of your progress.

Slowly you come alive again, learn to savour smells and fragrances, textures, the desert air, the inky silhouette of palms; and wonder at the strangeness of the neon signs beaming messages in Arabic, a sinuous calligraphy so beguiling that its meaning is unimportant.

In fact, whether you are allowed to enjoy these experiences depends on your cabbie. I was lucky; mine was sensitive and sympathetic. He didn't ask me if I wanted to see the pyramids, or if I wanted to go to Sahara City or if I needed girls or boys. He left me alone and I was grateful.

But when we turned off the Salah Salem highway into the medieval city he turned and asked: 'Where you go?' It was only then I realized I had forgotten the name of the hotel, together with the Arabic for the post office, the police station and the dentist which might conceivably have helped me out of my predicament. 'Talaat Harb,' I said, 'I know.' But I didn't know. Modern Cairo looks disconcertingly the same late at night from the back of a taxi and I couldn't get my bearings in the one-way system. We drove once, twice, three times down Sharia Talaat Harb without anything about the street registering in my mind. I racked my brain. I knew the name of the hotel was vaguely oriental. 'Sphinx?' I ventured. 'Mandarin?' No reaction. Finally we narrowed the field down to the Tulip or the Lotus. However, I had it fixed in my mind that the hotel did not bear the name of a flower. The driver was becoming fretful. We had been round the system at least four times and by the law of diminishing returns the chances of locating the hotel were diminishing. Then I recognized the building; it was indeed the Lotus.

The haggling began. I knew the price of a taxi from the airport to the town centre was normally 75 piastres, but we had been a long way round. As a starter I offered one Egyptian pound (E£1). The driver laughed, shrugged his shoulders and spread his hands. 'Should be 75 piastres,' I said by way of encouragement.

'Twenty minutes we....,' and he drew a circle in the air. 'One fifty.'

'One twenty,' I replied. He looked aggrieved, but when he saw it was my last offer he laughed and with good grace helped me out with my bags.

At one thirty in the morning Sharia Talaat Harb was as quiet as a pharaonic tomb. Seven floors above the inhabitants of the Lotus Hotel slumbered. It was a slumber I was about to disturb as I began the major operation of removing my belongings from the pavement to the hotel.

I burst on the Lotus like a returning tribe. The doorkeeper and the receptionist leapt with instant recognition although it was eighteen months since I had last passed through. I was shown to a room, the bed made up, foreign cigarettes asked for and received and bidden goodnight. It was two o'clock in the morning of January 27 1973.

****

Groppis is an Egyptian institution. It was established by Giacomo Groppi, a Swiss businessman from Lugano who settled in Egypt in the 1880s. He made his name and his fortune making chocolates which Egyptians bought and devoured in such quantities that he was able to found a confectionary empire, three teahouses and become in time the caterer to kings.

Foreigners knew Groppis for the teashops. For most Egyptians, however, Groppis meant ice cream. If you went to the cinema in Cairo you would be regaled in the interval by the familiar cry: '*uskreem groubies*' – a phonetic corruption necessitated by the difficulty Egyptians have in distinguishing between p and b.

Groppis in Soliman Pasha Square was the best-known. It had survived the Allied occupation, the revolution and nationalization in 1961 more or less intact. The confectionery stall still sold cakes, ice cream, chocolates and other bonbons. Inside, in a kind of inner sanctum. there was a restaurant where you could escape completely to another era. For 85 piastres, to which a 10 per cent service charge was added, you could eat a three-course meal on starched linen, a freshly picked rose at each table with cutlery which, if not quite silver, was comfortably solid. Immaculate waiters with Italian airs served with solicitude. You could give an order in any of the major European languages and these bandbox maestros would oblige with a flourish and a verve that left you breathless with admiration; their talents were clearly wasted. But then Groppis Restaurant was one of the best-kept secrets of Cairo.

Not so the coffee lounge which was normally crowded. However, at ten in the morning it was a different story. At that hour the only sound was the rustle of papers, walls of privacy concealing burrowed heads and hands which reached blindly for the coffee pots. It was to the coffee lounge I went my first morning back in Cairo with a copy of the *Egyptian Gazette*, the local English language newspaper.

The main story in the *Gazette* was a painstaking account of the president's movements the previous day. It was later explained to me in all sincerity that the reason for this obsession with the minutiae of the president's day lay in the Six Day War of 1967 and its aftermath. In the interminable post-mortems that followed the war Nasser was unable, embarrassingly, to account for his movements at critical moments. This had been ammunition in the hands of his detractors who had been quick to suggest the president had been caught napping. Thereafter Nasser ordered his movements be chronicled in detail, preferably with photographs so that there could be no doubt where he was at any given time.

Then the weather forecast written in the strangely poetic language Egyptian meteorologists use by way of concealing the fact that they have nothing to say. 'Cloud forming over the Delta. Mist may thicken early and spread south, perhaps reaching Cairo by dawn. Light northerly winds cover the country and will tend to strengthen in the Western Desert causing sands to rise.' The talk of cloud was to relieve the monotony. The sky was as innocent of cloud as it was of other blemishes. So I found on stepping out into Cairo and the sun.

One's first walk in Cairo after London has an unnerving strangeness about it. Sights, sounds, colours, people bombard you from all directions and there seems no avoiding them. The cosy encapsulating bubble in which I had immured myself against the weather, the next door neighbour, the next door neighbour's dog evaporated. It was an outrageous assault on my privacy but no one paid the slightest attention. The barriers were dismantled willy-nilly, defences a lifetime in the making, a pantheon of hurts, slights and inhibitions real or imagined, a whole schema of checks and balances, countermeasures and civilized behaviour were laid bare in a kind of psychological striptease that left me feeling naked and vulnerable. They wanted to know about me, all about me, more than I had ever thought it decent or politic to divulge.

So did the touts who, by some sixth sense and by dint of a good bush telegraph were on my tail with clear intentions to take away a little of my goodwill, preferably in coin or banknote.

They followed me up the side of Abdin Palace where I was accosted by a shoeshine man who drove me cowering against a wall.

'English, my friend,' he barked, as he attacked my shoes.

'Indeed,' I ventured, 'I am happy to be your friend.'

'Good people,' he continued. 'English, French, good people.

American shit.'

The conversation came to an abrupt halt. He had finished. There was a moment's silence, a silence pregnant with expectation as he put away his shoe cleaning equipment. I had no idea how much to pay and the gathering crowd was going to ensure it was not below the going rate.

I produced a 10 piastre note. 'That enough?' I enquired.

'What you think I am?' he demanded in disgust.

'OK. Fifteen. Here you are.'

But he would not have it. So plucking up the courage to put my foot down in an indifferently shone shoe, I told him he could take it or leave it. He took it – in bad grace. Only later did it emerge that the price of a shoeshine was 2 piastres.

Unsettled by this disturbing insight into the darker side of the Egyptian soul, I returned to the hotel and to bed. The hours passed, the light mellowed, and when next I looked out the sky had lost the grainy heaviness of noon and cleared. Everything was golden. I was still upset; but as the short dusk gathered momentum my spirits began rising and there was no way to hold them down.

Out on the streets the sun had already gone. Over the far end of Talaat Harb the crowds milled on the pedestrian overpass consumed in a moving fire dance of melting silhouettes which jumped and flickered against a glowing blood red sky. I walked towards the Nile past the bus station in front of the Mugamma; the oil slicks in the bus bays gleamed. On the Kasr el-Nil Bridge with its imposing stone lions sitting guard that leads to Gezira Island the crowds thinned. The sky was immense over the river.

****

It was the first of many walks and many sunsets as I got my bearings. After the first excursion into the hinterland of Cairo I went more carefully, expanding my knowledge of the city street by street, day by day. This was more difficult than one might imagine because of modern Cairo's disconcerting anonymity. To make it worse the French town planners who built the modern city at the turn of the century did so on two radial points: Midan Soliman Pasha (now officially Talaat Harb, although by some anomaly the street is known as Talaat Harb while the square has retained its old name – presumably to distinguish it from the street which often loses the 'Sharia' prefix) and Midan Mustafa Kamel. Each has a splendid statue: Soliman about to deliver an oration and Tariq on horseback.

They came to hold a near hypnotic power over me, Soliman and the equestrian Mustafa, as I tried to break out of the labyrinth of side streets and main thoroughfares. It seemed impossible to escape their gravitational pull, to launch into orbit as it were, for no matter how resolutely I put them behind me one or other would always pop up around the next corner, way off, slight and slender and at night dimly lit in an alluring orange glow, beckoning me back like some flute playing Krishna to the centre of the maze.

So it was a wearying footslog establishing landmarks. But in time the Central Bank became fixed on the corner of Sharia Kasr el-Nil and Sharia Sherif; you couldn't miss it because there was always a scruffy policeman in blue with a machine gun loafing around the entrance. Maison Thomas, a pre-war grocery store put Sharia Sarawat on the map while the main synagogue, boarded now and dusty with desuetude, established Sharia Adli. If all else failed there was always the Nile. One only needed to venture a little way across one of the many bridges that straddled it to glimpse, across the skyline of the modern city, the Citadel and the crusty ridge of the Muqattem beyond.

Downtown, as the sign on the Nile Corniche describes the central area, has redeeming features: the Sicilian palazzo on Sharia Sarawat, for example, now a store which, despite a false front and concerted attempts to bury it in graffiti, still manages to look like a Sicilian palazzo. But you have to look quite hard for the pre-War city behind, or preferably above, the kitsch boutiques and cheap stores that deface these noble edifices like an unsightly rash.

Elsewhere the skyscrapers soar in blank anonymity, their lifts creaking and slowly breaking down for lack of servicing and spares. They dominate the area around Sharia Kasr el-Nil and Sharia Sherif. You rarely see the sun at the bottom of the deep wells between them where the blue rinse fumes swirl noxiously over the traffic and the shuffling crowds.

Central Cairo suffers from a desperate lack of space. The city and its suburbs were built for three million inhabitants and now house eight. The press on the pavements at certain times is such that the crowds occupy the roads, snarling the traffic. It is in fact safer on the road. On the pavement one faces unnatural and unexpected hazards: street signs set lethally at chin level; flagstones laid over manhole covers; and the brick walls, a hideous legacy of 1967, built ostensibly to provide cover in the event of an invasion, which effectively paralyze pedestrian movement.

They suffer, Cairenes, with such stoicism and good humour! Once I saw a young mother with a swaddled babe trip on a flagstone. The baby parted company with her and went bouncing down the street. The woman got up with a grimace, her nylons gashed, picked up the baby who was mercifully unhurt and, after nods to helpers, continued her journey, still stunned, nothing said.

Egyptians keep their flair for display for the barrows and the street stalls. The bigger stores occasionally have window displays. Hanneaux, on Kasr el-Nil, once had a special offer on chandeliers that were stacked in the window like refuse awaiting collection. Sednaoui, on the corner of Midan Soliman Pasha displayed its choicest cloths as if attempting to clear substandard linoleum.

For foreign goods you go to Sharia Shawarbi which is always conspicuously stocked with foreign goods as the rest of Cairo isn't. In Sharia Shawarbi a little bit of Beirut comes to Cairo at prices as fancy as the frilly nighties and the nylons at E£4 a pair. There you can order anything.

Sharia Shawarbi is way beyond the means of the ordinary Cairene. He satisfies his craving for foreign goods by buying knick-knacks at the street kiosks that sell foreign tobacco, cigarettes and chocolates when available, or by window gazing in the dozen or so small multipurpose boutiques along Talaat Harb. These always draw a crowd, especially when a consignment of imported goods has just arrived. The crowds are always deeply preoccupied making choices, doing sums: hair shampoo or Lux soap; and if not these then nail clippers, tins of Duraglit, combs, razor blades, toothpaste, Nescafé. A thriving black market in contraband makes it worth the while of the *tigara al-shanta*, the suitcase salesman, to commute regularly to Beirut to buy colour films, unobtainable in Egypt, liquor and tobacco.

The authorities make half-hearted attempts to keep this trade in check. The most concerted effort to clamp down on the black market came to be known as the May Purge. In the late spring of 1972 Cairo was swamped by a tidal wave of contraband. Kellogg's cornflakes fell to 50 piastres a packet, a medium sized tin of Nescafé to 40 piastres. The shops were awash with Heinz ketchup. The kiosk owners and the multipurpose shopkeepers were worried that the bottom might fall out of the market; so was the government, for other reasons. The official view was that black markets were a blemish on the good name of the 'White Revolution' (Egyptians were proud that their revolution in 1952 was bloodless). The authorities, therefore, not wishing to hurt pockets, announced that all contraband handed in before a certain date would be covered by an amnesty. Egypt, being a socialist state the goods would be offered at cost price to the public who would thus be the principal beneficiary of this malfeasance, while the traders would recover their original outlay.

The amnesty did indeed bring in a good haul and Cairo keyed itself for the sale which was to take place simultaneously at four big stores. However, the night before the sale the police, tipped off or not no one knows, did a spot check on the goods and found everything sold - bought with post-dated cheques by the stores' employees, their families and friends. The May Purge was the last of its kind.

****

By the end of the month I had mapped out the centre: Sharia Champolion with its car workshops and hashish dens where the slums of Bulaq encircle the European city to the north; Babeluk with its cavernous cafés and clanking trams; Abdin, the monumental palace that once housed the Khedival court and is now the President's official residence; Opera Square once the hub of European Cairo over which Shepheards Hotel had presided before being burnt down in the riots of 1952, and the Opera House, built for the first performance of Aida in 1871, and now a car park after being mysteriously gutted by fire and pulled down in 1971; the adjacent Ezbekia Gardens where starched nannies once pushed prams under the palms and where now dogs scavenge on grass as scabbed as their skins. Walking from Ezbekia Gardens down Twenty-sixth of July Street (ex Rue Fouad) towards the Nile you entered what used to be Cairo's most exclusive shopping district and, bearing right at the intersection with Talaat Harb, you came to Midan Orabi and the Cecil Bar, formerly the British Officers' Club and symbol of the Raj, conveniently located a short walk from the nightclubs, cafés and restaurants of Sharia Elfiddin and the vegetable market of Tewfikiya.

This exploration was an evolving within as much as an expanding knowledge of the city around me. I picked my way through new sensations as I did through the Cairo back streets, the rubble, the rubbish and the smells. I slept a great deal, drugged on the high pressure and the sun, and looking back I realize that this drowsiness was an adjustment to a new condition. As one beautiful day followed another I was like a child waking into the warmth and security of its mother's arms. Days spent wandering; days that waited like patient

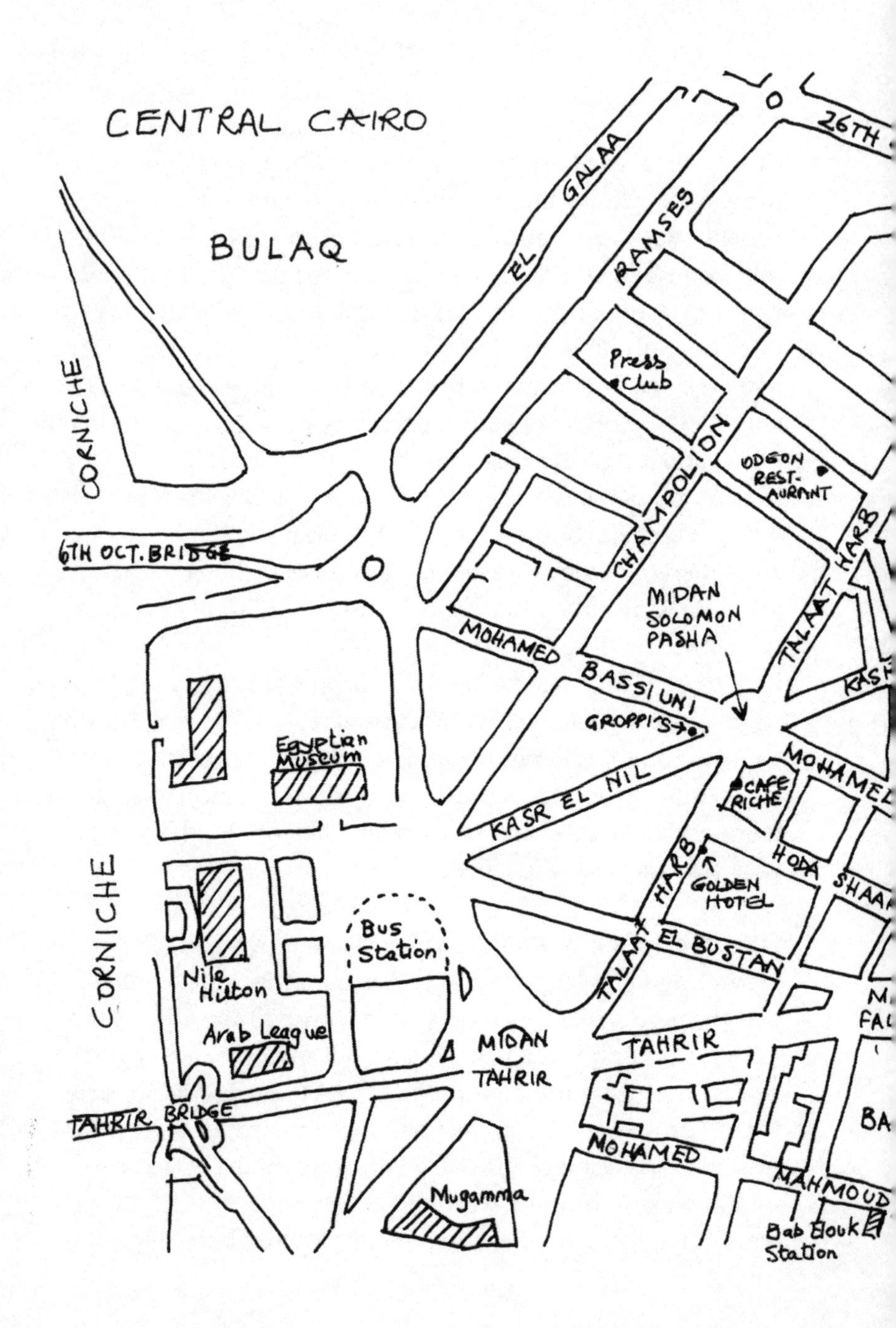

CENTRAL CAIRO
BULAQ
CORNICHE
EL GALAA
RAMSES
26TH
Press club
CHAMPOLION
ODEON REST-AURANT
TALAAT HARB
6TH OCT. BRIDGE
MIDAN SOLOMON PASHA
MOHAMED BASSIUNI
GROPPI'S
Egyptian Museum
KASR EL NIL
CAFE RICHE
MOHAMED
HODA SHAA
GOLDEN HOTEL
CORNICHE
Bus Station
Nile Hilton
EL BUSTAN
TALAAT HARB
Arab League
MIDAN TAHRIR
TAHRIR
TAHRIR BRIDGE
MOHAMED
MAHMOUD
Mugamma
Bab Elouk Station

MOHAMED BEY EL ALFI
EL DIN
26TH JULY
EMAD
ADLI
GOMHURIA
EZ BEKIA GARDENS
OPERA SQUARE
ABDEL KHALEK SARWAT
NIDAN MUSTAFA KAMEL
SHERIF
MOHAMED
GOMHURIA
SHERIF
RUSHDI
ALAM
ABDEL SALAAM MOH. AREF
MIDAN EL GOMHURIA

handmaidens on the glory of blood-crazed evening skies and the release of dusk. Everything else seemed a prelude to this. I remember once coming out of a cinema on Talaat Harb at this hour to see the workmen silvering the lampposts. Daubed with spatterings of silver paint, they danced like elfin creatures from the Mountains of Kaf while the light around sizzled and cracked from the static, which comes with the heat changes of dusk. Above the Hilton Hotel, like a neon trace, a blush of alizarin spread across the sky. It spread slowly over the city and for a minute or two, the city glowed pink from within. It was a moment of sheer magic, a move into a different order of reality. For out of the dead gritty sandstone, dead as pumice, dry as shed snakeskin something quickened, a spark which made for a moment the distinction between animate and inanimate a fiction of the mind.

So it was in the rhythm of the days that I began to know the city, in the street incidents, the markets and the hawkers' cries, in the vignettes of daily life that told its story more eloquently than the street names, the imposing buildings and the official guides, vignettes which were already forming the nucleus of my experience.

But it was the 'other city' to which I was drawn more and more: as the European city began to settle in my mind and I could move around more freely: the city glimpsed briefly coming down from the Salah Salem highway through the medieval city and the markets of Khan al-Khalili to the town centre, a city of prayer tents, mosques and fairy lights. New names crept into my ken: Bab Zuweila, Sharia Mu'ezzidin Allah, Ibn Tulun and Sayidda Zeinab. And it was acceptance into that city which had so brusquely dealt with me on my first day that was to be the high point of my first month.

It was a Sunday afternoon I remember, no different from a dozen other lazy afternoons in the way the sun turned slowly, gathering in its gold. It was the kind of afternoon I was to realize later that distilled the very essence of Egypt: a warm winter sun which, in easing you gently into the stream, asked nothing more of you than to trust, to put away all conditions and aims and to be. It was on one such afternoon that, stuck for anything to do, I took my first walk through the grimy back streets behind Abdin Palace to the Citadel.

I walked by the wall where the shoeshine man had accosted me that first day, my heart in my mouth, wearing my rudimentary Arabic like a talisman and a rather too cheery smile. I came to a junkyard, a children's fair, gaudy merry-go-rounds crudely painted, a jumble of tatty swings. A group of men were bringing the creaky carousel to life, a pathetic beautiful creature fashioned from odd wood, a rough place to sit and the owner at the centre pushing it round.

And no one noticed me.

As I gained confidence my inhibitions fell away. My heart was as open as the sky. I had nothing to hide, nothing to lose and I felt welcomed as one of their own. I realized then what had set me apart on that first day was not my white skin but a bundle of preconceptions I had taken with me.

I felt like Mohammed bin Louissan, Bark the slave in St Exupery's *Wind, Sand and Stars*, who is bought his freedom and let loose in the streets of Agadir. Delirious with joy at finding himself treated no differently from other men he spent the small sum he had been given to tide him over on bangles and beads for the children. As evening fell the citizens of Agadir had wondered at the strange spectacle of a Pied Piper to whose tune their children danced.

They must have wondered too, the blacksmiths, the shopkeepers and the housewives, at the spectacle of a wild-eyed European in their midst. But I hardly noticed them. I walked the back streets of Cairo drunk on a joy Mohammed bin Louissan alone knew, a freed slave with a retinue of street boys.

Chapter Two

A few days after my arrival I changed hotels. The Lotus was a little too grand and I had had an introduction to Fares Sarofim, the proprietor of the Golden Hotel across the way on Talaat Harb. I felt bad about leaving the Lotus; in Egypt one immediately establishes personal relationships. The receptionist hid his disappointment (the loss of a customer is a loss of potential business and in the way of Egyptians he had led me to believe I was promising material), and four men were delegated to accompany me across the road.

At the Golden I was taken to Room 31 on the third floor, the bridal suite as it was known I discovered later on account of its popularity with honeymooning couples from Khartoum. I never found out what it was about that room that worked such a potent charm with the Sudanese. It couldn't have been the plumbing. The plumbing preoccupied a deaf plumber who kept himself in a comfortable living servicing the hotel's loos. Nor could it have been the view. The room overlooked the street and a large dusty town house that seemed incongruous and cowed by the high-rise apartment blocks surrounding it. It was also overshadowed by a huge white wall which for me was its saving grace, that and the room's monastic simplicity. To wake to the sun splashed prodigally across that wall, a blank canvas on which to measure the tread of the hours in the spreading shadows was heaven.

In the house across the street, so legend had it, lived a certain Mrs. Green, a Jewish lady of great age and philanthropic associations. It was her family that had established the foundation that kept and preserved the rare Talmuds and other ancient Jewish artefacts in the synagogue in Old Cairo. Despite the Arab Israeli dispute her family had stayed on like a few other Jewish families of that class for whom Egypt meant more than race, creed or ideology, and who were prepared to put up with the antagonisms and petty bureaucratic persecutions which sometimes made their lives difficult.

Her family had been hit, as everyone had been, by the social reforms of the '60s. But the law allowed every individual to own one house, so they had been able to stay put. On Talaat Harb the family is vividly remembered; in particular one brother, a dapper dresser who used to walk each morning to Groppis for his coffee sporting a carnation in his buttonhole. But that was more than ten years ago. He and the rest of the family had died leaving Mrs. Green alone in this town house, one of the last surviving in the centre of Cairo. The place was permanently shuttered. The only sign of life was when a sweeper in powder blue *galabeya* would appear to water a few tired plants.

The Golden was a semi residential hotel. That is to say it had its regulars as well as passing trade. The Golden had seen it all: Palestinian guerrillas, mothers placing daughters at the University, Indian commercial travellers, Baathist Syrians, Libyans with the mannerisms of Texans, even the odd penny-pinching Kuwaiti, or, a very rare bird indeed, a Saudi. There was also a good turnover of European and American students en route east and south. We all rubbed shoulders in the narrow reception hall where everyone was welcome to sit and pass the time of day with a fresh orange or mango juice brought in from the fruit parlour next door, or a tea or *karkaday* brewed in the kitchen at the end of the corridor. It was in the lobby of the Golden that all the burning issues of the day and the great conundrums of human existence were discussed without ever really getting anywhere. Not that it mattered. What mattered was to be in a cool place surrounded by *mashrabeya* screens knowing that the hot, loving Egyptian sun was burning a path of gold in the afternoon. It was at such times that my nature was forged: like a Camus description of the Mediterranean, like an old and loved prayer, the repetition of the same old mantras soothed and reassured.

The hotel was run by an intense young Copt called Amin Simaika who had the tortured air of a Spanish hidalgo contemplating death. Amin had been a schoolteacher in a Delta town where for E£17 a month he taught adolescents French. The experience had killed his idealism and tested the foundations of his Christian faith with its heavy overlay of duty and devotion. Teaching in a predominantly Muslim school in a small Delta town demanded much of these with little spiritual recompense. No one it seemed had much notion of duty, sacrifice or justice in that particular Delta town. The teachers fiddled the curriculum so that pupils were obliged to take private lessons to cover the syllabus. And there was, he said, prejudice against Copts.

He was saved by his call-up into the army. However, he soon found he had exchanged one hell for another. He became an interpreter and was kicked around for the next six years. Then he had a slice of luck. Under the law one son is exempt national service if there is no other breadwinner in the family. Only sons are exempted altogether. As his father had died he or his brother had the right of exemption. He had gone into the army to allow his brother to continue his studies. The brother emigrated and, by a new interpretation of the law, no longer qualified as a breadwinner. Amin was thus released from the army to support his mother.

He was through with teaching but what was he to do? Fortunately his uncle, Fares Sarofim, was able to offer him a job as manager of the Golden while, having decided to emigrate, he arranged his papers, official releases from the army and the Ministry of Education, which still considered him a teacher although he was not registered in any school and drew no salary. It cost him a lot of time and some money to be sacked.

The wheels of the hotel were kept turning by the *bowab*, Am Mohammed. The *bowab* like Groppis is an Egyptian institution. Nearly every large building has one. The *bowab* ensures it doesn't fall down or go up in smoke and that undesirables don't get in. In theory it is a responsible if not a particularly onerous job: in practice it is one of the cushiest numbers in the Middle East. Many *bowabs* make fortunes collecting anything from 25 piastres to E£1 a month from each flat and a retainer from the owner. Some of the larger buildings contain sixty to seventy apartments. So a top bowab can earn E£100 a month or more. Amin conceded he had missed his vocation. *Bowabs* become men of affairs; some buy property. For those that have graduated into high finance a 20 piastre tip no longer suffices; they have long ceased running errands. The more conscientious hire others to perform their menial duties; the rest abandon their charges to their own devices.

In the small hotels it is different. Am Mohammed looked after our morals as well as our possessions, a duty not required of apartment *bowabs* who would happily procure for those in need of companionship. Vice in third-class hotels and pensions is for some reason anathema to the powers that be that impose on them all the restrictions and inhibitions necessary to maintain the community's sense of propriety. It meant that at the Golden you couldn't have visitors in your room.

It was difficult to guess how old Am Mohammed was because of his slight stoop and deferential manner. His grizzled pate suggested great age. He slept on a wooden bench near the door. He preferred the bench because it afforded him a clear view of the front door. There, in the evenings he entertained his friends to *shisha* and swapped reminiscences of old times on the servant circuit. Am Mohammed was, of course, Nubian. All the best *bowabs* were. The Nubians at that time had cornered the market in domestic situations because they made such good servants. Legend had it, a calumny perpetrated by the Delta people, that the Nubians had little brain. Sheer jealousy! They were sought after because they were honest and tidy.

Am Mohammed's neatness was a revelation. Sometimes you would catch him opening up the cubbyhole beside his bench and glimpse the immaculate orderliness of his lair. The comb, the piece of broken mirror, the alarm clock, the bundle of correspondence ringed with an elastic band, the tobacco laid out on the small shelf behind: everything in place.

Am Mohammed could have gone onto great things for he was trusted and much respected. But he preferred to remain at the Golden; as *bowab* of the Golden he was his own man. He was chairman of the local citizens' committee, a semi political organization which combined, as well, the functions of a magistrate's office. This was the extent of his ambition.

Am Mohammed had a son who must have been a genetic throwback. Where Am Mohammed was the soul of discretion, Fathalla personified fecklessness of a high order. Indeed, he was the nearest thing I ever saw to an Egyptian drop out – not in the name of CND, anti-vivisection or anything like that – but in the way life simply washed over him.

Occasionally he was moved to work and then he worked well; but it was only in short bursts, after which he relapsed into good-natured loafing. His father, thinking marriage might improve him, had found him a pretty cousin. But Fathalla was inclined to forget his wife as he was to wash the stairs. One morning past eleven o'clock, hunger having overcome her modesty, she crept down from their rooftop cabin to complain that Fathalla still hadn't produced the breakfast.

Am Mohammed pulled strings to get Fathalla accepted in the army. As an only son he was by rights exempt. Army life didn't agree with Fathalla. So one day he changed into his grubby pin-striped *galabeya* put on his size fourteen shoes which left an inch between heel and back and clumped to Cairo. Am Mohammed sent him back. However, the army refused to have him. He was discharged – according to his discharge papers on account of his flat fleet. What to do with him? In mortification Am Mohammed finally agreed, despite his deep reservations, to have him work in the Golden. Fathalla would probably have been happier minding the family sheep in Aswan.

Only one thing interested Fathalla: football. His eyes would light up at the mention of it and you could almost track his brain working as it regurgitated dates and names. He never missed a match on TV and would rush into the foyer of the Golden showing the whites of his eyes to announce another goal.

Last but not least on the Golden's payroll was 'doc' Mohammed. He was called 'doc' on account of time he had spent as a medical orderly in the army. He was imprisoned behind a pair of pebble-lensed spectacles and looked like Beelzebub. He was said to have fathered an enormous progeny which accounted for the feeling one had with him that if it wasn't for the mercy of Allah and your kindness he would have sunk a long time ago leaving a trail of untold suffering. There was a child-like vulnerability about 'doc' in his baggy blazer, just a little too short, hanging awkwardly on his paper-thin shoulders, a vulnerability accentuated by his pigeon toes. It was one of the routines of the Golden to start the day with a Boy Scouts salute from him. 'Good morning Meester Alan. *Sabah al-kheer*,' he would grate as he manipulated the antique lift, his face creasing into a Fernandel smile, his huge lips cracking like an overripe pomegranate.

'Doc' had a flair for delegation. He was great advocate of self-help especially when it came to over demanding customers whom he appeased with assiduous and ineffectual courtesy. He did the same with Amin and it got on Amin's nerves. Amin had given an order that he alone was to monitor incoming telephone calls as no one else could be trusted to take them properly. 'Doc' would trot half way round the hotel to tell Amin the telephone was ringing. Amin would shout at him for doing exactly what he had been told to do. In fact this dysfunctional symbiosis suited them both: it satisfied Amin's need to feel indispensable and 'doc's' latent fear of getting involved. But it encouraged bad habits in 'doc'. He behaved the same way with everyone, making his presence inescapably felt (when around) by dusting the reception desk, the telephone, the tops of chairs, and looking after the Greeks.

Everyone said 'doc' had the misfortune to look after the Greeks; they didn't know that the Greek couple were his perfect foil. They were always complaining about everything and as they complained about 'doc' this somehow gave him credibility. He had tried ensnaring them in a web of obligingness – 'doc' had a way of rubbing his hands together as if he would throw himself under the nearest bus if that be your wish – but the Greek couple were not fooled. So he would run errands for them: collecting medicines, bottles of milk, bananas, newspapers, and consequently could never be found.

Monsieur and Madame Christoferides occupied a converted box room on the second floor. They lived in considerably less exalted circumstances than 'doc's' constant ministrations suggested. Mr. Christoferides, a former accountant with the Suez Canal Company had been unable to repatriate his pension – not that it would have bought much outside Egypt. Their ties with the mother country were in fact tenuous: the wife's family originated in Albania; his had vague connections with Thessalonica. So they had moved on retirement from Ismailia to the Golden where they eked out their days taking the afternoon sun and window-shopping. In the evening they cooked the miserly harvest of 'doc's' foragings on a primus stove, splashing out at weekends on a bottle of Stella beer.

Each morning they descended to the hall for the post. Mr. Christoferides would greet Amin with a courteous 'Bonjour, Monsieur Amin. La poste, est-elle arrivée?' At that hour a truce was called to their guerrilla war. Then turning to me. 'Bonjour, monsieur. Comment allez-vous?' Nothing more. And Mr. Christoferides would go and sit next to his wife on a seat facing the entrance.

Their dress never altered. He wore the same black coat, the same grey trousers and spotted tie while she was always in black for a brother who had died four years previously. They sat each morning, David Hockney figures, an intense passivity about them, their hands folded. He square, heavy jowelled; she angular, pious, her eyebrows drawn carefully on pallid skin. They sat awaiting a letter from their son in Australia. After the postman had arrived, exchanged loving embraces with Amin and left them nothing, they would get up and dust themselves. 'Eh bien,' he would say, shaking his head, 'peut-être demain.'

Azzam had a room at the Golden. He was Palestinian and in his last year at Cairo University studying commerce and economics. He couldn't wait to leave. Five years in Egypt was enough, he said. 'No one takes any notice of Palestinians,' he would say. 'We have neither the rights of Egyptians nor the privileges of foreigners.' The precariousness of every day living got on his nerves. Once on a bus the man behind him told him not to step back; there was a gaping hole. He told me a pregnant woman had lost her child falling through the floor of a bus. The perils of Cairo transport epitomized his feelings for Egypt.

Surviving did not allow Azzam the time or energy to relax and enjoy the zanier side of Cairo life. His burgher instincts, the product of a solid upbringing built on thrift and hard work, didn't rub too well with the ebullient charm and inherent flakiness of Egyptians. In fact Palestinian students were generally welcome in Egypt although the quality of their lives was conditioned by the level of terrorist activity elsewhere in the Middle East and the official attitude to it.

But if Azzam was rather grave he was not dull and he had, in common with a number of Palestinians I met, a quiet dignity and generosity of mind. He had been brought up inevitably in a legacy of violence – a cruel irony, for of all people in the Middle East the Palestinians least deserve it. Azzam, a Christian said he had never known tension between Christian and Muslim in Palestine. He had Muslim friends who used to take part in the Easter processions; frequently they worshipped together. He had a cousin who was married to an Egyptian airline pilot, a Muslim; the family had raised no objection. In Palestine, he said, religious distinction was never mentioned; it would have been bad manners. In fact it was not until he came to Egypt that he became aware of sectarianism; and he didn't like the religious quizzing almost before saying 'hallo' that can occur in Egypt.

Azzam's people came originally from Haifa but his family had settled in Jerusalem where he was brought up. His father had died young and he had been reared by his grandfather. One incident from his childhood sticks with him. In a shop one day he had taken something he liked without paying. His grandfather found out, made him return the article and said if it happened again he would be out on the street. He said it taught him not to covet what wasn't his.

There was a certain irony in this. For with Partition in 1948 his family had to evacuate their home in what became the Israeli sector of Jerusalem and move a stone's throw into the Jordanian sector. So Azzam was brought up within sight of other people occupying his home. 'You can't imagine what it is like,' he told me bitterly, 'watching other people in your house doing everyday things like putting out the washing, dusting the carpets, watering the plants and knowing there is nothing you can do about it.' He understood how young Palestinians became guerrillas; for himself he didn't have the guts.

This seemed strange, for all Azzam's instincts, one would have thought, would have been against violence. 'Why?' I asked.

He thought for a moment and then said: 'I don't approve of violence. But this is a case of violence breeding violence. No matter what the reasons or excuses you have to appreciate that Israel is an occupying power. We are second-class citizens in our own country. They lack the common courtesies with us.' For a man so fastidiously polite (indeed, for Arabs generally politeness is more than a social norm; it is the recognition of another human being), this must have been the last straw. And it nearly was. Once when summoned to see an official at the Town Hall in Ramallah on the West Bank where his family eventually settled he asked an Israeli soldier the way. The soldier ignored him; he was talking to a friend. And then, suddenly realizing his existence, snapped: 'What are you doing here? You are supposed to go in the back entrance.'

Said Azzam: 'I didn't care whether they put me inside or what they did with me. I shouted at him, asked him who the hell he thought he was and told him he might at least have the decency to answer courteously.' Azzam wasn't locked up and he got to see his official, which might not have happened in many other occupations. But such incidents didn't endear Israelis to him. 'They say they want to be friends with us. But they make no effort to meet us on our ground. After all they came here; they should at least respect our way of doing things. Their lack of sensitivity makes a difficult situation worse. As far as I am concerned I would be polite to an Israeli but I would find it hard to be his friend.'

'Would you be prepared to live and work in an Israeli governed state?' I asked.

'No,' he replied. 'There is no future for me there, unless I wanted to dig roads.'

Azzam's instincts were almost English. Get him talking about London and he lightened up. He had relatives there and felt at home. 'It's such a relief to get out of these bloody Arab countries,' he'd exclaim 'and be sane about women!'

Relations between the sexes in Egypt are tortuous, and complicated by the tangled web of religion that dictates sexual mores and the huge undercurrent of frustration imposed by economic conditions. It feeds the myth of every self-respecting Arab student that the streets of Europe are paved with beautiful and available blondes.

Sex in Cairo is expensive. It is the one item in the price index which bears comparison with the West. Prostitution is illegal and virginity valued. The price of a scarce commodity rises. It is higher still because when the Libyans, Kuwaitis and Saudis came to Cairo they want girls and are prepared to pay for them. The money is good, so good that some respectable young girls, employees of the airline and tourist offices, students and shop assistants who find their money doesn't stretch to essential accessories like nylons, lipstick and hairdos, succumb to temptation, while others, perhaps with dependants who can't possibly make ends meet otherwise, are forced on the game.

Marriage is expensive too and becoming more so. Tradition dictates that when you marry in Egypt you do so with all the necessities of life. The groom provides his fiancée with a *shabka*, usually jewellery which even for people of modest means can cost E£300-400 (the idea being that should the marriage break up the wife had something to fall back on) and brings a dowry which reflects the social and financial status of the couple. Usually the bride's father matches the dowry. Three hundred Egyptian pounds used to be thought enough to set a couple up in a modest way; that figure has risen to nearer E£600.

Most Egyptians girls are brought up to believe marriage is the goal of their existence. They flop into matrimony, usually with a man ten years older, breed babies and get fat. But attitudes are changing under the pervasive influence of western ideas and culture, and with coeducation which is throwing the sexes together as never before. The generation gap is a popular theme in Egyptian films and television plays. But there is a widening gap between these expectations and the realities of life. As marriage becomes more expensive the young become more dependent on their parents and will continue to as long as conventional patterns of behaviour hold and incomes fail to keep up with inflation. It is why Europe for young Egyptians has become the great escape hatch: from the grinding poverty and the lack of opportunity – and the throbbing heat of summer afternoons.

Amin had girl problems; he wasn't on their wavelength, which made it difficult sometimes with customers.

Once when Amin wasn't on duty a Japanese businessman came

to the hotel and enquired the price of a room. The proprietor told him E£1.20.

'If I take it next week as well? Once a week. How much?'

'We can make it E£1.'

'If I have it week after. That is 80 piastres?' enquired the Japanese businessman, warming to negotiations.

'No, I'm sorry, we can't go any lower,' said Fares, who discouraged weekly arrangements.

'Well, I want room for three hours once a week for E£1. I come back,' he said and left.

A few days later he returned and confronted by the redoubtable Amin declared he wanted a room for three hours.

Amin responded well to incisiveness. It brought out his latent talent for efficient service. 'No, I'm sorry, sir,' said Amin. 'We don't rent rooms by the hour.'

'Old man said room was E£1,' pursued the dogged Japanese businessman. 'I want room for E£1. Can have it in one hour?'

'Very well,' Amin conceded.

So he went. And he would have got away with it had I not let the cat out of the bag. Amin's pencil moustache twitched and he went very stern. Not wanting in his heart of hearts to think such ill of anyone he protested: 'We have many people who want a room for a couple of hours to rest and change.'

An hour or so later the Japanese businessman reappeared and asked for the key. Amin bustled busily. 'Please could you step inside a minute,' and with birdlike steps he hustled the hapless fellow into the inner lounge.

His companion, a rather pretty girl in glasses, ceased looking at the ceiling and asked sharply: 'What's going on?'

'He wants to speak with me.'

She took to looking at the ceiling again and affected boredom. Azzam recognized her from one of the airline offices on Talaat Harb.

Moments later the Japanese businessman came storming out, his glasses glinting. 'They have no rooms,' he squeaked. 'They are cleaning the rooms.'

Amin was of an unfortunate generation that never met girls. Education at a Jesuit school in Alexandria, university, schoolteacher in a God forsaken Delta town and then the army had effectively isolated him from the fairer sex. When he moved to the hotel he was given much more scope, especially with foreign girls, and as he wanted to emigrate this suited him.

Amin didn't believe in 'coup de foudres' but was for ever having them. He was reticent about these short painful encounters muttering that they were 'bad, very bad'. One never knew whether it was his passion for Nat King Cole (I can see him now walking two steps ahead, one foot in the gutter, breathing heavily over his companion as he crooned 'Unforgettable') or the disarming way he would serve himself up on a platter that started him off on the wrong foot. Being a Copt he couldn't divorce. On this he was adamant saying he believed that marriage should be 'for keeps'. Yet he gave one the feeling that he was going about it as he might buying a car.

He nearly married once. He had just come out of the army and had asked an uncle if he could find him a match. His uncle knew a suitable girl. Amin met the girl's mother at a wedding reception and was invited home to meet the family. He arrived bearing flowers. It was like an interview for a job, he said. Eight of them round a table and he in the middle. He wondered what the hell he had let himself in for. He wanted to call it off there and then but his uncle was involved and it would have embarrassed him.

'Give it one more try,' his uncle urged, 'and if you still don't like the set-up, well and good.'

So Amin did. This time the mother sensed he was stalling and to force the issue demanded a E£1,200 bracelet as the *shabka*, a car and E£6,000 dowry. Amin was a dreamer – in his mind's eye he had already built his bride a penthouse flat in Alexandria – but his pretensions fell well short of a E£6,000 dowry and a car. However, it did at least offer him the opportunity to bow out gracefully.

But that wasn't the end of his brushes with matrimony. Amin was full of surprises. Once when walking down Kasr el-Nil with him he stopped suddenly. 'Go back and look in the jeweller's shop on the corner there,' he told me. 'You will see two girls. Look at the taller one.'

When I came back he told me someone, a business associate,

had actually suggested he marry her never having clapped eyes on the girl. She was Armenian he said and owned buildings. Amin came from a good family it would be an ideal match. Amin demurred. He said he wasn't interested in the money or the buildings; he wanted to marry for love. 'Go and have a good look at her in any case,' counselled the business associate. So he did and didn't take it further.

Helmi, like Azzam was Palestinian, but his family lived in Kuwait. He, too, had a room at the Golden and girl problems – but of a very different order. Helmi was devoid of all modesty, a surprisingly engaging trait. He told me without the slightest hint of braggadocio that he had won a scholarship from the Kuwaiti government, a grant from Fatah, the Palestinian resistance group, to travel to East Germany and a scholarship to study in Albania. He had also held down a high powered job with a Saudi company and a lucrative position in Kuwait. His prolific talents and craggy good looks made him irresistibly attractive apparently to girls.

His girlfriends in Kuwait had apartments and cars; in Egypt they had neither, which was irksome. It required he make the running, a state of affairs for which he was not temperamentally suited.

One morning I met him in the Filfilla restaurant just round the corner from the Golden, bleary eyed from lack of sleep.

'Hey Helmi,' I called, 'You're looking rough, what's the matter? Come and have a beer.'

He came and sat with me, refusing the beer and launched into a tirade about the complications in his life. He was currently involved with a physical training instructor who lived in Maadi, a suburb some ten miles south of Cairo. 'I'm furious with her,' he droned. 'I told her not to ring this morning because I was working late last night and she rings at ten just to say 'hallo'.' He talked in a ponderous drawl as if nudging the words to speak for themselves. The drawl was as dead as the look in his eye. Indeed, it might have been a fraction slower this morning on account of his disturbed night's sleep.

'I just said *zift*.' He raised his chin slightly as he said it. 'You know what that means don't you?' A slow reflective smile spread across his handsome hooked features, cigarette smoke steaming from his nostrils; it was a smile of recognition for his consideration of my lack of Arabic. 'And then she started crying.' He shrugged his shoulders, stubbed out the cigarette in a gesture of mild distaste. 'It's no good,' he sighed. And one felt the weight of those words hanging over the girl like a death sentence. 'She lives in Maadi and she hasn't got a telephone.'

Sex played an overt part in Rahman's life. He was a South African of Indonesian and Irish pedigree. Tiring of a comfortable life running his own interior decorating business in a middle-class coloured suburb of Durban he decided to go on the Hajj. He decided he had neglected his soul too long. 'You see, basically I'm a religious person but I knew nothing about religion and I thought I ought to,' he told me. He had continued on from Mecca to Cairo to pursue his religious studies and took up with a *sheikh* at Al Azhar. His Arabic had made spectacular progress, whether through the efforts of the *sheikh* or his diverse range of contacts was a matter of debate.

Rahman was a paragon of conscientiousness. Though admitting to being 'naughty sometimes', he nevertheless kept a tight rein on his peccadilloes. His naughtiness never interfered with his prayers and he didn't drink. He would refuse politely but emphatically if offered alcohol. 'It would take me forty days to purge myself and as I pray each day it would be impossible,' he pronounced.

Amongst other tendencies was one to dress up. His taste in clothes was as flamboyant as his religious fervour. He appeared once in the foyer of the Golden in a dazzling white *galabeya* and red silk turban as if off to audition for Scheherazade. It was magnificent and slightly preposterous – as was everything about Rahman. One never knew whether he was taking the micky or whether this zany sense of humour masked an existential sense of the ridiculous.

There were always two or three messages waiting for him in his pigeonhole from a positive telephone directory of Ahmeds, Ibrahims and Zakis, a network of shady contacts who came but never stayed or else phoned from public telephones and never left a number. He read all the messages intently looking for the hidden clues as to which Zaki, Ibrahim or Ahmed it was. Occasionally a bewildered young waiter or bartender would wander in and say he had been sent for.

Rahman, as I have observed, certainly liked people but people sometimes betrayed his trust. Once he and a friend called Hassan went to the Blue Mosque near Bab Zuweila to pray. Rahman had with him a new imported sweater and a bag in which he had a radio. These he left, together with his coat, at the entrance to the mosque while he and Hassan went inside. Hassan had less to discuss with Allah and left early. When Rahman had finished he found the sweater, bag and coat had gone. The *bowab* said Hassan had taken them. Rahman had a terrible tussle with his conscience but finally went to the police. Now he only had a vague idea where Hassan lived, nevertheless he marshalled a posse of the law and went to confront him.

Hassan answered the door. 'What's all this about?' he enquired.

'This man says you have some things of his,' said the police inspector.

'What do you mean?' retorted Hassan outraged. 'I've never set eyes on him in my life.'

If you mentioned the incident Rahman went quiet. He has wrestled with his faith, so far unsuccessfully, to find the grace to forgive Hassan.

Chapter Three

Lappas was just down the road from Groppis on Sharia Kasr el-Nil. Less select and more Egyptian, Lappas wasn't really a summer place. It came into its own on crisp winter mornings, the breath rising on the still air, resurrected overcoats turned up against the cold. Then it was good to walk into the warmth and the clatter of plastic cups and savour the smell of croissants and the hiss of the Espresso machine belching steam as you took your coffee and newspaper into one of the pools of sunlight flooding in from the high windows.

In summer there was always the inner lounge. The inner lounge opened at ten thirty in the morning and was a great place in which to read newspapers. One morning, deep in my *Egyptian Gazette*, a voice startled me with: 'D'you mind?' in accents which oscillated between Stepney and Peckham Rye.

'No,' I said, and burrowed deeper into my newspaper.

After a second's pause. 'D'you come from London?'

'Yes,' I said, trying to hide my churlishness. It's not done in Cairo to be churlish.

'Thought you were. I'm just back.'

No doubt about it. His freaky frizzy hair, wispy moustache

and beard, pebble spectacles said it all. Two weeks away from washing dishes and lugging suitcases at the Kensington Palace Hotel had kindled a warm nostalgia in Maher for all things English and that, apparently, included me. 'Very nice people,' he volunteered. 'Got everythin' in London.'

London must have been like Shangri-La for Maher. He had tripped through a catechism of vices with a concupiscence that Flaubert or Baudelaire would have admired and had come through apparently unscathed. 'I just like to feel good,' he said. Hashish and liquor made him feel good; and so did girls. He loved girls. And girls apparently loved him. He had spent a large slice of his working time in London chasing chambermaids. They must have found him irresistible, for he had a kind of demonic fascination about him, an ugliness which was quite original. In appearance he was a sybaritic Pan, the high forehead, great myopic eyes, the slightly pug nose, the full, cruel lips and strong chin, the sense of wispiness given by the straggly facial hair and the lithe body. But the resemblance to the goat god did not end there. Maher was ageless. He was old at fifteen and would be young at forty five. Experience ran through him like water running through a drainpipe, neither checked nor balanced, registering nowhere.

Maher's stamping ground was half a dozen European capitals and the larger cities of the Middle East. He kept tabs on them by using the world's airways with the insouciance of a head of state. There were no plans, no schedules for Maher's peregrinations; they had the flavour of a highjack. Signals came in from time to time whence you could sketchily chart his movements. The odd post card helped pin him down further. But usually you had to wait for his return for the full story. He returned when he had run out of money, or with a girl, to the poky flat his mother ran in Falaki. It would therefore be incorrect to say that Maher was completely without ties. He was tied to his mother, who paid the bills, and in a strange way to Cairo. He had a trace of remembrance for the city; otherwise he was without remembrance or conscience. It was the secret of his charm, the way he lived so totally and unremittingly in the instant. But he needed the city, its ambience, the web of contacts and associations. He was happiest in the backstreet cafés behind Sayidda Zeinab or Sharia al-Qala'a, where he could rely on finding a table for cards and where he was accepted as if he had never been away.

Maher was in his element and he wanted me to share it. His hand went up to adjust his formidable spectacles and he leaned forward. 'You're my freend,' he said in a voice like gravel sliding from a dump truck. 'We're gonna have a good time. I'll show you Cairo.'

I didn't doubt it. But with him...? He was about as potent as a hallucinogenic drug and you had no way of knowing whether it was going to be a good or bad trip.

'OK,' I said finally.

'Let's meet this evening. Come and see my mother's play, she's an actress. Afterwards, maybe party.. drink.. girls..' and his eyes gleamed. So that evening we met at Lappas.

The play was a farce. Three brothers had each to produce a male heir to inherit their father's fortune. Their wives could not oblige so they had to look elsewhere with hilarious and time consuming consequences. It seemed slightly risqué given the straight laced attitudes of the Egyptian middle classes. But the rather thin audience laughed heartily and kept it up for three and a half hours on hard seats with only one break. The play finished just before midnight leaving one wondering how everyone was going to get home.

No such problem for me. Maher guarded me with the solicitude of an impresario with a new-found star. It was a small birthday party. The guests were actors and actresses in their late thirties and early forties. With the grilled chicken and the delicious accompaniments came bottles of whisky which by four in the morning had mellowed us for Um Khalsoum.

The effect of Um Khalsoum was electric. A large woman in a white dress rose from her seat, found a chiffon scarf to wrap round her and while the others sighed and swayed launched into a belly dance. Like an elephant getting up she slowly heaved and pivoted her ample breasts and tummy until she was into the dance. The music and the undulating hips reminded me of the gully-gully man of my childhood and the way the hooded cobra would sway to the tune of his flute. She danced to Um Khalsoum until the cocks began to crow, the spell was broken and we all went home.

We arranged to meet the following Thursday to see a friend, a police inspector. 'But first we have a little smoke. OK?' said Maher.

So we met as usual at Lappas. 'Where are we going?' I asked as he bundled me into a taxi.

'Sayyida Zeinab,' he said.

He told the cabbie to stop in one of the streets that run

down to Kasr el-Aini, paid, hauled me across the road and disappeared inside a café. There were shouts. A waiter appeared and went behind a counter, followed seconds later by Maher, seething. 'He's a thief that man, E£3… for this,' he growled, withdrawing a small pellet from his anorak. 'Each week it goes up. Never mind. Quick.' He whisked me across the road to a junk yard and into a shed where seats were arranged around low tables. Travel posters of palm fringed beaches lined the walls. It might have been a travel agency or a dentist's waiting room.

Pipes were brought out and laid on the tables. A large elderly Nubian came in and busied himself with the pipes. Maher talked to him and then turned to me. 'This is Abdul.' Then, looking at Abdul, 'Abdul's the other way. How do you say when men like other men? Queer? Abdul's queer.' Abdul modestly continued cleaning the pipes. Maher laughed. 'Abdul hopes you come and see him again.'

A rack of six clay pipe heads was laid out and Abdul carefully placed a blob of hashish on each. We smoked for twenty minutes in silence. Then Maher said it was time to go.

We took another taxi and after what seemed an interminable journey turned off a long, congested thoroughfare into the backstreets. The taxi could go so far and then we had to walk through unpaved lanes to a crude brick apartment block no different from thousands built in Cairo as part of Nasser's housing redevelopment programmes. We climbed five flights of stairs to the top floor.

It was a small flat and a large family occupied it. A poky vestibule served as a living and reception room, there was a dining room inside and cubby-holes for bedrooms led off the central area.

'Do you want to marry Gold Meir?' I had hardly set foot inside the door.

'No, not my type.'

'I'd like to eat her,' said Grandma, with a cackle. 'What about one of the girls?'

'Now that's different ....' There were two girls, about seventeen and nineteen. The elder spoke excellent English and wanted to practise it but her father had other ideas. Walim, Maher's police inspector friend, was seated on the couch in the vestibule, his pale blue *galabeya* tucked up under him hiding the discreet bulge of a paunch. 'Come and sit here, Meester Alan, and Maher, you explain.'

Walim searched me with shrewd, heart-troubled eyes. After listening to an account of my coming to Egypt and happy that I wasn't up to anything sinister, he said: 'Do you know Mr. Fitzpatrick?'

'Who's Mr. Fitzpatrick?'

'Mr. Fitzpatrick of Scotland Yard. I worked with him during the War. Mr. Fitzpatrick was very thorough,' he paused, and then. 'Tell me, what do the English think about Egyptians?'

I told him the English didn't know much about Egyptians. 'There were the old Colonial administrators and the British soldiers who were here during the War. Most of them hadn't asked to come and they weren't exactly made welcome. Then there were the boat passengers passing through Suez. They met spivs and they think all Egyptians are spivs. It's absurd: as if an Egyptian went to Piccadilly Circus, had his wallet stolen and thought all the British were thieves. But there we are.'

He hung intently on my words, his koala bear eyes registering nothing.

'Is there a black market in England?' he asked.

'No,' I replied. He couldn't grasp the notion of going into a shop and buying what one wanted.

'But there must be some things you can't get.'

'No, nothing, except hashish. There's a black market in hashish.'

Maher laughed and delved into his sock for the remainder of the pellet. It wasn't a melodramatic precaution because the possession of drugs can earn you a stiff prison sentence. It was a question of contacts and observing the proprieties. There was nothing wrong it seemed in having a joint with a police inspector in the privacy of his home.

****

It was through Maher that I met the El Gamals. Always concerned for my welfare he had been 'shocked' at how much I was paying at the hotel.

'Too much,' he said. 'If you stay with a family you pay E£10 a month, no more.'

'Where's the family?' I asked, 'and in any case I'm very happy in the hotel. It's central. And the price is very reasonable for what I'm getting.'

'I have an uncle who takes lodgers. You must see him. He lives in Shobra – you know, where Walim lives.'

So we arranged another cloak-and-dagger meeting in Lappas. When we arrived at his uncle's house, Mohammed el-Gamal and his family were lined up to meet us: Atar, the only son, Buzeina and Malak, the two girls and Mrs. el-Gamal who had prepared rabbit heart's soup, *kishk*, cold roast rabbit, *molokhaya* and *ful* with mulberries for desert by way of a casual lunch. The table was laid with the remnants of the King Fouad silver dinner service. The King Fouad silver dinner service was only brought out, Am Mohammed (as Mr. el-Gamal was more familiarly known) assured us, on state occasions. At other times it was locked away in the bottom of the wardrobe in his bedroom.

The history of the King Fouad silver dinner service caused Am Mohammed much pain to tell. It had been presented to his father, a Port Said school teacher, by King Fouad long ago and had remained intact until the party he had unadvisedly thrown to celebrate the birth of his only son and heir. That was eighteen years ago and the memory still rankled. On that day the King Fouad silver dinner service was brought out and displayed in its pristine splendour for the last time. For the guests, as well as eating him out of house and home, departed with forks and spoons, leaving Am Mohammed to clear away the remains of the dinner service with the leftovers.

Am Mohammed prided himself on his English. He laid it out

as it were to see what I thought of it, sang Humpty Dumpty and Twinkle, Twinkle Little Star (he gave up serious English at five, he said) and a lewd army song about a fanciable bint walking down a Cairo street, which seemed to owe more to Port Said affiliations than to the nursery. He kept up a running commentary meanwhile with his family in Arabic. They looked at me with wide-eyed incredulity at the childishness of the English.

'Atar speaks French,' said Am Mohammed, suddenly conscious of the fact that he was hogging the conversation. 'You speak French? You speak to Atar in French.'

'Really?' I said, turning to Ali. 'Vous parlez français?'

Atar smiled amiably, revealing grimy teeth. 'Oui, je barle français.'

'Ou étudiez-vous?'

The smile didn't waver. 'Dré beu,' he said. 'Je barle français dré beu.'

The solemn processions I was to witness, of Atar escorting the tutor into the guest room (my room, the only room respectable enough) for French and other instruction, were to prove a charade.

A large portrait of Nasser hung in the dining room gathering dust. The family ancestors in the guest room were treated with more respect. The guest room was dominated by a picture of Am Mohammed's father, the Port Said school teacher, rimmed in black with curriculum vitae and date of death. There was Am

Mohammed at military academy, his military associations were shrouded in mystery and not often talked about, and pictures of the family. He showed them all with pride.

The family was scattered. One sister, Maher's mother, was Malak el-Gamal, the well known comedienne; another had married a Saudi Arabian minister. The men had done less brilliantly: a school teacher, an engineer and Am Mohammed, master glass blower first class.

Am Mohammed had moved with his young wife Fatheya to Shobra from Port Said about twenty years ago. Shobra then still retained a little of its pre-war élan when Rod el-Farag and Sharia Shobra were fashionable. Time and the relentless population explosion put paid to its breezy suburban spaciousness and it has acquired the dubious distinction of being home to over two million souls, or a quarter of Cairo's burgeoning population.

As Shobra's population has risen, so its social standing has declined. It is now more truly representative of Cairo than any other district and the dreams and aspirations of its middle class and lower middle class inhabitants set the pattern of Egyptian urban life – and to a degree the Egypt of the future. In Shobra, Egypt tries to come to terms with modernity against insuperable odds. Little renovation has taken place for decades and the pressure on essential services: water, electricity, sewage and transport grow daily greater. Shobra's students diligently read up the theory but have little opportunity of putting it into practice.

Nearly half of Shobra's inhabitants are Copts, which means Shobra accounts for one fifth of Egypt's Coptic population. And their industriousness and regard for education set the tone. The gleaming pharmacies (in Cairo the pharmacies are invariably spotless even in the dingiest slum), the shambolic down-at-heel department stores and the ephemeral street trade hardly measure up to White Plains or Wimbledon but disguise an interesting sophistication.

In Midan Shobra, opposite the railway station, you might find the odd copy of *Le Progrès*, the French language newspaper, but at the intersection of Sharia Kholosi and Rod el-Farag, a mile and a half up Sharia Shobra, it is the Arabic newspapers or nothing. They read them in the bright tiled parlours, the radios blaring in competition with the street, the jangle of carts, the honking of traffic and the clang of the trams, where everything conspires against concentration. They even read them on the buses. They read them and inwardly digest them, turgid columns of ministerial happenings; not only inwardly digest them but they read between the lines. And, in a sense, their judgement is surer for that.

It was into this Shobra that Am Mohammed had gently come down in the world, to the ground floor flat of a crumbling four floor apartment block in a small side street behind Sharia Kholosi, a stone's throw from the open air cinema. There, on most mornings, you would find him in his dressing gown leaning on the balcony, a Cleopatra cigarette in hand, watching the world go by. It didn't seem to bother him that he and Shobra had fallen on hard times. Nor did it bother his more successful brothers and sisters, who found nothing incongruous turning up in their Mercedes at the festivals. Am Mohammed was head of the family and therefore it was to Shobra that they came – although Am Mohammed did not actively encourage these demonstrations of familial solidarity as he was left to foot the bill.

I met Maher in Lappas the next day. He urged me to move out to Shobra.

'Where would I sleep?' I asked.

'You go in the room where we were first.'

'With the family ancestors?'

'Yes.'

I mulled it over and thought: 'What the hell. Family ancestors or no, it's worth a try.'

'How much should I pay?'

'I don't know. You must arrange that with Am Mohammed, but less than the hotel.'

*****

I moved in with Am Mohammed on a day of *khamaseen*. Such displays of affection! There was no hiding anything from these people; they demanded total spontaneity.

And they wasted no time. My bags were produced and unpacked. Nothing was spared the minutest inspection. They knew how many pairs of underpants, pyjamas and socks I had, and shirts, even the number of batteries to my cassette recorder. The camera was inventoried together with books and pads. And when it was done and everything stacked away in places they knew and I didn't Am Mohammed said: 'Don't worry, there are no robbers here.'

It had been a long eventful day so I decided to turn in early. The heat made sleep difficult; the activity in the dining room made it impossible. Glass partitions in the doors meant the rooms were never really dark and there were people up all night. They took it in turns, the five of them, to sleep in the one free bedroom.

That first night I must have dozed off at about four o'clock, in a nightmare hum of low voices, to wake at seven to a dazzling new day and the cries of the street vendors. The air was alive with birdsong and cocks crowing.

'Sleep well?' Am Mohammed enquired, as I moved timidly towards the washbasin.

'Yes, thank you.'

'Have you razor blades?' he asked, looking up from his newspaper.

'Yes,' I said. I had taken the precaution to stock up with razor blades and tea bags before leaving England. Out they came and were received with a nod and a cursory 'Thank you.' After a further pause Am Mohammed looked up with a quizzical, preoccupied expression, much as one imagines a surgeon might ask for a scalpel in the middle of an intricate operation. 'And cigarettes?' I produced a couple of packets of Benson & Hedges. He seemed disappointed. 'Haven't you got big box?'

I felt mean. 'No, sorry, they are all I've got.'

'Never mind.' He said graciously. 'Have you whisky? I'll pay for it.'

The question was redundant. He already had a complete rundown of my effects and their prospective value. Perhaps he thought I had whisky somewhere else or could put my hands on some. A bottle of Scotch in the Duty Free shop in Cairo Airport would cost around £2 sterling and he could get twice that or possibly more for a bottle on the black market. All was grist to Am Mohammed's mill.

Then he took me into the back yard where we were almost run down by a couple of large, sloppy guard dogs. Am Mohammed limped archly in pursuit, waved his stick, kicked and cursed them. They retreated with yelps. Am Mohammed mopped his brow and started off again.

In the back yard he kept chickens, rabbits and pigeons which lived in apparent harmony with the dogs. We chose an egg for breakfast and, while I dressed, Am Mohammed, who was the supervisor of breakfasts, cooked it, laid out bread, *ful medammis*, olives and white cheese and warmed the bowl of water for my shave. The breakfast fare never varied.

No sooner had I left my room than the girls began turning it upside down. After the *khamaseen* all the rooms were scrubbed. The girls worked quickly, Malak, the younger pulling faces. Atar was not in evidence; he rarely was, and when at home, he sat.

The girls let Atar's regal habits wash over them; his mother was less complaisant. Am Mohammed's wife, Fatheya, was a rotund little woman with a shrewd foxy face and a huge girth which made her waddle. It was difficult to communicate with her, for it would never have occurred to her to engender understanding by any other means than through the language Allah had given her, or to make any concession to the fact that the other party, less gifted than she, might be struggling to keep up. If she had anything to say she would gabble happily; then, seeing it made no impact, collapse with an 'Oh' and a kindly wrinkle-nosed smile. Fatheya was an invaluable bench mark against which to measure my progress in Arabic.

Fatheya was not all peaches and cream. In fact she had a vile temper – one of the vilest it was possible to imagine. Periodically she was prone to headaches, the result of a diabetic condition. She was also a good barometer of the weather. She spent a lot of time shouting at Atar when he was at home. It was a good way of knowing Atar was at home. She and Am Mohammed also had rows occasionally. Am Mohammed had never really overcome a childhood habit of raiding the kitty for money for his cigarettes. Fatheya was thus sometimes left with 5 piastres with which to feed the family, and had the demeaning task of asking me or someone else to lend her money.

I had tried a number of times to broach the subject of how much I should pay for my lodging. Each time Am Mohammed dismissed the request with an airy wave of the hand and a 'Take it easy, take it easy. Plenty of time.' Then one day he was unmasked.

He had been visiting relatives and returned visibly cast down. It must have been an important meeting because he was wearing his dark suit and non-matching waistcoat, an apparel which became him but wasn't to his liking. He wore it on such occasions as it was necessary to give the impression of a sober, upright citizen of education and means. It went with a pair of smoked glasses and a walking stick and was so impressive that he could have passed muster as a retired general or a senior member of the People's Assembly.

However, there was no pretence at any such illustrious disguise in the Am Mohammed sprawled out in front of me in an easy chair, splayed legs exposing one prominently undone fly. He took a 20 piastre note from his pocket and laughed ruefully.

'I ask my sister for money and look what she gives me. I wanted two, three, ten pounds.' He waved the grimy note with an air of impotence. 'What can I do with this?' He sighed and leaned on his walking stick. 'In hospital they came with fruits and flowers. Some flowers from Mrs. Wonderful in Midan Soliman Pasha cost E£5.' He spread his hands. 'Can't eat flowers. I need money.'

After his obscure flirtation with the army, Am Mohammed had been trained as a glass blower. It was a good job, well paid and secure. Even when he was bringing up his family there had been plenty of money, for he had supplemented the E£46 a month he earned as a glass blower by running an agency for patent medicines. This contributed, on average, another E£20 a month, bringing his total earnings to around E£70 a month, a very respectable wage.

Then three years ago he had fallen and ricked his back. He was in bed for six months, virtually unable to move. Although he could walk now with a brace, his doctor forbade him to work. His company had put him on half pay meanwhile, but because of his lack of mobility he had lost the patent medicine business. Overnight his income shrivelled from E£70 to E£23 a month. It looked as if Am Mohammed was about to join the Cairo masses on the breadline, for he still had heavy commitments. He didn't admittedly have much rent to pay but his children had to be educated. Their free state schooling had to be supplemented by private tuition and that put him back E£18 a month.

He had soldiered on until such time as he had been forced to take lodgers. Ibrahim, who had the room next to mine, was a pleasant but embittered Palestinian from the Gaza Strip. He couldn't afford to pay much, said Am Mohammed. His father had been killed when he was a small child. He was now the breadwinner of the family and obliged to work in his summer vacations in the Strip to pay his way. He took the room without board and hardly ever ate, it seemed. Fatheya gave him an occasional meal.

'What would you like me to pay?' I asked. Maher and others had said a room in Shobra with board should be E£10 a month, although for a European this seemed unrealistic.

Am Mohammed left it entirely to me, suggesting what I had paid in the hotel as a guideline. 'You know,' he added, 'if I was fit, must not take one piastre from you. You know you are one of the family. You must tell us what you want to eat each day. Elen must say: 'I want chicken, I want rabbit'.'

So it was decided that I should pay E£5 a week for my full board. The matter settled, Am Mohammed found another cigarette.

'It is difficult for Fatheya,' he continued. 'Sometimes I am depressed, nothing to do. I can't sleep. I get up early. I feed the chickens and the rabbits. I make the breakfast and smoke a cigarette and wait for the newspaper. I can't go out. With my back I can't go on buses. And taxis? No money. I smoke too much, I know, but what can I do?' Am Mohammed's life appeared to revolve around making the breakfast and doing the crossword puzzle.

'Am Mohammed, you have problems,' I declared a trifle earnestly.

Am Mohammed went soft and concentrated. He always went soft and concentrated when asked to consider things he did not fully understand.

'But, Elen,' he said, 'everyone has problems.'

After this we were friends. He showed me a few of his mementos, the box in which a bottle of whisky had arrived from a counterpart in England in 1937, his shaving brush which, he claimed, had been with him for forty years.

He was forever telling jokes. He was happiest telling jokes. 'Do you know what is *baksheesh*?' That was one of his favourites. He would be in his white *galabeya*, perched in his favourite armchair. 'Say a man wants money but must not steal it,' he chuckled, raising himself on his elbows and spreading his hands. 'He comes up to you and says, 'May I show you the pyramids?' 'No.' Am Mohammed draws on his cigarette. 'Then, may I be of service to you? Do you want to see the tombs of Qait Bey or do you want to go on the Nile, and can I do all these things for you?' He was well into his stride, his crinkled apple cheeks glowing, his eyes twinkling, gurgling with glee for all the world as if he had stepped out of one of the Cow & Gate baby food advertisements that dotted Cairo.

He gave me advice about the city, a welter of information about bus services. He said that if I wanted to visit the City of the Dead I must let him know as he had a friend who ran a coffee shop near one of the big tombs. 'Sells skeletons,' he intimated darkly. 'If caught, in prison.' He exhorted me to go to the Islamic Museum on Port Said Street and the Kutubkhana beneath to view the Korans and other priceless Islamic texts. This literate Am Mohammed was a far cry from the Am Mohammed who struggled with the *Al Ahram* crossword.

And there was another, who emerged when the children were around the dining room table in the evenings with their homework that expanded eloquently on his life and loves. The girls sat through his picaresque accounts of life and elementary physics without comment. Out would come the atlas, innocent of all reference to Israel, to illustrate some lurid tale of adventure in Ethiopia or Yemen. No one knew why or how he had come to be there or the origins of his other forays in the Middle East.

It was inevitable that at some time we should touch on the Arab-Israeli dispute. My view having satisfied him, the matter was dropped. But not before he had said he wasn't against Jews. 'There is plenty for everyone but they took our land. Not right,' he said, and shook his head. 'I married *yehudi* woman ... Yes, long time ago, before Fatheya. She left in 1948. I told her: 'must stay.' Her family said: 'must go.' So she went. She was very sad, I was very sad,' he sighed.

There was a constant stream of visitors, neighbours making or taking telephone calls, friends of the family and others. Tradesmen came and invariably left empty handed. The *makwagi* (the ironing man) was a small stumpy man with thin bristly hair and blue Coptic crosses tattooed on his forearms. There was always a slanging match when the *makwagi* called and he usually retreated, like the guard dogs, in a hail of curses and imprecations. He was much abused and loved. Once, after one of these performances Am Mohammed turned to me with a chuckle and said: 'He is very good man, very old friend since twenty years. Very honest.'

Am Mohammed was always roaring at the girls, who paid as much attention to him as Atar did to his mother. And Am Mohammed roared at their girl friends, especially Nadia, who was always calling round. Nadia had Circassian blood for she had grey eyes, frizzy brown hair and a pale skin, and a deep husky voice which Am Mohammed said came from too much talking. One day she came in far from ebullient. It was a day or two after her birthday. She had been cock-a-hoop then because her grandmother had given her a pound with which she had bought a voluminous handbag made of mock crocodile, so big that when she searched inside it she almost disappeared. The handbag was with her and she was dressed for the handbag in her best lime green dress and ill-fitting high-heeled shoes; which made her tears and agitation all the more incongruous. She sat opposite Am Mohammed who had adopted the composure of a compassionate Buddha as he wrote slowly, looking at his handiwork over the top of his spectacles. Nadia, meanwhile, dabbed her eyes with a black lace handkerchief. Then, the note she had come for written, she fled in a flood of tears.

'What on earth was all that about?' I asked.

Am Mohammed laughed. 'Her father will beat her. So I write a letter to her father to say 'Don't beat Nadia. Nadia is good girl today. She is shopping with Buzeina.'

'Why is her father going to beat her?'

'Oh, Nadia is *magnoon*, crazy. Must beat her, otherwise Nadia get too big.'

No one had ever beaten Atar as far as one could tell. Atar properly thought, as do most firstborn sons in a Moslem family, that the home was run for him. He took to shouting at me, not out of any disrespect, but because that was the way he normally behaved. It was he who spearheaded the family's war of attrition on my possessions. After a few cursory enquiries as to how it worked, he requisitioned my tape recorder and, before long, tapes were being lent out amongst friends in exchange for other tapes of *frangi* (Western) pop music. He was very fond of Englebert Humperdink and Tom Jones and was at a loss to understand how others didn't share his enthusiasm, especially at four in the morning. He liked 'Oh Mammy' and 'Shalala oh oh' which he intoned in a tuneless croak, his head swaying orientally as he punctuated the 'oh oh ohs' with glottal stops. He liked 'Shalala' because it was devoid of content, a little refrain that ran easily off an Arab tongue. With 'Je t'aime', Serge Ginsberg and Jane Birkin's hymn to their mutual passion, however, it was very much the content that interested him. Atar tackled 'Je t'aime' with the cold determination of a code breaker confronted by an intransigent code. Each morning the honeyed opening bars would be a prelude to another session. He went over each note lovingly, stopping at the difficult bits for a re-run until he was near word-perfect.

However, he didn't have the slightest idea what it all meant. He knew the song was naughty; there was a lot of heavy breathing and the record had been banned. So he came to me with his gormless smile, lips curled at the corners, thick, black curly hair slicked down at the side, and mumbled, 'what's this mean?'

He handled the tape recorder dextrously. The grunts and sighs came intermingled with a shortened glossary of *Gray's Anatomy* in French. It was neither titillating nor appetizing but I gave him a faithful rendering in Arabic. Slowly his expression of thoughtless amiability turned sour; he couldn't see what all the fuss was about. As for me, I was a disappointment.

With the girls it was different, especially with the elder, Buzeina. She was plump and unbelievably good natured. It had to be something very aggravating indeed to upset Buzeina and then she went quiet and sad. It wasn't dullness but a sunny, subtle nature. She was always getting into trouble for her homework, and once Am Mohammed forbade her to go out for a week which provoked a rare outburst of temper. But for a girl, avowedly with little brain, she had a way of drawing you up sharp. An example of this was during the *khamaseen* when Atar, in a rare moment of introspection, complained that he was having difficulty getting himself together. 'I don't want to use my mind,' he wailed. 'Then why did Allah give it to you?' quipped Buzeina.

In accordance with Am Mohammed's admonitions I accompanied him to the police station to register. Shobra Police Station was like most police stations, bare and seedy, although morale was high that day as the Cairo police force had shed its shabby blue winter serge for smart white summer kit. Shoulders were straightened, paunches drawn in.

Am Mohammed and I were shown up to a small room at the

end of the corridor on the first floor. The room was crowded with people seated on the floor in a semblance of a queue which stretched out into the corridor. Three rickety tables, a filing cabinet, an upended bicycle and a lot of open files stood or lay around a kindly, elf-faced man in *galabeya* and woollen cap who ushered me to a seat and asked over steel-rimmed spectacles where I was staying and with whom. Solid as the Bank of England, Am Mohammed stepped forward. He was wearing his dark suit. No further questions were necessary.

We were on the point of leaving when a man sitting at one of the other desks, asked: 'You smoke *shisha?*' A man sitting at another table leaned over. 'Hubbly-bubbly – at Walim's.'

'Oh, yes,' I said. 'Walim's.' And they smiled and winked.

The family felt it incumbent upon me as a Christian to visit the shrine of St Theresa in Shobra. They were a little disappointed I had not paid my respects the moment I had arrived. Malak and Buzeina would not let it rest. Each day they asked me if I had been and then one day they took the matter into their own hands and marched me there.

St. Theresa in Shobra is credited with many miracles and the plaques of the grateful and the healed cover the walls of the small antechamber above the tomb. The church itself is an oasis of order and cleanliness in the outer reaches of Sharia Shobra close by the police station.

We joined a file of pilgrims and stood respectfully in front of the tomb, the girls deep in contemplation. Then, when they had kissed the tomb, Malak said: 'We'll see the priest now to have you blessed.' They took me upstairs, pinioned between them, and we found the priest who blessed me to their satisfaction. Then they said we could go home.

*****

It was nearing the festival of *sham el-nessim*. 'You will be coming with us, won't you?' enquired Buzeina. 'We take a picnic to the gardens in Shobra el-Kheima by the Nile.' The invitation was irresistible.

By tradition, *sham el-nessim* falls on the Monday after the Coptic Easter. This is for convenience. *Sham el-nessim* is really a pagan festival with its roots in deepest antiquity. It is said to celebrate the discovery by Isis of her husband Osiris's remains and resurrection after their cruel dismemberment at the hands of his jealous brother, Seth. Modern Egyptians, dim on their mythology, celebrate in less exalted fashion with picnics and piastre rides on the Nile. They welcome the first of the Spring fruits, especially the apricots, eat a pickled herring called *fesikh* and in, their prodigal enjoyment, pay their respects to any deity that happens to be at home.

Sham el-nessim means literally 'The sniffing of the air'. At *sham el-nessim* Cairo bus drivers exchange bouquets, stopping their buses in midstream to salute a friend and to select roses and carnations from dashboards carpeted with flowers. The accident rate doubles, a kind of spring madness grips the city. From early morning, as if driven by some sixth sense, Cairenes make for the green spaces. They stream down to the Nile, they occupy the traffic islands, storm Gezira Island and spill over into Giza, into the zoo, into the Botanical Gardens where the fire eaters, jugglers and the musicians sweat through their acts, and the pagan prolific crowds frolic under the tall, grave palms the long day through and deep into the evening. They stay until the park keepers drive them out and start the massive task of clearing up the litter from the bare, devastated earth. The rape of the green places for the fecundation of the mind: that is *sham el-nessim*.

We assembled in the flat in the morning with hampers and baskets, and Atar was sent to find a taxi. The taxi could not hold all of us so the children went by bus. I travelled in the taxi and when we arrived at Shobra el-Kheima Am Mohammed asked, 'Elen got money?' Alan had money.

The crowd was already stupendous, camped on the ground and under trees. We picked our way to a café under a banyan tree. An enterprising crone had set up shop there by the side of the Nile, stretching a tarpaulin between the trunks of the trees to establish her patch. There she sat amongst her pots and pans, minding a fire and her kerosene stove, brewing tea for her customers, whom she enlisted to keep out the unwanted riff-raff. She didn't have to move. The cups were in a small cupboard nailed to the tree above her head and there were ladles for the farthest pans. She presided over a circle of privilege and reason in the prevailing anarchy.

For outside it was quite different. On the right, encased in the trailing banyan trees, the *feluccas* tacked, taking people for ten minute rides on the Nile. On the left, an infernal magic theatre threatened the mind's capacity to absorb, and carried it kicking and screaming into a primitive dance of atoms.

The seething pressure of colour grew in intensity as noon approached, the kaleidoscope of humanity out in the sun, in the bright, bright sun, so bright now that the eye could no longer take in the contrast of light and dark but saw spots and stars in jiggering play, so bright that as the wind raised the dust it turned to star dust, which in turn set the carousels dancing in the light haze, and the shadows dancing in the rubbly stones.

Three young girls in identical day-glow dresses, blue and purple to match the spots in the eyes, rode the carousel. Another in grubby green, her hair matted, spread her legs as the horses turned and flaunted her slit as her skirts lifted. *Baladi* women, their chiselled Durer features set off by blue shawls, flipped plump, veined breasts from flowing robes for their suckling infants. A magnificent loose-limbed 'alley cat' prowled amongst the crowds. She stood apart with henna bleached hair and broad, silver-toothed smile and as she moved about in her tatty white dress, you knew how the *ghawazi*, the gypsy dancing girls, amassed fortunes and ruined kings with their right subtle mix of lasciviousness and refinement. The sensuality was tantalizing...

On the *felucca* a small girl with enormous eyes pressured me to dance. '*Sahen dahen bu*' she mimed, contorting her comic face and rosebud mouth. The packed boat took up the refrain of the old folk song that had been revamped into a pop song. '*Sahen dahen bu. Edli wadla bu*' they chanted as she began to dance, moving her hips and her hands with an eroticism that left nothing to the imagination and had one wondering where the treacly, airless imagery of Um Khalsoum, that other Egypt of static emotion, belonged in this... '*Ein il-wad be'eia...Sahen dahen bu*' they chanted holding the beat as the boat tacked and listed dangerously.

We hit the bank with a thud and they spilled out taking the refrain with them into the crowds. It spread like wildfire until the whole fair was moving to *sahen dahen bu*. It encompassed the

khawal, the male impersonators of the *ghawazi*, as they ground their hips and clicked their steel castanets for attention; it encompassed the *sa'eedi* groups as they danced their fluty dances, the clowns loping above the crowds, the *araguz* (the Punch and Judy show), the colony of *kosheri* stalls and the peddlers with their candy floss and maroon balloons.
Then the radios took up the refrain. '*Sahen dahen bu*' they shrieked in splintered pain. But the mind was freaking slowly, planing with the feluccas as they arched like winging swans over the glittering waters, spinning with the whirligig as the world blurred to the stillness of dangling legs, to the stillness of girls' dresses, still at the centre, straining with the children on the swings as they tried, tried to remain there, motionless, upside down...

It was just then that Am Mohammed, who was unaffected by *sahen dahen bu*, the light and the din, settled his walking stick by him and tucked in his *galabeya* ready to play *tawlah* (backgammon), chasing away the kids as he did so. And that was how one died half an hour later not forty yards from us, being chased away to fall into one of the locks of the Ismailia Canal. We only heard about it through rumour, slowly substantiated in the din of the fair. Fatheya said afterwards it was a tragedy. He was only fourteen.

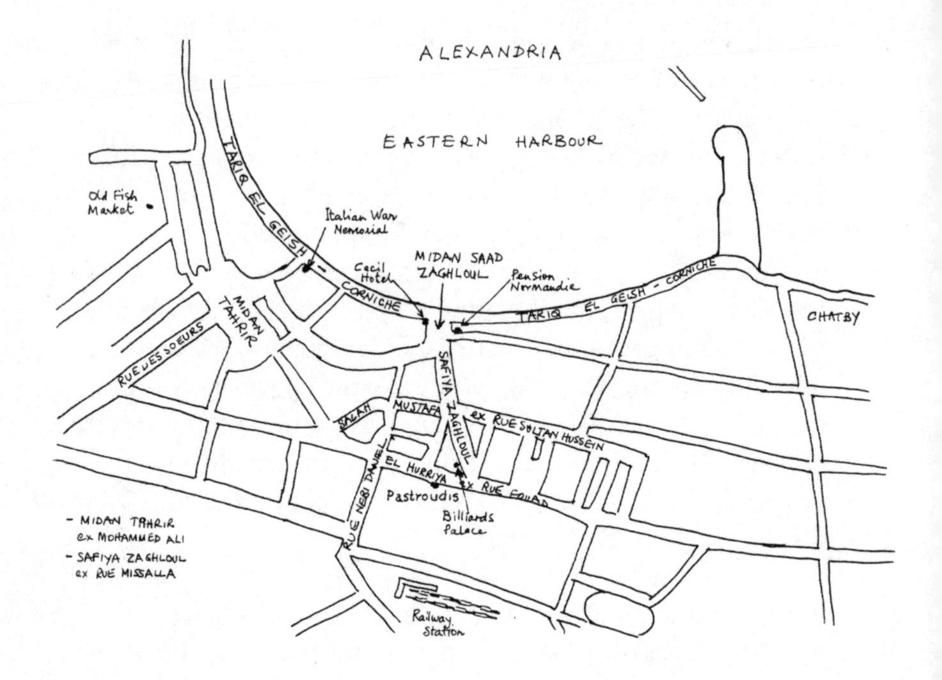
ALEXANDRIA
EASTERN HARBOUR
Old Fish Market
TARIQ EL GEISH – CORNICHE
Italian War Memorial
Cecil Hotel
MIDAN SAAD ZAGHLOUL
Pension Normandie
TARIQ EL GEISH – CORNICHE
CHATBY
MIDAN TAHRIR
RUE DES SOEURS
SAFIYA ZAGHLOUL
SALAH MUSTAFA
ex RUE SULTAN HUSSEIN
RUE NEBI DANIEL
EL HURRIYA
ex RUE FOUAD
Pastroudis
Billiards Palace
Railway Station
– MIDAN TAHRIR ex MOHAMMED ALI
– SAFIYA ZAGHLOUL ex RUE MISSALLA

ALEXANDRIA ENVIRONS
Maamoura
Aboukir
Montaza
Eastern Harbour
Stanley Bay
Sidi Gaber
Mahmoudia Canal
ALEXANDRIA
Western Harbour
Agami
Mex
Fish Restaurant
Lake Mareotis

Chapter Four

ALEXANDRIA

A little over a month after arriving in Egypt I made my first trip to Alexandria, the city of western myth invented largely by the fertile and wonderfully erudite imagination of the Greek poet Constantin Cavafy who inspired E.M. Forster and a literary renaissance with ties to the Bloomsbury Set in London. E.M. Forster went on to publish his groundbreaking *Alexandria: A History and a Guide* which combined contemporary scholarship of a high order with his personal reflections on the lost city of antiquity to create a new genre of travel guide. Forster's Alexandria was deeply infused by his own sexual awakening in an affair with a young tram conductor who was to be the great love of his life. A generation later Lawrence Durrell in his masterpiece, *The Alexandria Quartet*, took the idea of portraying the city through the Alexandrian women he had loved, creating an emotional landscape against which to explore relationships and the human condition.

There is of course another, more prosaic Alexandria, the modern city that underwent a commercial renaissance in the first half of the nineteenth century with the building of the Mahmoudia Canal which reopened the Rosetta branch of the Nile to maritime navigation and the city to its hinterland, enabling the development of the modern port. The country's second city is now the inspiration for a different kind of myth making in which modern Egyptians are rediscovering a taste for hedonism.

March

You don't possess Alexandria. It is too mercenary to love; obscene in its giving and its withholding. Yet it is easy to see why Alexandrians are so attached to their city: the softness of the climate, the light, its location. But it is above all to do with the almost unbearable sweetness felt when the city is its most venal. It is this sweetness, most times cloying, occasionally pristine, that distinguishes Alex.

****

Behind the bus shelter across from the Cecil Hotel I almost step into a pool of swimming excrement and involuntarily wretch – God, you would have thought they could have found somewhere else – only for the stench to be cleansed within moments by the breeze off the sea.

The Corniche sweeps away beyond the breakwater where the surf rolls on metallic sands. In the grey twilight the shadow of a street lamp dances like a marionette in the wind; ruffled puddles; the melancholy of winter in a seaside town.

On Casino Chatby pier couples cluster by the plate glass windows saying nothing above the roar of the sea.

In Alex there are these constant lapses into oblivion.

****

I have come to Alexandria at Amin's invitation. He is an Alexandrian, proud of it and anxious to reveal to me the beauties of his city. It is my first time back since my sensational initiation to Egypt with Linda in 1965.

On Thursday we took the road to Agami past orchards of fig trees half buried in drifting snow-white sand. The sea was a pellucid bottle green, the beach deserted save for the *bedu* girls collecting seaweed or fluffy balls of algae shaped thus by the wind. We swam and as we dried ourselves afterwards we drank the bottle of wine I had buried in the sand.

That night I slept with the sound of the sea in my ears and the tingle of the sun and the surf on my skin. It was March 1. And the next day the weather crucified my impertinence in supposing it was Spring. Softened by the sun there was no resistance in me to the wind. My teeth chattered uncontrollably.

It was bitterly cold again on Friday with the raw damp of the sea. The wind strengthened during the night until the whole city rattled with the clatter of dustbins and loose shutters. I woke at five, at the height of the storm, and heard faintly above the roar of the gale the hoarse call of the *muezzin* rising and falling, like a great ship ploughing through rough seas, the wind whimpering in the pauses before the rhythm of the prayer caught on again.

****

We visited an uncle of Amin's who lived in the family villa in Maamoura. A truly Tolstoyan character, visibly decaying, who complained as we entered that no one had been to see him for two months and he had been ill. A kerosene stove lay abandoned in the corner amongst a stack of newspapers. He apologized for the mess and said he would have changed and cleared up if he had known he was having visitors. Amin was sad to see the villa so.

A neighbour called and as if ashamed of the squalor invited us up to his apartment to see how it might be. His sitting room was furnished in imitation Louis Farouk. Two fine ormolu clocks stood on a side table and a sideboard. In the backs of the richly brocaded chairs frock-coated youths proffered roses. On the walls a painting of trees in glowing autumnal colours embowered a rushing mountain stream and in another a chalet lay buried in an Alpine winter. The neighbour shuffled over to a low cabinet, lifted a canopy of gold velour to reveal a stereo. 'Do you like Verdi?' he enquired.

To the strains of Aida we sipped tea seated on gilt thrones while our host brooded. Then he played Um Khalsoum and there seemed a logical connection between the two, Verdi and Um Kalsoum: the orchestra of a thousand and one strings. But Um Khalsoum had something more, the incomparable alluvial heaviness of the Nile, heavy as the spreading thighs of young mothers scoffing ice cream in Groppis, heavy and soft with the incomparable softness of epicene young men fingering prayer beads in ministerial antechambers.

And we sat listening to this strange odyssey through the landscape of the heart, such was the effect of this drowsy alluvial heaviness, a heaviness that stilled wind and embalmed the least breeze, the mighty storms of passion to the most intimate whisper, distilled them into crystal fruits for the delectation of poets and song writers, the orchestra of a thousand and one strings and Um Khalsoum.

Our host was the head of the criminology department of Alexandria University. The homicide rate in Egypt was neither high nor low. It was about average; that was to say about the same as the UK Most homicides took place in the country, the result of land disputes or vendettas which in Upper Egypt ran in families for generations and were as brutal as anything known in Sicily or Corsica. Crime in the towns is almost entirely larceny and petty thieving, he continued. Bank robberies and holdups are virtually unknown. 'Our criminals are unsophisticated,' he said. 'Just give them time.'

****

Conversations. I remember one, undoubtedly on Amin's obsession with unrequited love, sitting in a café on the Corniche, interminable dissections of his latest affair, watching the spray rise and hover over the breakwater and thinking dimly how the city moved to the languorous rhythm of the sea.

****

Bakoos. The Greek gods have lent their names to the tramway stops. A wet evening: wind and sporadic rain, the spattered drops glistening on the windows of the clattering trams. It recalled Venice and the comfort of lights on the damp canals. Only a city encompassed by lagoons feels quite so acutely the seeds of its own mortality and has a measure of the sky.

****

It was at Pastroudis that Amin and I had our most fruitful conversation. We had fought our battles in the city's cafés, skirmishing with each other's ideologies and glowering in impasse. It was at Pastroudis we agreed to differ. He believes in God, a primitive Christian God, an almighty bank manager who makes sure his books are balanced each day; in his way as picturesque and caricatured as old Jehovah. And Amin is as unforgiving as the bank manager. The blue-boned Copts, they say, watch their pennies and never forget.

The Copts live in a society which, though not ideologically hostile, has made life difficult for them. Persecution has been sporadic rather than systematic, invariably the result of individual caprice. Now their problem, and especially the problem of westernized Copts, lies more in themselves and their ideological antipathy to Islam which, as well as challenging Christianity's claim to be the unique way, resists the spread of the West's secular values.

The Copts are a minority in a society which has a less exalted view of Man than their own, a view that stretches him less between his mortal coil and heavenly aspirations; they live in a society which is, therefore, more relaxed and less ambitious. However, this only spurs the Copts to think of Christianity as being intrinsically more civilized and makes them feel doubly obliged to distinguish and promote their standards. To the natural sensitivities of a minority they add the sensitivities of their own view of themselves as Keepers of the Light. The cross of Christ lies heavy on their shoulders.

I myself have come to Alexandria as an erstwhile Christian in search of my European roots. A month in Egypt and the unrelenting 'difference' of Cairo is beginning to rub against the grain. I miss the feel of Europe, the sense of solid buildings, order in the shop windows, moderately clean streets and gardens; all those things that ratepayers get up in arms about.

The ratepayers of Alexandria are constantly writing to *Le Progrès*, their local paper, about the lack of amenities in their city. Occasionally there are rumblings of revolt. But they could no more stop what is happening to Alexandria than stop the sun. The European city is being eaten by a creeping blight.

It is in the centre that the clash of style is most evident. Alexandria is resisting the Arabization of its centre as a last gut reaction to a terminal disease; but the process is so far gone now that you feel the sooner it is over the better. As the Greeks, the Italians and the Armenians move out, the Egyptians, Saudis and Lebanese, with their predilection for chandeliers and white plastic, move in. Scratchy Arabic calligraphy supersedes the more prosaic Latin; the plain, sombre, interiors, once the repository of Alexandria's dreams (Cavafy's city) are disappearing and with them the last vestige's of the European city.

Yet those qualities that make modern Alexandria depressing, the lack of sympathy, the uncaringness of the Arab mind for material things and the absence of an instinct to preserve, has saved its spirit. Alexandria evokes its past like a deserted graveyard; down the same decaying streets you walk the city of the *Quartet*. And as if to contradict the supposition that the ghosts of that city were dead, a strange thing happened soon after I arrived.

A young man was walking hand in hand with his wife along Nebi Daniel to the intersection with Rue Fouad when the ground gave way. She disappeared. They never found her or any trace of her, though they brought in the excavators and turned the street into a building site. For a week they dug, paralysing the traffic in the city centre. The theory was that she must have fallen into the conduit of an old Greek well.

The incident was widely reported and aroused much sympathy for the young man who was taken to hospital in a state of shock, still clutching his wife's wedding ring which had come away in his hand as she disappeared. But once the hole had been filled in and fresh tarmac put on the road the city seemed to bury the incident too.

****

Madame Balankeya received visitors between five and seven on Wednesday evenings. We were thus stretching etiquette arriving at four on a Thursday afternoon – or so thought Amin who felt it wrong to take liberties with the domestic arrangements of Russian émigrés, especially émigrés of noble birth. Nevertheless we were received and taken down a long marbled veranda flanked with potted palms to her room. She was almost totally blind and made no effort to rise as we entered. But she had us in her mind's eye in seconds. 'Now you are in the chair on the right and Mr. Amin is on the sofa.' She pronounced it 'soofa' but otherwise her English was flawless.

Madame Balankeya had fled from the Ukraine to Alexandria in 1920 before the advance of the Red Army. She had married and settled there. Now, her husband dead some years and her children married, she had ended up in the Peleuzheim Nursing Home, a home run by nuns for gentlefolk such as she.

She talked of the Alexandria she had known. 'Of course it has changed,' she said with no trace of nostalgia at the way Egypt had gone under Nasser. That she accepted in the natural course of events, an expression of the aspirations of the people, even though it had destroyed her world. Then she described how she had arrived.

'One thousand five hundred of us in a boat made for five hundred. The British didn't know what to do with us. It was a fine old mess.' She laughed a clear, girlish laugh. It was striking how contemporary she was; still a young girl in her movements, in the agility of her mind. She was still engaged and it gave her a kind of immunity against what life had thrown at her. 'They couldn't send us back,' she continued. 'We had nowhere to go. Nor could they leave us on the streets where, in fact, most of us were. There was terrible suffering....

'Then someone had the bright idea of putting us in the General's Camp. It was called the General's Camp because it had just been vacated by a group of German officers awaiting repatriation to Germany. So we were put there and told to get on with it.

'My fiancé arrived on the next boat from the Ukraine and we were married in the camp. We had nowhere to go and no ties, so we decided to settle here. You see, it was paradise then.'

A pleasant faced rubicund nun came in with Madame Balankeya's supper. 'See how spoilt I am? She's coming for my hot water bottle.' And hardly pausing, 'I hear things are getting very bad in England with the railwaymen's strike and now the hospital staff.'

We left her to her supper, two summer dresses hanging behind the door, her other possessions packed in suitcases behind the washstand – still in transit.

****

April

Mist and the dream of sails on a flat landscape; house clusters shored up into domains, the stupa shapes of the pigeon lofts; the lustrous tresses of the eucalyptus tumbling in the wind; the glitter of sunlight.

I returned to Alexandria a month later by the agricultural road (it was the only one open then to foreigners), and in the monotonous eating up of the miles, the changing panorama of the Delta, the slow trip back into memory began anew. It was spring. And in Alexandria the lettuce carts rumbled through the city leaving an aroma of hay behind them. One moved through eddying currents of scents and airs, awakened to an ancient sensuality rubbing at the interface of two worlds: the desert and the sea.

I woke early next morning to the bellow of an ass, a noise like ropes strained through awnings, and a calm of glazed water and light clouds in which the city lay suspended.

A removal van had been abandoned in a street off the Corniche. 'Societé Éoudite, Meubles de toutes destinations' proclaimed the legend on its sides in floral lettering. Around it the rubbish lay exposed like the smells.

In every underlay of sound, or smell, or colour there is invariably a memory... and sometimes on certain afternoons an intimation…

In the sun-kissed streets of the Gumruk district, walking

through the fish market of Hag Hazada the following afternoon I sensed it … snatched fragments from the intermezzo to *La Traviata* wafted from the café radios. And for a moment the Sicilian balconies, the crumbling plaster, the garlic bunched among the washing became a theatre set, the music swelling and surging the length of the street in waves of sound that carried all before it, before subsiding and being taken up again by the radios at the next street corner…

'Come, have a look.' They were baking bread in a kiln, sliding the dough on long-handled paddles having first coated it with flour. They kept up the rhythm without pause, never missing the batch to come out. The pats emerged like cushions straining at the seams.

There was a bull's eye stall just beyond the bakery, air rifles propped against a wall and a battered target on which, crudely painted, and badly scratched and pitted, a familiar bald dome above an eye patch. They say Dayan is from Alexandria, an Alexandrian Jew. They say anything.

And why not in a city built on myths?

****

The Grand Café Commercial de la Bourse on the Corniche is a place of silences, steamed windows, tarbushes and ivory dominoes. The clack of the moves echoes in the gaunt, neon-lit hall. The chairs lie stacked in rows pointing out to sea.

Here, in the gradual slippage of time, the sea pulls you…

To Agami beyond.

The crush on the bus was stupendous. At one point the driver stopped and refused to go further until some passengers got off. We were then miles from anywhere and no one felt inclined to walk. Finally, the driver won over with cigarettes, we started again.

The fig trees are now in leaf; but on the beach there is no trace of the seasons. Here time passes by another measure, the periodic regurgitations of the sea, jetsam washed up by the storms or the slicks of oil that dribble in from the ships anchored off the harbour bar.

For an hour I lay there as the *bedu* girls stooped to their eternal gleaning and the beach dogs gambolled in the haze. Slowly the sun and the warmth seeped in, washed over the mind, licked at its farthest reaches, till it was scoured and smoothed in the ebb and flow of the sea cleansing the sands – erasing the last traces of my intentions.

At Agami without a car the city time is the next bus. I asked a man on the beach when the next bus was due. 'Quick, quick,' he said, 'there is just one coming.' I floundered through the soft white sand to the bus stop. There was no bus.

'There will be one soon, perhaps in a quarter of an hour, perhaps in half an hour. There will be one soon.' They fetched chairs and we sat in the sun. The children clustered round and were shooed away. But one refused. He stood astride his improvised go-cart, a surreal creation made from spare parts and bits of metal, and watched. Then he raced off and wheeled round looking back with mocking brown eyes. Everything about him was studied, the comic, self-possessed way he walked, the strident sobs at being thwarted. At eight or nine he was a little grown-up clown. But he was more than a little grown-up clown, for he knew something about the forces between humans.

Nothing else could explain his extraordinary self-consciousness: the clear coffee-coloured skin, the milk-white teeth, the smile in profile with the thick locks falling on the forehead bespoke his beauty and he knew it. It was his self-consciousness that struck me, so rare in the Middle East and yet so grounded in this child. He saw the possibilities – but didn't force them.

He kept us amused as the bus took its time. But by then I didn't care, for I was mesmerized by this hour of magic and what had conspired this gratuitous piece of theatre. It had to start with a human intelligence and a culture, an intelligence left unconditioned so that it could observe and manipulate the flow without effort or artifice, so raising it to the level of spontaneous dance. Then environment: for the mind has to be settled and still to pick out the lines. Agami gave you this – a clear mind, a mind wiped clean by the sun and this feeling (and how does one begin to describe the feeling Agami engendered in you of being dismantled bit by bit of culture, memory, everything, and set free?), this feeling of deep-rooted contentment.

It is from these white shores of the northern littoral that Alexandria gets its sense of the clear light, currents of another consciousness which filter through the thick cocoon of the city's parvenu pretensions and western values. It is this intimation of immortality that touches all in Alexandria with the bitter-sweet of a great romance which has within it the promise of a new, indescribably more beautiful order of things.

They talk of their city personally, Alexandrians, as a woman who bewitches them without their understanding and in so doing haunts them with their inadequacy.

In Alexandria Europeans dared the clear North African sun. They came, those seekers after fortune, from the northern lands a little over one hundred and fifty years ago, with the development of the port. They came with their paraphernalia of trade and prosperity, a bourse, shipping lines, their sports clubs and endless cocktail parties, their organized games and municipal gardens; the British with their institutions and an unassailable belief in their superiority, the French with their language, the Italians with their edifices and the Greeks with their gods. In their wake came Lebanese, Jews, Syrians and Armenians, a veritable crucible of the Levantine bourgeoisie.

And there was no one to stop them; certainly not after Napoleon made landfall in the late eighteenth century, for Alexandria had shrunk to little more than a fishing village under Ottoman rule. These new Alexandrians wasted no time forging links with the ancient city and claimed as theirs its European heritage. But they were without roots, a synthetic culture, nourished, protected and insulated by their wealth and their northern ways.

Pre-War Alexandria was without context, a microcosm of western civilization stranded on the shores of North Africa, a living social organism isolated in laboratory conditions. This was Durrell's master stroke in choosing Alexandria to set the *Quartet* – a location where his characters inhabited a no man's land between myth and time, an isthmus haunted by the surf licking its seaward face with the unseen shores of Mareotis behind: that other, harsher elemental reality that made no concessions to the city's reality but branded it with the venality of its social games and mediocre aspirations and mocked its seriousness. They have mostly gone now, the inhabitants of that city.

'You should have been in Alexandria before the War. It was paradise.'

She sat at one of a dozen tables, her hands folded on the floral tablecloth without expression or humour in her eyes, a small neat woman. The cowbell jingles on the main door and the manager rises from the corner where he is making up the bills. Through the wood-panelled sitting room you can glimpse the sea. A wash-basin has been installed in the corner of the reception room so that it converts easily into another bedroom; these days you can't afford to turn anyone away. From the kitchen behind the manager emanates a faint whiff of olives and kippers that competes with the odour of carbolic soap and stale urine from the passageway. The notice in the lavatory asks you to leave it as you would wish to find it: a sign of the times – the lack of self-respect – and reflects the difficulty in finding plumbers. The threadbare furnishings are another sign of the times; prices have been frozen this past decade and there is nothing left for renovation or repairs.

The grave French lady, who took over the running of the Pension Normandie when her husband died, soldiers on from day to day. But the pride has gone out of the undertaking. Now it is a question of gradual amortization and hanging on, hoping till grim death she can keep the manager and staff from pilfering everything.

'Twenty years ago. Then Alex was something! You could walk

along the Corniche and hardly ever meet an Arab,' a friend chips in. She is buck-toothed, blithe as a sparrow chirping in the palm trees of Saad Zaghloul Square below. That kind of remark raises eyebrows even amongst the old guard. For Alexandria has decidedly moved on.

However, the Revolution never cured Alexandria's taste for the sweet life. The gharries continue to work through to the closing of the nightclubs, so do the flower sellers and they do good business. The new elite vies with the Arab sheikhs for the lavish villas of Maamoura and Agami which in the height of summer fetch E£500 a month. It is a mystery how, in socialist Egypt where a Cabinet Minister earns no more than E£150 a month they manage to, but they do, and they set a trend which is mythologized in films and magazines. A summer holiday in Alex is the status symbol of modern Egypt's middle class. There is no better barometer of social change than the size of this annual migration to the sea – one million Cairenes swelling Alexandria in summer to twice its normal size.

With a taste for the sweet life goes a taste for money; it percolates through to all levels. Alexandria has never outgrown its commercial origins, never acquired the graces that sometimes come with wealth; it lacks, they say, the warmth of Cairo, its inhabitants are harder, more superficial and mercenary.

Durrell's city at least had the counterpoint of West and the city's situation. Now there is no West, just westernized Egyptians; it isn't the same. Yet you can still taste the elixir on those afternoons when the light is golden, so golden that the glories of the journey dispel all thoughts of Ithaca and evoke instead intimations of an immortality uniquely Alexandrian –

underscored by a clear-eyed recognition that all endeavour ends in disaster or inevitable decline, which is the very essence of the legend.

Chapter Five

CAIRO DIARY

Great cities have no need to flaunt their charms. They inhabit a self sufficient, occluded world of tradition and ingrained habit that shields them from the prying eyes of strangers. Their denizens go about their business like nocturnal animals in a zoo, the plate glass as likely to throw back a reflection of the spectator as provide a glimpse within. It is why the exploration of great cities invariably becomes a voyage of self-discovery.

However, the brute amoebic energy of Cairo, its size, its unconstrained humanity, rarely affords the luxury of such introspection.

In recorded history there has always been a settlement at the confluence of the Nile where it fans out into the Delta. The pharaohs established their northern capital at Memphis some twenty miles south of the modern city. The Romans later built a strategic fort a little further north on the opposite east bank of the Nile at Fustat. After the Arab colonization in the seventh century the city expanded north from Fustat along the fringes of the flood plain where in 968 AD the Fatamid caliph Mu'ezzidin founded a new capital and named it Al Qahira. Two centuries later Salaheddin built a fort atop the hill that dominates the city. Al Qala'a, to give the Citadel its Arabic name, was not only the seat of government for many centuries;

it became a national icon like the Statue of Liberty, Windsor Castle or the Eiffel Tower, vying with the treasures of pharaonic Egypt for prominence on the nation's postage stamps. To this day the end of the daily fast in Ramadan is signalled by the boom from a cannon fired from its ramparts resonating across the city.

Contained by its burial grounds to the east and south the city expanded westwards towards the river, encroaching on and eventually absorbing the pleasant orchards that abutted the Ezbekia Lake, where the prosperous merchants in medieval times used to escape the stifling heat of life within the walled city.

By the time Napoleon invaded Egypt in 1798 and billeted his army in a slum called Bulaq – an infelicitous corruption of Beau Lac – the city had put down tentacles by the river's edge. The taming of the Nile had begun – a process only completed with the commissioning of the Aswan High Dam in 1970 and the elimination of the annual flood. Increasingly released from the constraints of the Nile, the nineteenth century city expanded northwards to the apex of the Delta and south along the valley until, in the early twentieth century, it started to overflow the valley itself. New communities like Heliopolis sprang up, creating a kind of urban Sadd, a human equivalent of the mighty swamp in central Sudan that saps the strength of the great-hearted river without ever extinguishing its flow.

This was the city the Free Officers inherited after overthrowing the monarchy in 1952 and which Gamal Abdel Nasser, the first native ruler of Egypt since Cleopatra, set out to establish as the capital of a regenerated Arab nation. Though the Revolution changed the social and economic face of Egypt, delivering

At the Golden Hotel everyone was welcome to take a fresh orange or mango juice brought in from the fruit parlour next door.

The telephone operator with cool grey eyes with Mr Badri, the *bowab* of 54 Sharia Mohammed Shaheen (holding child), and his assistant Hussein.

It was the trees that distinguished Sharia Mohammed Shaheen.

The swings at the 'slum' end of Sharia Mohammed Shaheen

Author with Buzeina and Fatheya el-Gamal in the backyard of 12 Hara Hadad.

Fatheya el-Gamal with Buzeina and Atar in the backyard of 12 Hara Hadad.

Am Mohammed with smoked glasses and walking stick in his dark suit, from the balcony of the flat in Hara Hadad.

The onion seller.

Summer in Alex: No better barometer of social change than Egyptians' annual migration to the sea.

Nadia, the flower girl of Agami.

The Luxor Corniche. The clip clop of the spent nags hauling the antique gharries along the road to Karnak.

Author at Agami.

Amin Simaika (right) at Agami.

On Sharia Mu'ezzidin Allah the inertial current carries a steady steam of commerce.

In the Street of the Tentmakers the light gleamed on the rafters as the crowds shifted beneath.

The Mosque of Ibn Tulun at prayers.

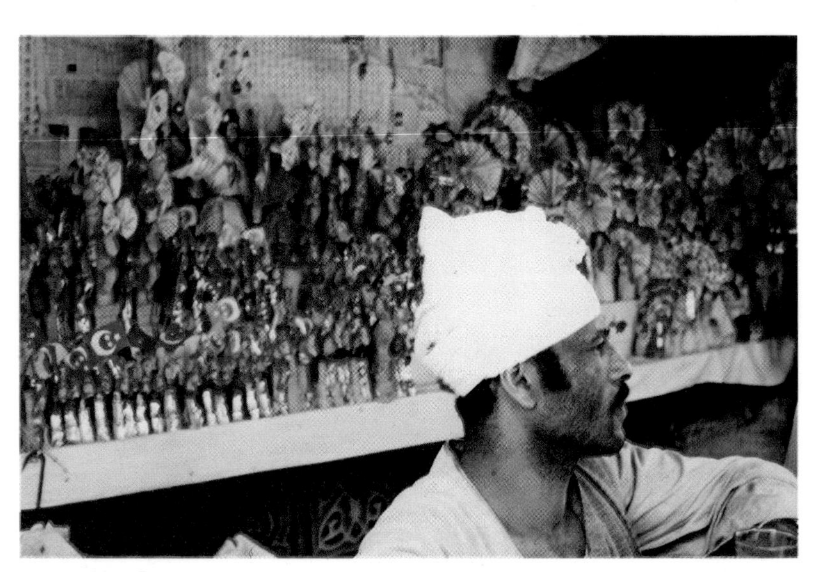

Arussa dolls, the sinister sugar dolls of the mawlid, painted with crepe fan bustles and iridescent ballerina's wings.

land reform and universal healthcare and education, Nasser did little to reform the apparat, the centralized administrative system that had run Egypt since pharaonic times. Rulers had come and gone: the Fatamids, the Ayyubids, the Mamluks and the Ottomans, and latterly the British without ever having done more than tinker with the bureaucracy which had, in a ramshackle but highly effective way, yoked ordinary Egyptians into a life of perennial servitude.

The power of the ruling order and the bureaucracy that underpinned it was only once seriously challenged. Mohammed Ali, an Albanian officer of the Ottoman army, seized power in 1811, putting an end to six centuries of Mamluk rule. The Mamluks were a military caste of ruthless enforcers introduced into Egypt by Salaheddin in the twelfth century. A century later they usurped Salaheddin's dynastic successors, the Ayyubids, and governed in their own right until forced into the Ottoman fold in 1517. Nominal fealty to the Porte in Istanbul did not, however, cramp their brutal, oppressive style.

Having ousted the Mamluks and confiscated their lands Mohammed Ali set about making Egypt the regional power. He was the first Middle Eastern ruler to appreciate that if he was to realize his imperial ambitions he had to promote economic and social development.

He sent his brightest technocrats to Paris to study government, and invited training missions to Egypt to establish new industries. He built, in addition to munitions, plants to supply his new army, textile mills to kit it out. He revamped agriculture, dug canals and strengthened irrigation systems and he transformed Egypt's economic fortunes by introducing King

Cotton which became a money spinning cash crop. Cotton production necessitated western finance and the establishment of bourses – which was fine in the good times, especially during the American Civil War when the price of cotton tripled, but deadly when conditions turned.

Mohammed Ali's successors lacked his fiscal prudence and the building of the Suez Canal, which opened in 1869, financially stretched his grandson, the Khedive Ismail. The sale of Egypt's share in the Canal to the British in 1875 failed to stave off national bankruptcy. Administration followed, jointly managed by the British and the French who charged a usurious 7 per cent interest – to be paid in gold – on their loans.

In 1882, following the murder of two Europeans in Alexandria, Britain took sole charge of Egypt and established a protectorate. It did so ostensibly to safeguard the foreign communities which each ran their own courts under the detested Capitulations, an Ottoman dispensation that gave foreigners immunity from Egyptian law. However, it soon became apparent the real reason for the British establishing a presence in Egypt – a presence that lasted to 1954 – was to protect the Canal and the all important trade route to India.

The first Consul General of what came to be known as the 'veiled protectorate' was the formidable Lord Cromer. Cromer did much to restore Egypt's finances. Agricultural production revived, thanks to ever more ambitious irrigation schemes and the bureaucracy was streamlined to incorporate the best traditions of the Indian Raj. The state coffers filled and foreign entrepreneurs flocked to Egypt. Many made huge fortunes. In a famous contemporary cartoon Egypt was portrayed as a cow with its head munching hungrily in the fertile Nile Delta while

its udder is simultaneously milked in Europe.
That said, and despite the scandalously thin veneer of development this wealth had created, the country the Free Officers inherited was not only agriculturally self sufficient, it was financially sound, with gold and currency to pay for at least six months' imports. A generation later, on the eve of the Ramadan War in 1973 the Central Bank could barely scrape together the funds to pay for the next wheat shipment, the country having several years previously slipped into imported food dependency.

The economic story of Nasser's sixteen years in power was one of systematic plunder: first the gold and currency reserves; then the foreign nationals' assets after the Suez invasion in 1956; and finally, in the early 1960s, the wholesale nationalization of the economy, when the regime adopted full-blown socialism with a military face. It was all done in the name of pan-Arab nationalism which Nasser inspired and Egypt was forced to bankroll. The Yemen civil war, which raged in the first half of the 1960s, pitched Nasser against the House of Saud and the forces of reaction in the Arabian Peninsula. It fatally overextended him (and Egypt) financially and logistically and was to provide his enemies in Israel and the West – who feared his power to galvanize the Arab masses every bit as much as the conservative rulers of the Peninsula – the opportunity to engineer his downfall.

That happened in June 1967. The Six Day War disabused the regime of any aspirations to lead a pan-Arab renaissance. It bankrupted the country and left Nasser a broken man. In September 1970 he succumbed to diabetes and died. He was buried in his local mosque in Abbasseya midst scenes of unprecedented public grief. The poisoned chalice passed to

Anwar Sadat, the Speaker of the People's Assembly, who was widely viewed as a stop gap for Moscow's favoured candidate, Ali Sabri, the leader of Egypt's sole political party, the Arab Socialist Union. However, Sadat had other ideas. In May 1971 he staged a coup which he grandiloquently dubbed the 'Corrective Revolution'. The Moscow clique was dislodged and the break with the Soviet Union sealed in August 1972, when all twenty thousand Soviet advisers, who had been seconded to rebuild Egypt's broken army after the June 1967 War, were sensationally ordered home.

It was an act of breathtaking recklessness, or so it seemed, leaving Egypt effectively defenceless with no countervailing western support to replace the banished Soviets, and bogged down on the Suez Front in a war of attrition with Israel. The country was locked down – foreigners forbidden to venture outside Cairo, Alexandria, Luxor and Aswan – the economy in limbo. This was 'no war, no peace', a suffocating paralysis, and it had many wondering in the early months of 1973 how long Sadat could hang on.

February 3

Woke at four. The cold was as sharp as the knife-edge new moon. To the east violet smoke palls hung in tatters across the rooftops, drifting in the wind currents. The streets echoed to the howls of dogs and cockcrows.

Yesterday evening by the Nile the cheerful 'hallos' of sailors greeted me. They were standing guard over an old naval corvette that had evidently come back to the Nile to die. Walking further along the Corniche past the headquarters of the Egyptian Long Distance Swimming Association, a dilapidated Louisiana style paddleboat, towards the tip of Roda Island, I had my first glimpse of the pyramids nestling between two riverside skyscrapers on the further bank.

Sadat's speech to the General Assembly on February 1 has triggered fears of a clampdown.

Mamdouh Yaccoub, a lecturer in archaeology at Al Azhar, dismisses the student protests as the work of troublemakers. He's indignant at the way Sadat's wife, Gihan, has been dragged into the fray. The disturbances are concentrated in the Faculty of Engineering at Ain Shams University, he says. Al Azhar is trouble free. He's as jovial as ever, collecting new jobs like postage stamps.

February 5

The prickle of early morning mist, the chilly feel of moisture alien to the skin. The Nile, where it widens past Gezira Island, is like a giant pond, becalmed. It has the light texture of Ile Saint Louis from the banks of the Seine in autumn. It comes with the promise of a fine day but for the time being the sun is struggling with the forces of cold. Sitting on the balustrade you can feel it nibbling beneath the skin and into the flesh....

Gradually the mist lifts, the glint of cars crossing University Bridge gives way to a. view of the bridge itself and by noon the world is material again. I took the launch to Old Cairo. On the river we passed an old sailing barge, a magnificent gnarled beast with the primordial quality of a pterodactyl, the helmsman in flowing blue *galabeya* bolt upright and motionless at the tiller, steering by a monolithic rudder.

In Old Cairo the army was massed, three lorry loads of conscripts and a water cannon. Troops started moving onto the streets and the crowds dispersed. A lorry broke down and five soldiers were delegated to push it. The engine coughed but failed to fire. They smiled, waved and abandoned the attempt.

But walking into the back streets the mood changed. I attracted a trail of children chanting: 'Halloo, halloo'. But then more seriously, more fiercely: '*Baksheesh, baksheesh*'. An old man signalled to me to return the way I had come. I didn't argue.

****

Peering through the looking glass of the daily round reveals glimpses of random anarchy, of mangled logic and disjointed action.

A leader in the *Egyptian Gazette* discusses the scandalous case of a tram driver who, caught in traffic, decided to nip across the road to buy a spot of lunch and had been run down. If the authorities had provided proper canteen facilities, the paper thundered, the hapless driver wouldn't have felt impelled by hunger to go looking for food and paid with his life.

The cinema newsreels feature interminable parades of dignitaries arriving at Cairo Airport, leaving Cairo Airport, being greeted, shaking hands, bidding farewell or seated at conference tables and in informal groups. The audience hoots, whistles and claps....

At the Garden City interchange there is a traffic jam. Drivers on the filter road suddenly realize what is happening and reverse 'en masse'. Pure Buster Keaton.

A policeman tries to hold up the traffic on Tahrir Square. A few cars slip through and then the line gives way. '*Ya salaam*....' he moans, throwing up his hands and retreating to the traffic island where he plonks himself down and eats his sandwiches.

Early evening and Talaat Harb hums with an electric vitality as youths amble hand in hand, two, three abreast, blocking the pavements. Around eight o'clock the cinemas disgorge the evening sittings – a lava flow of humanity that stops the traffic. It prompts the thought that someone should make an aerial survey of the pedestrian flow, feed in a rumour, like dye into the bloodstream and plot its course....

****

During Nasser's time Fares Sarofim was obliged to travel frequently to Upper Egypt to administer the remnants of his estates. Like most expropriated landowners he was tailed by the *mukhabarat* (secret police).

One bitterly cold night in February, having caught the last train back to Cairo, he was scurrying across the deserted station concourse to find a taxi, when a tap on the shoulder brought him face to face with a complete stranger close to tears who asked him if he wouldn't mind in future catching an earlier train as he had a wife and children to get back to.

The Egyptian security services assume *khawagas* (foreigners) do not speak Arabic.

Stopped late one night outside the Semiramis Hotel an American, who had been delving a little too deeply into the wartime liaisons of a senior politician with a belly dancer (in this case Sadat), was asked where he was going.

'Who are you? ' he demanded.

'I am a policeman.'

'Can I see some form of identification, please?'

He flashes a pass. 'You aren't a policeman.'

The security agent is totally confounded. 'No one told me you could read Arabic.'

For a *khawaga* a modest working knowledge of Arabic is an 'Open Sesame' into the magic theatre ....

Once in a communal taxi from Cairo to Alexandria – a bargain in those days at E£1 – I found myself precariously wedged in the front seat next to an expansive woman who occupied the centre place, which left her companion squashed in the corner and the driver steering from what seemed like a foot outside the left side door.

The lady matched girth with volubility and was subjecting her discomfited audience to the tribulations of a neighbour who had become matrimonially entangled with a playboy who appeared to advocate a kind of conveyor belt system for his wives to ensure variety and new blood. The unfortunate lady had worked her way to the end of the line and was about to be discarded. Her friend thought this scandalous.

I came in half way through this unwitting peroration in the cause of Women's Lib and asked my neighbour, an engineer with the Harbour Board in Alexandria, what all the fuss was about. He explained; I thanked him. Then he did a kind of double take. He looked at me, six feet two and fair, and asked in his politest Arabic: 'Excuse me, Sir. Are you from Syria or Lebanon?'

****

In Khan al-Khalili to the west of the Hussein Mosque I came upon a community centre where the custodian, a young man in soiled pyjamas, asked me in. He had an open face and stubby teeth and was training to be a doctor.

He told me the previous night the hall had been used for civil defence training; learning how to make bombs. Today an ombudsman would hear local complaints.

He had no time for beggars and malingerers. There were subsistence allowances for the really needy, he said. He himself would earn E£20 a month when qualified. I asked whether he had ever thought of emigrating, given the lack of opportunity and the low salaries. He looked at me blankly. 'These are my people. I want to help them,' he said.

His transparency disarmed me. In a western context the guy looked to be a complete no hoper; in an Egyptian one he was a true hero.

****

The *baladi* woman beckoned me, 'Very sweet,' she said. The grubby urchin in front concurred. 'Ten piastres.'

'Nice oranges,' I responded. 'But too expensive.'

The price came down to a more respectable 7 piastres a kilo. But when she had been given 7 piastres she demanded one more. I walked away in disgust without oranges or money. Consternation! I could be chiselled but not robbed. '*Khud, Khud*. Take them, take them,' she screeched. I collected my oranges, pleased with the success of my stratagem, to find she had taken out one and left me with three.

****

He must have been over sixteen as he mentioned applying for an identity card to find proper work. However, if he did that he would be eligible for the army draft.

He had been lucky finding a patch at this restaurant where he earned between 30 and 40 piastres a day – not a bad income for a shoeshine boy. However, his takings went straight to his father who was too fond of the bottle – the reason he wanted to cast out on his own. He saw his mother perhaps once or twice a year when either she would make the nine hour train journey to Cairo or he would go home.

****

Five o'clock at the Semiramis Hotel: the tinkle of the baby grand, the clink of cups amongst the hushed Venetian splendour. Armenian matrons bandy reminiscences as outside, beyond the Corniche and the silver ribbon of the Nile, beyond the crumbling, spiky palms, the sky turns mauve.

****

February 21

At one thirty this afternoon Israeli fighters shot down a Libyan civilian airliner with seventy people on board. The plane had strayed into Sinai. I heard the news in a taxi en route to Zamalek. The taxi driver made no comment. For the rest of the day the news broadcasts were taken up with it and the Israeli raids on Lebanon.

February 22

Cairo is grimly calm this morning. Out on the street you wouldn't know that a full scale crisis had blown up. Incongruously, the flags are flying to celebrate the twelfth anniversary of the Syrian union. On Talaat Harb a small crowd is gathered outside the Libyan Airline offices where a list of passengers is posted. Since last night friends and relatives of the victims have been collecting at the Red Cross office to confirm the worst. They take the news stoically, almost matter-of-factly. There are no displays of grief. A well known television announcer was on the plane; most of the passengers were Egyptian.

There is little surprise at what has happened. It is what Egyptians have come to expect, although there is public outrage that the victims' bodies were returned in packing cases, unwashed. They see, in this disrespect and inhumanity, the nature of the people they are dealing with. They remember Deir Yassin and the gloating publicity given to the photographs of shoeless Egyptian soldiers running 'like rats' across Sinai after the debacle of 1967. 'We have done bad things,' they will admit, 'but can anyone claim *they* are more civilized?'

It is against the West that the bitterness and the cynicism are primarily aimed. 'You wait.' said Azzam, of the airline disaster, 'they will whitewash the whole thing.'

But the western Press did not. *The Times* of London likened the shooting to the sinking of the Lusitania. The New York *Daily News* said the Israeli philosophy of 'fire first and ask questions later' looked uncomfortably naked now. The majority of the British and American newspapers called for full compensation, a full investigation, punishment of the guilty and a public apology. The general view was that at best it was a tragic blunder, at worst callous murder.

Sadat and Mahmoud Riad, the head of the Arab League, unaware of the strength of feeling, trotted out pro-forma statements condemning Israeli aggression. Khedaffi kept his counsel.

Egyptians feel the incident has won them credibility, the lack of which, together with what they see as an innate western prejudice to the Arab world, has made the presentation of their case well nigh impossible. The main propaganda victory is the exposure of the Israelis' initial attempts to whitewash the whole affair; it backfired badly, leaving Egyptians feeling as if they had nailed a policeman on false testimony.

February 24

An evening stroll with Amin near Bab Zuweila, on the southern edge of the Fatamid city, took us just outside the city walls into Sharia al-Khayamat, the Street of the Tentmakers, a timbered arcade lined with box stalls, each offering an intimate window like an advent calendar into a medieval trade: a cobbler's workshop, an alchemist, a tailor surrounded by yards of cloth measuring a broad-girthed gentleman wearing a tarbush for a *galabeya*, and a blacksmith working his glowing irons.

Then – suddenly – the electricity failed and we might have been back four hundred years, so soft were the cries, so intense the stillness.

With the lights restored – and as instantly as they had been extinguished – life snapped back to normal.

'Have you heard what the Israelis have done?' The *fatatiri* (pastry cook) was dextrously dripping dough in concentric circles into a burnished copper pan to make *khanefa*, a shredded wheat like pastry. 'A terrible tragedy; all those women and children.'

I asked Amin why people didn't talk much about the plane disaster. 'They are resigned,' he said. 'And anyway, we still don't talk too much. People got out of the habit under Nasser.'

****

They swaggered into the fruit bar, two windcheatered characters built like nightclub bouncers and a seedy fair-haired youth wearing dark glasses and an oversized naval blazer. They entered in that peculiarly offensive way by which some Europeans make their presence felt, in a place where they feel that by rights they shouldn't have to be, but in the cause of needs must. The need in this case was milk shakes all around which the youth ordered as though the bar was empty and the bartender should quit fiddling on the other side of the counter and serve.

They were talking, very loudly and indiscreetly, cracking jokes about gunrunning, African revolutions and derring-do on the Front which, if they were to be believed, made nonsense of Egyptian claims that they were confronting anything more threatening than the Vatican Guard.

Then they spotted the two of us, a European friend and myself having lunch, two white faces trying hard to lose ourselves in the crowd, and with a 'Stanley meets Livingston' look, came over.

'And what do you do here?' demanded the youth in dark glasses....

I shuddered to think what an imaginative wall would make of these hucksters and my nebulous occupation. I stalled and countered, 'And what are you doing?'

'UN.' He squared his padded shoulders.

We had both been wrong. My companion thought they were mercenaries; I contract workers from the Canal.

The youth, it transpired, was the son of the local UN commandant, South American of Spanish origin. The other two were Scandinavian soldiers who had volunteered for UN peacekeeping and been deployed in a number of African hotspots as well as Cyprus and Bangladesh. They had witnessed disasters, famines and civil wars, events they had been largely impotent to deal with, and on occasions had found themselves caught between warring factions with orders to fire only when fired upon – an instruction that ran so totally against the grain of natural instinct as to leave them nerveless and slightly unhinged.

The commandant's son, who had never seen war and was never likely to, made up for their lack of sensitivity by glancing round the bar and declaring: 'I don't think we should talk so loud in here, The enemy might hear us.'

The enemy had. An Egyptian approached and said: 'You have been very impolite.'

The youth took the hint, called the others and, with a leer in our direction, beat a retreat.

Outside we bumped into the Egyptian and apologized for the gross display of bad manners. He laughed. 'When the boy went to order the drinks he shouted back to his friends, 'Watch those bags' – as if I was about to run off with them.'

****

Any stay in Egypt over a month requires an extension to your tourist visa. To obtain an extension you must have first changed £30 sterling for each month you intend to stay. You then go to the Mugamma (the Kafkaesque headquarters of the Egyptian Interior Ministry) in Tahrir Square and to the non-Arab visa application room on the second floor. You take with you two photographs and a certificate stating that you have changed the requisite amount of money.

You may have thought the receipt you are given when changing money sufficient evidence of the transaction but you would have overlooked the chronic overstaffing problem in Egyptian banks. As it is virtually impossible to be sacked (some employees leave for several years without ever having resigned and resume work again as and when they feel like it), and as no self respecting employee is ever likely to resign, the banks are crammed with 'lifers' on meagre salaries supplemented by the odd *baksheesh*. They ward off boredom by dealing with unmanageable queues, shuffling forms or doing the crossword. As a way to justify this masterly and pointless activity, the management and the Mugamma have devised the 'certificate' which is issued against currency receipts specifically for presentation at the Mugamma.

This is where the fun begins. You return to the branches where you changed money to get a certificate only to be told certificates are only issued at head office. If you have changed money in several banks and are someone for whom time is money, you will do what the authorities expect of you, head for the nearest head office, change what is required, so doing your bit for the country's depleted reserves, and a certificate is produced on the spot. But if, like me, you are someone for whom time is elastic and of marginal value, someone invested with principles that balk at such overt blackmail, you have taken the first step on a long and stony road.

I had changed money in three different banks and so had had to make six separate journeys in order to pin down the three head offices. One head office gave me a certificate in twenty minutes; the second issued me with an identity disc and shunted me from one office to another for an hour before producing one; the third informed me certificates were not issued at head office but at a dedicated branch in Heliopolis.

Heliopolis is situated some five miles out of Cairo on the airport road. It is a spacious flower filled suburb. Well-to-do Cairenes with a yearning for space and privacy have to thank the foresight of a certain Baron Empain for Heliopolis. Baron

Empain was an enterprising Belgian nobleman who realized the only thing needed to turn desert into prime real estate was water. He piped it in, developed Heliopolis and made a fortune.

It was, therefore, a combination of Baron Empain's vision and the whimsy of the third head office which accounted for Amin and me riding the Nozha Metro on a gorgeous spring morning, mission almost complete, £25 sterling's worth of certificates under the belt and an insidious exhilaration creeping up from the guts at the thought of reaching the end of the trail. As we trundled and clanged out of Cairo into a crisper more brilliant sky, I wondered why all the clerks in the third head office hadn't put in for transfers to the certificate branch for a taste of Elysium. The sun played on whitewashed walls, there was shade, trees, grass and colours: oleander and apricot blossom, gushes of bougainvillaea, and the vivid splash of the euphorbia tree in flower, scattering orange shellfire against the blue, blue sky.

We reached the bank about half an hour before closing time and were attended to with courtly courtesy. The currency receipt was inspected and we were asked to step behind the counter. There, a cashier completed a form, signed it and asked me to do the same. The form plus currency receipt then went to another man sitting behind a glass partition who scrutinized them, countersigned them and sent them back to the cashier for stamping.

'Come this way, please.' And we entered an antechamber where a table, four chairs and a ravished looking safe did duty, apparently, as the manager's office. The manager I guessed to be the self-absorbed man seated at the table.

We smiled and we waited. Five minutes later we smiled again and this time we drew a smile from the bank manager. We were just about to pay our respects and leave – they could have all gone home for all we knew – when a clerk came in and said: 'Please don't go. It is nearly ready. Have some coffee while you are waiting.'

'Don't worry,' said the bank manager, having elicited the reason for this invasion of his privacy, 'these things take time.'

A moment later the clerk came back. 'Have you got the currency form?' he enquired.

'What currency form?'

'The currency declaration form you sign when entering the country.'

'No. They didn't want it in the other banks.'

Well. I'm sorry,' he said. 'We require it here. We have to record the issuance of the certificate on the back. What the other banks did wasn't strictly correct.'

So there was nothing for it but to return the next day with the offending currency declaration form. '*Bukra fil mish mish*' as the Egyptians say: 'Tomorrow in the apricot' which means, as the apricot is a notoriously fickle fruit to flower, that it might happen, but don't bank on it.

****

March 5

Three Palestinian guerrillas belonging to Black September today held a number of ambassadors hostage at the Saudi Arabian embassy in Khartoum. When their deadline for an aircraft to be made ready for them was not met (it was in the middle of one the worst dust storms to hit Khartoum in living memory), they killed three of the hostages, the American ambassador and his chargé d'affaires, and the Belgian chargé d'affaires who, as it turned out, was half Egyptian. Black September later accused the American ambassador of having been a member of the CIA, a charge that was never taken seriously.

Egyptians are very upset that the guerrillas should have mounted such an attack so soon after the Libyan airline incident. They feel that much of the good that came from that has been undone.

So bitter is the feeling about the Black September incident that rumours are sweeping Cairo it was engineered by the Israelis.

****

Mid March

It was full moon and after dinner a group of us decided to visit the Giza plateau. We walked the perimeter of the Great Pyramid in silence, picking our way over the bone white ground out of the wind. Boulders lay strewn like chippings in a giant builder's yard, as if the Titans had upped and gone without bothering to clear up.

Compared with these first generation giants of the pantheon, who are the gods of the enlightenment? Greece, the seedbed of reason, only gave us a simulacrum of their raw, archaic power.

****

I was late and, of course, Mamdouh was on time. Mamdouh's life is a perpetual time and motion study where minutes, seconds, lost could wreck the averages so you felt you were personally letting him down if you kept him waiting. But he took my tardiness in good part and we were off, lurching round craters in the road, the horn peeping in afterthought, collecting vegetables and colleagues along the road.

Arrival at Sakkara produced the familiar kick: the dramatic end of cultivation and the start of the sands, the Cinerama effect of taking off into the desert with the sudden change in perspective as you rise out of the valley. It was a beautiful day, the desert air crisp and clean, the sky a mild, mild blue. Sakkara smoothes out the crinkles in the mind with the sky's blues and golds and the desert's plastic curves.

It was to Memphis, twenty miles south of Cairo on the western ridge of the Nile Valley that the early sorcerers in eternity repaired some four thousand years ago after abandoning Abydos in Upper Egypt. They didn't do too badly according to their lights, though they had a lot going for them – especially the weather. Sakkara is as safe as a glacier when it comes to preserving things.

Sakkara boasts the famous Step Pyramid of Zoser, the oldest stone building in the world and probably one of the earliest to be excavated by archaeologists. A wooden beam at the centre of the pyramid, which was used as a prop in one of the first digs for the tomb, dates from the third century BC; in those days there was little to distinguish an archaeologist from a tomb robber. According to Mamdouh, and despite the best efforts of the tomb robbers, there is a positive Atlantis of buried treasure under the sands, hundreds of noblemen, thousands of the fabled ibis, an arsenal of alabaster jars of perfume, 'We've only just scratched the surface,' he says. 'What we lack is money.'

The evidence was plain from his bucket shop operation. Each week he goes to Sakkara in his capacity as Head of Works there. He takes with him two or three packets of Cleopatra cigarettes which he distributes on his rounds in exchange for loyalty, affection and good intentions. His team's latest find causes some excitement. It is a many-tonned marble slab with mysterious inscriptions on its underside. They would like to have a look at the inscriptions. The slab is at the bottom of a sixty foot shaft. They only have a couple of rickety winches, a danger to the slab as well as to the men who would work them. The intention is to extract the slab without scratching it.

In his capacity as Head of Works, Mamdouh held a conference in his office. Slouched at his desk, legs sprawled across the back of a chair, he inspected the books, twiddling his keys (symbols of authority) round his little finger while meting out justice and retribution to those caught pilfering, skiving or crashing one of the mission's antique vans, and bribing the honest with honeyed words and cigarettes. Then, almost coincidentally, he got up and told us to come with him as he had something to show us. And what he showed us brought the magic of ancient Egypt absolutely alive.

We entered a complex of tombs and came to a battered, padlocked door. An attendant produced a key and unlocked the padlock. 'Come,' said Mamdouh, 'two at a time.'

The tomb belonged to a young man called Nefer who, long ago, had been head of the orchestra and chief steward at court. Scenes from his life were depicted on the walls: Nefer conducting the orchestra and supervising the kitchen; the calving as it is still done in the Nile Valley to this day.

'Have you the mirrors in place?' Mamdouh asked the attendant.

Then he unlocked the padlock of a trapdoor and asked us to go down. It took a second or two to adjust the mirrors; and there was Nefer in a small niche, the wooden lid to his coffin propped at one side. He lay as he had been found and as he had lain for the past four thousand five hundred years.

He was so well preserved that he still had his fingers and toenails; you could discern the dark aureole of his nipples and his jutting sex. His features were serene, his mouth set in a slight smile. You felt that if you touched his shoulder he would stir. And I would have gone away under the spell of a timeless sleep but for one chilling detail. A small necklace of lapis lazuli had broken and scattered over his throat and jelled into the skin.

Mamdouh then took us down into the little pyramid of Imher and into the central burial chamber. The walls and the triangular arch of the ceiling are made from slabs of granite twelve feet thick. The ceiling is engraved with blue stars and the walls with hieroglyphs and the keys to eternal life. Imher had been interred in a narrow burial chamber under twelve feet of granite – yet it felt as if he had been buried under the stars with all the space of the heavens above him.

The journey back to Cairo, imbued with the spirit of the tombs, is always a great affirmation of life – and so is Mamdouh as he helps the car with a touch at the steering.

'Heepies?' he growls, his sparse, spiky moustache bristling like his sparse, lank hair. 'Heepies? What do we want with heepies? They come with their fahncy cloth-es. Why the fahncy cloth-es? Here, everyone is heepy. But we don't have fahncy cloth-es.' Then, after a moment's reflection. 'Do you think Khedaffi likes us? Khedaffi says heepies are good people.' He breaks into a huge belly laugh which threatens to rock the car and the fragile course we have set north to Cairo.

And the Nile Valley flows past, the Nile Valley that has seen it all and in whose perennial rhythms – the sowing, the harvesting and the winnowing of the corn, the cycle of seasons, birth and death – can be discerned the pattern, the eternal cycle, the link that has bound Egyptians to their land from Nefer's time to the present day, through flood and famine. And this massive physical and emotional bond has bred in them an élan, a sense of savour that makes of their lives one long love affair, an astoundingly rich, deep marriage with their environment.

****

It was hot, humid and uncomfortable. This, they said, was the *khamaseen*.

The papers talk incessantly of the *khamaseen*: a slight flush of heat and they say it is the *khamaseen*; an iron cold sandstorm off the Libyan Desert and they say it is the *khamseen*. The *khamaseen* has somehow come to signify any weather that is hot and disagreeable, any weather that is cold and disagreeable, so long as it brings the sand.

The *khamaseen* is in fact a season (the word is derived from *khamseen*, the Arabic for fifty, the number of days during which, traditionally, it occurs) when hot winds from the south upset the pattern of prevailing northerlies heralding the end of winter. Days of dust, dirty fingernails and short tempers. Days of sudden puffs of hot air; colloidal days which have you gasping for air. Such is the *khamaseen*: nothing spectacular, just a bloody nuisance.

But today was different. For it became hotter, and the dust thicker and yellower, like a gently curdling custard stirred occasionally by a ladle. The city turned the colour of a photograph yellowed with age. And it got worse, the gusts of wind more frequent, sudden puffs from unseen bellows raising the dust. The sand infiltrated the city like an insurgent force; the silence was unnatural.

Then, as it got dark, it seemed as if the city had caught fire. A reddish glow suffused the sky as if the city had been put to the torch, the whole tatty skyline of Talaat Harb thrown into lurid relief. The wind was quite violent now, slaps of stinging heat which left the throat parched and burning. Only when the extreme heat had passed, hours later, did the dust subside.

Next day the city was grizzled with sand.

****

Mid April

Not a breath of wind: glassy waters in which the barges scythe

the reflections. The heat is testing the tempers of passengers and the stamina of buses.

One broke down on the bridge. The driver had to be won round to an understanding that there were more effective ways of registering protest than by staying put; the policeman sweating, the driver making operatic gestures. Another bus came from behind and gave the stationary vehicle a friendly nudge. The engine coughed and spluttered to life, gears protesting. The kid in *galabeya* who had been watching from the sidelines takes up his station again on the back bumper and beckoned his friends to join him.

To alight a moving bus is a mark of manhood. Middle aged men and cripples do it. Once a one-legged man dropped from a moving bus in the middle of the rush hour traffic in Ramses Street; he dropped like a leech shaken from a tree, picked himself up, dusted his crutch and wove in amongst the traffic to the other side. A bus hopper will never be turned away – such is the generosity of Cairenes.

****

Walked up into the hinterland of Sayidda Zeinab where preparations were being made for the *mawlid al-nabby* (the Prophet's birthday). Outside the mosque the crowds gathered to watch two men perform the stick dance. They were dressed in *galabeyas* and the *ameya*, the woollen head cloth worn by the *sa'eedi* of Upper Egypt. To the drone of the flutes they wheeled and twirled, the sticks clicking as their arms arched and curved and met in parrying blows. In another circle a gypsy boy, muscled like an armadillo, puffed and preened as if preparing for a wrestling match.

Then I wandered up a side street into the wasteland of Amr's pillaged city. Cairo is built on its cinders. There are places where the scars refuse to heal. On these mounds, the city's true burial grounds, you can walk on ash a millennium old. Only the most desperate go there. The City of the Dead, the burial grounds that encompass Cairo to the east are preferable to these bat infested ruins. Atop one of these mounds of solitude I espied the mosque of Ibn Tulun and decided to have a look inside. Well outside the walls of the medieval city, it has endured centuries of neglect and today rises out of a sea of slums and bomb shelters.

It was dusk, a faded grainy dusk, the silence punctuated by the *aisha*, the evening call to prayer. Tired stone and weeds; Ibn Tulun seemed to be going the way of the rubble heaps.

****

But I was to see Ibn Tulun in different circumstances, a different light, and marvel at the magisterial symmetry of its arcades, the complexity of the shifting planes of the pillars as one moved, the effect of moving through a dense forest. I was to marvel at how such tired stone could evoke such strong form.

It is a question of atmosphere. Mood has a counterpart in impression. What part in reality?

****

The Luxor train was late and there was a rush for the couchettes. Childish excitement. The station bell clanged and the train pulled away. Wow, it was hot! A soft, palpable heat that turned the roads to putty and dulled the mind.

Then, as we walked away from the station, Amin produced a mouth organ and started playing: reedy sounds on an evening that had the feel and colour of freshly washed grey cashmere. And suddenly it all begins disintegrating, you're off the ground and climbing, the heaviness falls away to a riveting lucidity; you have the gift of tongues and the city is yours, all of it, a crumbling ant heap of magic.

The Zen masters call this *sartori*, the leap of consciousness that takes place when the mind is presented with a logical, physical or emotional impasse from which there is no way on and no way back. The smallest catalyst can cause the conscious mind to disintegrate, the ego with it, and in this moment of breached defences the mind perceives without conditioning.

****

It is a public holiday. Cairo is deserted, exposing the wall advertisements, Sasso Olive Oil, 'Glaxo builds up bonny babies,' cracked and peeling relics of the 1940s.

The empty streets allow the mind as well as the feet to wander and to see above street level to the city's structural elegance – to the bone structure of a beautiful face devoid of makeup. Perhaps because the chaos and the squalor are now so much part of the experience I no longer notice them and can claim with all sincerity that the European city has a style to match London, Paris or Rome. If the city were a woman, would not this quick vertiginous slide into subjectivity be called 'falling in love'?

Subjectivity is thus a necessary starting point to understanding – provided it is open-hearted and not self-absorbed. For it is only through risking and learning from knocks to the ego that we grow. With vulnerability properly harnessed comes a new kind of appreciation of others, a sensitivity that transcends self-pity and a desire for vengeance and only indirectly has to do with pain.

I remember once, hurt in love, walking back to Shobra and discovering how the city compensated me. I had walked out the pain of rejection to the point where I felt raw and free. And for the first time I felt myself of the same grain as these people: first things first and don't try to force events into patterns that don't fit. Go with the flow.

Sharia Shobra is ugly. Hell, it's ugly! A straight, scythed scar on the face of the city like the avenues of Harlem. But it is alive, so alive it hurts.

I stopped in a café half way down the street. The din was crazy. A scratchy radio vied with the noise of the traffic and the clang of the trams; the parlour glittered under the fluorescent lighting oblivious of the bright sunlight outside. And I felt I had a place here in the order of things. It was on the street that I would begin to see through the looking glass into the city's inner life.

It is good, sometimes, to have to find one's resources elsewhere, in the city, in the people, and in the sky.......

****

The sky is a huge piece of faded denim in which the building opposite is sown like a neat patch. While the light was still luminescent the rectilinear lines cast a clear white shadow.

It was a day like a stream of others we have been having recently, the temperature balanced on a knife edge so that the changes seemed to come from within, pitted against the mean of sun, clear skies and the gentle north wind. This afternoon I went on a trip of my own making. Lying on my bed on this balance of sensation, I could feel the air like a numbing ether dissolving my skin into the skin of the world and my body being eaten away, skin, flesh, bone, absorbed without trace as the nerve ends spread in this new element, like those weird, vegetal growths in water tumblers the street boys hawk on the pavements of Talaat Harb.

Then I was off with all the oceans of the world beneath me, secure in the deep-sea equilibrium of a preternatural calm, set sail into the stillness, into the great heart of the centre..... soothed, lapped into a forgetfulness which was neither waking nor sleeping but a gradual corrosion of feeling for something more complete, more blessed.

And as the airlocks opened one by one, I felt the experience flowing through me, mindlessly, noiselessly, a river flowing into the unconscious....

****

The clip clop of the spent nags hauling the antique gharries along the sandy moonlit road to Karnak; the flutter of bats over the sullen waters at dusk; the white heat of the sun going down over the Valley of the Kings, an iron fist gloved in velvet: Luxor takes you perilously close to the fire.

It took Luxor to break finally the introversion that Cairo had been telling me in different ways to shed, the self-absorption of my culture. After Luxor I knew that magic was a question of concentration, a lifetime's work to realign the outer and the inner eye. But it was not until I was on the night train coming back from Luxor that I was actually taken by the shoulders and turned round.....

I woke at three. The train had stopped in a village, an old village which lay the other side of the window under a layer of silver dust, palms and houses embalmed in the moonlight.

I wandered in a time continuum that stretched back two thousand years while the village slept, fixed in space, open to the dreams which alone could unlock the glacial stillness.

And the train remained there a full ten minutes until the mind could take no more and I closed the blind.

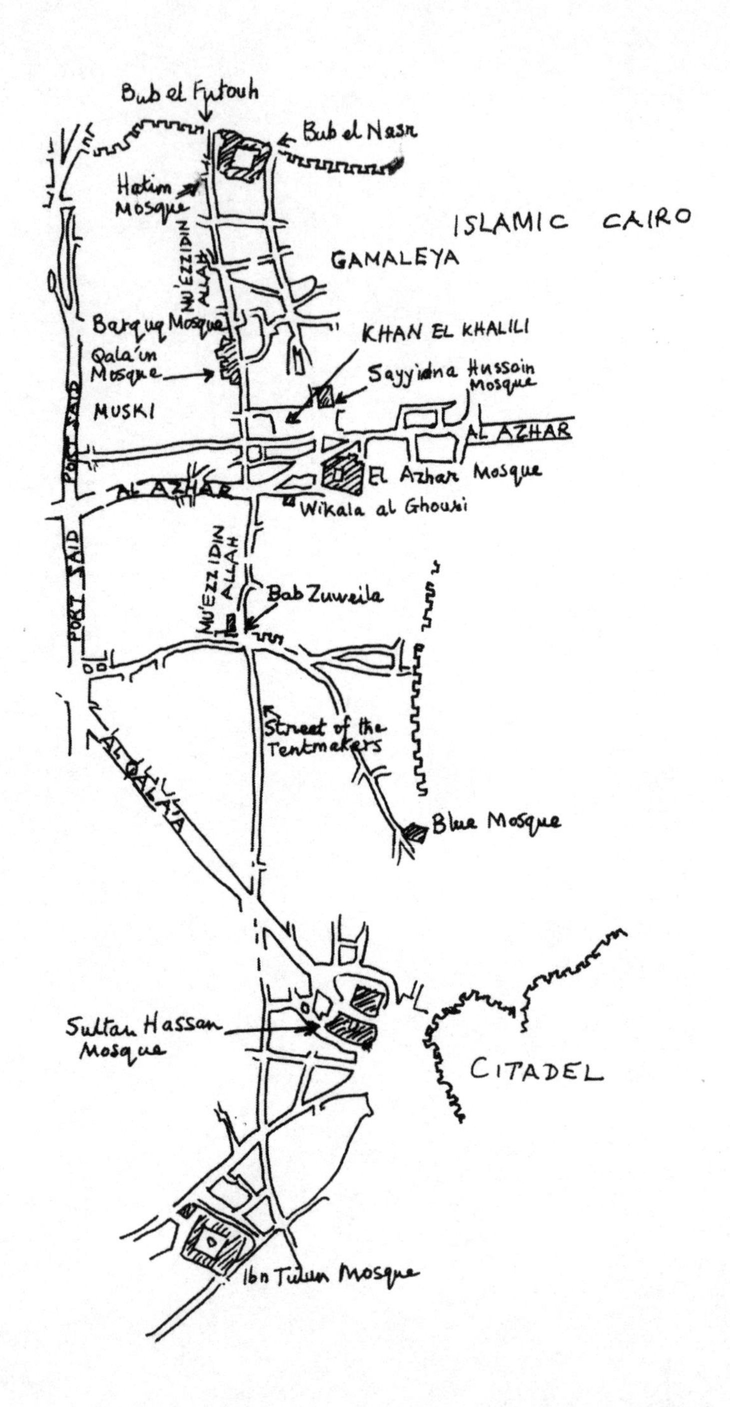
Bub el Futouh
Bub el Nasr
Hatim Mosque
ISLAMIC CAIRO
GAMALEYA
MU'EZZIDIN ALLAH
Barquq Mosque
KHAN EL KHALILI
Qala'un Mosque
Sayyidna Hussoin Mosque
MUSKI
PORT SAID
AL AZHAR
El Azhar Mosque
AL AZHAR
Wikala al Ghouri
PORT SAID
MU'EZZIDIN ALLAH
Bab Zuweila
Street of the Tentmakers
AL QALAA
Blue Mosque
Sultan Hassan Mosque
CITADEL
Ibn Tulun Mosque

Chapter Six

There is a street in the Fatamid city called the Sharia Mu'ezzidin Allah. It runs the length of it from north to south and is its spine. Around it grew the medieval city – as a cursory glance at any map will show. It is an archaeological compendium of its history.

The casual observer, however, starting at the southern end, would be hard put to think it so. Once past the imposing gate of Bab Zuweila and the Al Mu'ayyad Mosque the street is rather unprepossessing, clogged with carts, seedy Indian stalls, sellers of pots and pans – all the bric-a-brac of the cheap bazaar. Here the medieval city is buried under slums, Mamluk mansions overrun with families, four, five to a house, or taken over by artisans. But if you persevere – and it is worth persevering – over the new road that cuts through the Fatamid city from the Salah Salem highway to the city centre, past the Jewish quarter, the spice markets and the bazaars of Khan al-Khalili, the street begins to open up; the shops and stalls give way to walls and domes, traces of Samarkand and Spain, the Abbasids of Iraq, the Omayyads of Syria, Circassians and Turks, drawing together strands of times and places and lives into the living street. The street was my escape hatch, an emotional earthing point. I never came to it without a tingle of anticipation.

There were many touchstones, of place and rhythm as well as time: biblical rhythms set by the ambling carts moving through the congestion and bustle on the unpaved road like boats on a slow moving river. The inertial current carrying this steady stream of commerce affected everyone: the street traders and the *fellaheen* huddled on the backs of the mule carts gliding by.

From a cart one saw the street as a pedestrian never could. It was a good way to touch its magic, for the mind, relieved of the consciousness of walking, moved unhindered, better able to make the imaginative leap.

Once I was offered a lift on a mule cart in the early afternoon, when the world slept. The way was clear, so the driver drove his mule hard and we galloped till the whole street spun. He dropped me outside the Qalaoun Mosque at a point where the street opens up after Khan al-Khalili. I had to look around to find my bearings. Dusty *mashrabeyas* embellished an old house across from me; apart from a dishevelled Victorian lamppost leaning drunkenly I could have been back five hundred years.

It was not just the street's antiquity – a thousand years of it – that drew me to it; it was the ease with which it conjured up its ghosts. I only had to walk through the massive portcullis of the Bab el-Futouh to relive the accounts of Edward Lane and Gerard de Nerval, two early nineteenth century travellers, watching the return of the caravan from Mecca.

Here the Hakim Mosque abuts the Bab el-Futouh, brooding behind crennelated walls – a fitting monument to the capricious innocent after whom it takes its name. Caliph Hakim was the grandson of the great Mu'ezzidin who founded Cairo. Hakim, so we are told by the phantasmagorical de Nerval, studied astrology, even building an observatory on the Muqattam, and was given to visions, discerning divine portents in his stars. Concerned that these might be prejudiced by his sister Setalmulk contracting an alliance with a mere mortal, thereby sullying the ancestral bloodline, he resolved to marry her. The prospect so horrified his sister she conspired with Hakim's advisers, who also had much to fear from his highly erratic and idiosyncratic behaviour, to have him put away. One night, wandering the city in disguise as he was wont to do to discover the true condition of his subjects, he was picked up on the orders of his Grand Vizier and placed in an asylum.

There, what tenuous links Hakim had with reality were broken. In the unhinged world of the mentally deranged, the norms and conventions of daily life, which had at least forced him to question his instincts, no longer obtained. Here, where they spoke a language of the heart, the unadulterated impulse, it took little encouragement from his co-inmates to persuade him he was indeed divine. When finally he escaped the asylum and reclaimed his throne – exacting condign retribution of his tormentors, the head of the Grand Vizier amongst others – he decided to put his ideas to the test. He proclaimed an amnesty and began by lifting the humiliating ordinances he had imposed on Jews and Christians; he allowed freedom of speech and encouraged criticism – even of himself. It seemed like the dawn of a new age. And with most such dawns, it proved to be a false one.

For Hakim disappeared soon after, never to be seen again. Some say his sister had him killed, fearing he might follow through on his intention to marry her. By this account he was ambushed and despatched. Others say he wasn't killed but, weary of court life, retired to the desert. After his disappearance his followers were driven out of Cairo and settled in the mountains of Lebanon where they founded the nation of the Druze.

Legend – and legend it is – attributes a cautionary tale to another of medieval Cairo's treasures: the towering *madrassa* (religious school) and mosque of Sultan Hassan, which nestles beneath the Citadel outside the city walls. Hassan was an unprepossessing Mamluk sultan who came to the throne as an adolescent and achieved little in his one score years and seven beyond establishing an undeserved reputation for personal extravagance; undeserved because the state's treasure was not squandered in riotous living but on a grand project: the construction of the greatest mosque the world had ever seen. True, he hoped that in dedicating this edifice to the glory of God, a little of its kudos would rub off on him, conscious that posterity was unlikely to remember him for anything else he was likely to achieve. However, Allah saw through Hassan's overweening pride and exacted a terrible vengeance. Exactly a year after completion the dome collapsed killing forty pupils in the school beneath. And forty days later Hassan himself disappeared in mysterious circumstances, never to be seen again.

In fact it was a minaret over the main entrance to the mosque that collapsed during construction, killing three hundred, which turned the fates against Hassan. The calamity was taken as a sign by the populace that Hassan's days were numbered, which indeed they were, for he was kidnapped a month or so afterwards and subsequently murdered.

However, Hassan can be said to have had the last laugh, for his mosque and *madrassa* are a triumphant vindication of his own bid for immortality and are amongst Islamic Cairo's finest architectural gems.

There were still other touchstones: the thrill of the call

to prayer with its evocation of a deeper, more primitive consciousness, a barrage of sound magnified by the tannoy system that stopped the street dead in its tracks, froze it before a simulation of the Flood. There were numerous dusks and nighttimes, each with their own atmosphere and mood; and there were the festivals.

The most important festival is the month long fast of Ramadan. During Ramadan, a display is staged at the Hussein Mosque just to the east of Khan al-Khalili that ranks amongst the world's great carnivals, a night long charivari of Koranic recitations and dancing with the haunting spectacle of Cairo's street theatre thrown in: the musicians, the dwarfs, the jugglers, the fire eaters and the *khowals* set against the ubiquitous *koshori* stalls, the lights and the charcoal fires. The war put an end to the Ramadan celebrations in 1973, but I was up at the Hussein Mosque for the *mawlid al-nabbi*, which fell in March that year.

The crush was intense. Weaving crocodile lines passed through the square and filed into the Hussein Mosque, into the glare of white neon and white marble, the signs of 'Allah' everywhere in fluorescent green. Blue smoke wafted in amongst the lights leaving fluttery patterns in the brain. The effect was psychedelic: the smoke, the neon lights and the dripping fairy lights over the stalls where, in yellow day brightness, they sold *arussa* dolls, the sinister sugar dolls of the *mawlid*, painted like Cinderella's ugly sisters with crepe fan bustles and iridescent ballerina's wings.

In the prayer tents they were limbering up for the *zikr* (the dance of remembrance), the *imam* reciting from the Sufi texts in time with the sharp *allahus* of the dancers as they stamped their feet and swung their arms. As the rhythm established itself, more joined them until there were some eighty dancers ranged in lines, swaying in unison, like trees before the wind. Just as it seemed the beat had tamed them into a single motion, it quickened; and while the majority strained to stay with it, a few went off into their own dance. The arms pumped faster in frenzied arcs until they gradually lost the battle to keep up with the pivotal swing of the swaying crowd. The lines of dancers regrouped and with arms raised, jumped and swayed on the spot chanting 'Allah, Allah', while the few continued to whirl and gyrate till they, too, lost the beat and dropped out one by one.

Slowly the floor cleared leaving debris as from a battle or a stampede. Most only needed a helping hand as they jigged and hopped, nerves jangled, glassy eyed, gibbering and foaming from the mouth; but there were a few beyond help, who writhed in paroxysms on the ground, overcome with hashish, or an excess of oxygen to the brain, or the sheer elation of being part of that throng, swaying in such all encompassing unison.

The *zikr* is supposedly a holy dance. The ascetics condemn this kind of exhibition as demeaning sensationalism that has nothing to do with the contemplation of unity, the true purpose of the holy dance, and is the very antithesis of that clarity of thought a true Muslim aspires to: the play of feeling in the 'what is so'. Nevertheless, the *zikr* is an integral part of the religious festivals.

At the *mawlid* Hussein, a month later, (the *mawlid* Hussein celebrates the birth of Imam Hussein, Mohammed's grandson, whose head is buried in the Hussein Mosque), I saw the *zikr* danced in the back streets of the Gamaleya district which abuts

Khan al-Khalili. It was an occasion straight from the Arabian Nights, without reference in time or space, a trip into the light fantastic.

Turning off the Sharia Mu'ezzidin Allah into the Gamaleya district there were no street lights; one had to steer by the odd pin prick of light and the glow of the forges. I walked along a side street where the houses almost touched above my head and down a dark lane. The beat of a drum, the tinkle of steel castanets; the crinkled, rouged face of a *khowal* appeared and was gone, flutes and tablas in his wake. Then silence. Further on in an alley lamps flickered on children riding the swings. Nearer the Hussein Mosque there was a fair. A dwarf stood by the peepshow, cockshies, dumbbells, surreal contraptions for gauging strength. And again, a total absence of sound.

Then, as I moved north towards the Musafirkhana Palace I came, in an open space hollowed out of a narrow passage, across a group of dancers huddled on mats. They hadn't seen me. A lamp flickered from the end of the passage; *mashrabeya* leered as if from empty eye sockets; above, a prickle of stars. The sound of a drum, then flutes, the music strong and sweet, the beat resilient; then like snakes rising to the music, two, three dancers from a cluster rose and began swaying. And as the beat strengthened others joined them, *Sa'eedi* folk or *fellaheen*, their heads bandaged, their *galabeyas* hanging straight from them, swaying like animated dolls to the rising swell of the *zikr*.

A hurricane lamp was lit and threw fluttering shadows on the wall. They started singing, the sound coming almost in spite of themselves, and with it a hiss as they lunged from left to right flailing their arms, the hiss changing to a hoarse, high grunt as the beat quickened. Then, when they could stay with the beat no longer, they burst into short, sharp cries of 'Allah, Allah' and sank to the ground, their billowing skirts subsiding around them.

More lights. I had been seen and the spell was broken. So I made my way back to the Hussein Mosque to find the workmen dismantling the prayer tents. And on the bus back to Babeluk, head cricked against the ceiling above a sea of others, I experienced Cairo as zones of prayer, mapping the city in the *muezzins'* calls.

****

Arabic was the touchstone to the people who were the human fabric of the street. I crossed that threshold one stifling evening in early June up by the Hakim Mosque when I held my first proper conversation in Arabic, with a bus driver from Ismailia.

He came over as I ordered tea in a café that looked out on the city's wholesale garlic market. Across the square against a long wall piles of cloves were stacked so high they dwarfed the shafts of the upended carts propped up against them.

He enquired my nationality. I said 'French.' It was always instructive to gauge an Egyptian's true feelings against his natural predilection to please.

'That's good,' he replied. 'We like the French. They understand us. We prefer them to the English.'

'Why?' I asked.

'We still think of the English as occupiers. They weren't popular here during the war. And they kept to themselves.' He took a sip from his glass.

'Not like the Egyptians?' I ventured.

'No, not like the Egyptians.' Then, after a moment's reflection, as if suddenly conscious of the enormous blessing life had bestowed on him by being born Egyptian, he declared: *'Lakin, fiy kulla haga hinna. Allah karim. W'andina al-shams.'* He spoke from deep in his throat, savouring the words lovingly. 'There's everything here. God is generous. And we have the sun.'

'Yes,' I concurred, reminded of Albert Camus' dictum that it was better to be brought up in the squalor of an Algerian slum than a grey industrial town in northern France. 'You have the sun.'

'People are poor,' he conceded, 'but not too poor. You can still get a meal for 5 piastres.....'

'Not everyone has 5 piastres.'

'Most people do. They manage. Anyway, we don't need all those things you have on Kasr el-Nil: whisky, rum, beer. Look, I'm happy with a glass of tea. So are you.'

'I am, you arc. But is cveryonc?' It was a simplistic vicw that resonated with many but ignored the difficulties most people faced in providing more than the very basics in life. It ignored, too, the undercurrents of familial discontent stirred by materialism and the unmet aspirations of the young. Living in Shobra I witnessed the nascent tensions between Am Mohammed and Fatheya and their children. There was no question of the children openly rebelling, the ties were still too symbiotic, but it was disingenuous to imagine Buzeina, for instance, taking at face value everything her parents told her, though she would obey them out of a sense of duty. I sensed her siblings would toe the line for more practical reasons, because they knew on what side their bread was buttered.

'Nearly everyone,' he continued conceding there were too many people and not enough space. Then added: 'We need development.'

'There's none to speak of,' I pointed out.

'That's the problem. How can there be development when all our money goes to the war? Egypt has no money. What can we do? Israel wants our land. We must have it back.'

'If you have your land back, what is to become of Israel? What do you want to become of Israel? Do you want Israel to disappear all together?'

'No, no, no.' He was vehement. 'They have a right to a place like anyone else. But they have turned out three million Palestinians who are now living with us (he was a little hazy on his facts). What is our population? Thirty-five million? And we have to take in three million more. It is like a house with five beds and six people to sleep in them. You can not go against nature. Sooner or later God will have his way.' And he pointed at the sky.

'Do you think there will be peace?' I asked.

'Not for a long time.'

I left him pondering on the lack of bellicosity of Egyptians and their stoicism, their ability to look disaster in the eye and face it down believing something would turn up. Despite the crippling cost of the War of Attrition and demographic pressures that are set to double the population in the next three decades they retain an optimism many might consider Panglossian. What sets them apart is their patience, the patience that comes with being an old people; they believe profoundly that the laws of nature if not of man are just and everything that goes round eventually comes round.

I walked down the street which was now a hive of activity and bright with lights. In the Jewish quarter they were packing up for the night; the scent of spices lingered.

Towards the Bab Zuweila it suddenly turned quite dark. It took a moment to register that it was another blackout. The garish cloth stalls were suddenly effaced as the lamps were primed behind the *mashrabeyas,* The street blossomed in a network of lace friezes. Beyond the city gate in the Street of the Tentmakers, a few of the tiered booths were still open for business. The subdued light gleamed on the rafters as the crowds shifted beneath in silence, a congregation of the quick and the dead, saints and sinners, knaves and fools bobbing through the smoke.

Chapter Seven

June

Dense dews on Gezira Island. Cool, crystalline mornings, deadly still until the heat aggravates the wind.

Then one morning you wake and there is no moisture, the air is thick, the outline of the Muqattem blurred and heavy. With the last gasp of the north wind the city loses its will to fight. The greens turn grey. Like a chameleon the city dissembles to survive; the heat stills everything to the dull blood throb of the world's pulse ticking gently. Summer is a kind of hibernation in reverse.

I had taken a flat in Aguza. Aguza – which means 'old woman' in Arabic – runs north of Dokki on the west bank of the Nile up to the industrial district of Embaba. It is a residential area of modern breeze block apartments and loosely asphalted roads, a district where the slums encroach casually on the middle classes and their hairdressers, boutiques and restaurants. It is not smart like Zamalek, Dokki, Garden City or Maadi, but it has character. I lived on Sharia Mohammed Shaheen behind the military hospital on Sharia el-Nil.

Having lived on Sharia Mohammed Shaheen carried a certain cachet among a generation of Arab students who had studied in Cairo. 'Ah, you lived on Sharia Mohammed Shaheen.' And there would be that tacit understanding of an experience shared.

The Arab Diaspora gravitated to Sharia Mohammed Shaheen because it answered many needs. It wasn't expensive, yet it was accessible and because of the high turnover of residents, there was a degree of privacy if you wanted it and always the street if you didn't.

It was the privacy that the visiting Saudis and Kuwaitis liked about the street, that and the trees. They longed for green. Come to think of it, it was the trees that distinguished Sharia Mohammed Shaheen. There were very few streets in Cairo with trees.

The Saudis and Kuwaitis arrived in May and June, descending on Cairo like flocks of migratory birds. One morning you would find them, wandering aimlessly down Sharia Talaat Harb or Sharia Adli, distinctive in their muslin *dishdasha* or *thobe* and *ghutra*.

Their presence was felt instantly on another barometer, the price of apartments. Cairo smelt money when they appeared. A house on Gezira Island which you could probably have rented for E£60 to E£70 a month in the winter shot up to E£300. These inflated rents included the decorator's bill; landlords could be persuaded to settle for less if they could be sure the place would be left more or less habitable when the flats were vacated.

In Aguza landlords weren't so fussy. Nevertheless, the price of apartments rose sharply even in Aguza and I was lucky to find a grubby little flat on the second floor of No. 54 for E£25 a month. It overlooked a junkyard where Mr. Badri, the *bowab*, was trying to grow a couple of mango trees. He had cleared a space to plant the seedlings and had dug an irrigation canal between them. It didn't look promising. But Mr. Badri watered them each day and mended the damage done by scavenging dogs.

The apartment had apparently been designed so that there wasn't a spot in it that wasn't overlooked. However, in summer the shutters kept out the heat and the dust, as well as the prying eyes. It had the bare necessities: a fridge, a table, five chairs and a gas stove. In the sitting room, which gave onto a poky balcony, there was an ornamental hat stand and a stuffed wooden framed sofa.

The bedroom had a matching rococo wardrobe and dressing table in panelled walnut with doors that lifted out on nonexistent hinges. They were a natural sanctuary for the cockroaches that emerged around ten in the evening, peeking out from the telltale crevices in the floor. After a quick shufti to ensure the coast was clear they would scuttle to the wardrobe where they regrouped until about an hour after lights out when they advanced into the rooms. I hunted them with sadistic pleasure, bought sprays to kill them in unspeakable ways and lay still listening for their scuffles before turning on the light and despatching them. Later, much later, when sleep was a notion you could at last entertain, I began counting dead cockroaches in place of sheep.

The nights were exhausting. At the height of the summer the heat didn't begin to subside until about two. Around four the cocks began crowing. In the uneasy silence which followed, the cats found time to settle their vendettas and the dogs joined them in a symphony of barks and caterwauling that echoed eerily through the tenements. At five it was dawn and the first tremulous quavers of birdsong brought hope of repose. Soon the roar of it drowned out the cats and the dogs and sleep could be entertained.

But as Aguza subsided into slumber there was a commotion. A van pulled up in the street below. A long shattering hoot; Aguza must have been sleeping with cotton wool in its ears for it didn't raise a snuffle. Another blast, an extended wail of excruciating pain like a knife turned at the base of the spine that continued until the battery ran down. Finally, shouts as the driver's mate emerges; doors slam, the engine revs reviving the horn and they set off hooting all the way to Embaba.

Mornings were thus spent recovering from the night before. A late groggy start and I would pop into the telephone office to establish contact with the outside world. The telephone operator presided over the chaos of his office with cool, grey eyes. It was quite possible to spend a morning waiting for a line. Yet you dared not demur nor stir seated on the wooden benches awaiting your turn. How well he had us trained!

Out on the street hawkers were assembling scales; melons and marrows lay dappled by the sun; fruits and vegetables glowed in the shade of the jacaranda trees.

Stopping for bread I launch into the ritual of a Cairo day.

'Sabah el-kheer.' I'd greet the bread seller handling the unleavened pats like discuses.

'Sabah el-full.' he'd reply. The morning of the jasmine.

'Sabah el-ishta.' The morning of the cream.

Despite everything it was undeniably a beautiful day. With the sun filtering through the flaming jacaranda trees, Sharia Mohammed Shaheen was a veritable playground for the senses, from my end of the street where the road petered out in slums and the children's playground, down to the taxi rank at the other end where the fruits forgot themselves, unable to be contained, and spilt over onto the pavement.

A kilo of tomatoes cost me 4 piastres. A flip of the breast for the suckling infant as the thickset woman chose and weighed the fruit, a full firm nipple casually swept aside as another tomato was added to the scales.

All these women, it seemed, were with child or suckling, handmaidens to the Goddess of Fertility. Mothers in black *malayas* over floral patterned dresses and scarlet tasselled shawls combed the matted hair of their young. Fathers in *galabeyas* held their children tenderly. It started here with this prodigality of nature. The women would take the stance of their pregnancies into old age, the arched back to counteract the heaviness of the child. They would spend more than half their lives with this quickening in the womb.

It was the best time to walk in the street, before the heat got up. The Great Heat. You steeled yourself for when the thermometer rose above blood temperature, when the tarmac softened.... The heat would usually build in waves, two to three days at a time and then burst with an inrush of cool, deliciously cool breezes, which would enliven the skin and permit sleep. But each time the north wind blew a little weaker, a little less certain and the heat would build inexorably hour by hour, day by day, week by week, until the city was finally without inner resources to resist it and the evenings brought no relief but something worse, a stifling draught of air from the desert. Dusk in midsummer is the hottest time.

There were two antidotes to the heat; cool drinks and showers. It was about this time that I established an intimate acquaintanceship with Stella beer which I bought from a woman near the telephone office. She charged 15 piastres a bottle and gave 2 piastres for returns.

Then one day I bumped into Mr. Badri on the stairs, about to replenish my supplies. He saw the empty bottles.

'Where are you going with those?' he demanded.

'I'm going to get more beer.'

'Where do you get it from?'

'From the woman across the road.'

'How much do you pay?'

'Thirteen piastres.'

'Thirteen piastres? No!' He laughed incredulously. 'Our beer is 15 piastres; it's the cheapest in Cairo. Call Hussein when you need beer.' It was an offer I could hardly refuse. So thereafter I used to go to Mr. Badri's assistant, Hussein, for my beer and paid 16 piastres a bottle. It was explained to me it was necessary to add 'baksheesh'.

Mr. Badri used to call in person at the end of the month for his money.

'What money, Mr. Badri?' I enquired. 'You had a tip when I signed the contract and I thought the rent included all other expenses.'

He waved his finger. 'Oh, oh,' he said. 'How can I and my family live if you don't pay me?' he asked disingenuously.

'How much do you want, Mr. Badri?'

'One pound.'

I didn't quibble. But a little bit of mental arithmetic in the wee small hours when I wasn't counting dead cockroaches persuaded me that Mr. Badri was making a small killing if he was taking the same amount from every flat in the block.

About eleven it was time to go into town. By then everyone was in his place. A shrivelled old lady ministered to the coals roasting the sweet corn. Another sat by her and opened a napkin containing a handful of unripe limes. Limes were sold individually for 2 piastres each. Geese, chickens and rabbits waited in crabbed, wicker cages for the knife and the bloodstained jerry can, always kept discreetly out of view but detectable by the swarm of flies.

'Gaz, gaz,' bleated the paraffin man with a hoot on his two-tone horn. 'Eeaw, eeaw, gaz, gaz.' He was the street clown, bent at forty-five degrees under his pack. The tabla man passed and banged at the flute seller who peeped back. A little girl in a yellow patterned dress joined in with makeshift castanets made from bottle tops jigging to the tabla. The street was strident with syncopated sound.

But Sayeed was nowhere to be seen. Sayeed was the 'fix-it' man through whom I had hired the flat. It was almost impossible to run the gauntlet of the street without bumping into him. With each step I would expect to be stopped dead by his strangled cry, 'Meester Elen, Meester Elen,' and run down by a little man with a big jaw and a small moustache on a bicycle with no brakes.

'Meester Elen, *izzayak*, (how are you)?' He would shoo everyone away.

'Very well, thank you, Mr. Sayeed. And how are you?'

'Kwaiss, il-hamdulillah. Inta awz haga? Good. Praise the Lord. Do you want anything?'

He looked at me earnestly.

'No, thank you, Mr. Sayeed. I have everything.'

'Kwaiss, kwaiss giddan, Meester Elen.' And having finally satisfied himself, 'Meester Elen, *habibi*,' before scuttling off.

This morning, mysteriously, he wasn't there. He was such a fundamental fact of life on the street that his absence caused a loss of bearings, like the sun momentarily passing behind a small cloud as I walked up towards the bus stop. It wasn't going to be a good day. And so it proved.

I usually caught a bus to Tahrir Square or, failing that, a trolley bus to the crossroads outside the Sheraton and changed. A 99 or a 174 would take me directly into town but they were capricious and usually came in pairs. But they were cheap: 1½ piastres in the front, 1 piastre in the rear. Breaking the journey was messy and more expensive; you had to weigh the odds: wait for a direct bus and chance anything up to an hour's wait or take the combination.

On Cairo buses you learned to make an art of travel, to sail, as it were, in place of motoring, and in so doing you acquired a new terminology governed by standing capacity, traffic flows, temperature gauges and service frequencies (and anomalies).

It was amazing how you came to feel for these leaky battleships. If you saw one on a hot day, gently boiling over in the middle of Ramses Street, snarling the traffic right up to Tahrir Square, you empathized. There was something especially poignant in witnessing one of these great-hearted beasts being towed away to the scrap yard. Cairenes did not treat their buses well. A self-respecting Cairo donkey got a better deal than a Cairo bus, and that was saying something. It wasn't therefore surprising that at any one time a third of the city's buses were off the road being repaired or serviced.

Cairo, in theory, was one of the best served capitals in the world for transport. If you looked at the routes and schedules, you didn't have to walk more than a hundred yards to find a bus, trolley bus, tram or Metro stop. But Cairo's transport was like its telephones: if you got a line, you still had to get through; if you found a bus, you had to get on it. There was no necessary connection between the theory and the reality. In practice Cairo's depleted and obsolescent rolling stock was insufficient and thinly spread.

Cairenes, nevertheless, adapted with ridiculous ingenuity. Not content with making human conserve jars of their buses they would take to the roof, running boards, bumpers, loose skirting, anything that offered a toehold or a crevice for a fingernail. The conductors kitted in gym shoes and khaki trews did battle with them. They were scandalously undervalued and underpaid, these Protean elves: to a memory for faces of a third generation computer they were required to possess the physical attributes of a Houdini, the perseverance of a storm trooper and the patience of a saint.

A conscientious conductor attempted to take all fares, a task worthy of Sisyphus, especially as he would announce his presence by tapping a lead tipped pencil on his ticket board and calling, '*Hat ya bey... Ersh ya effendim... Aiwah ya ustaz... Ya ukhti, khud.*' It made everyone feel wanted to be called professor, sister, lord and sir, but gave determined bilkers ample time to burrow further into the human fastness. Despite the heroic efforts of its conductors, Cairo Transport lost about a third of its revenue in unpaid fares.

It was not surprising that I was late for my appointment with Fawzi. I had met Fawzi Wafei through mutual friends. He was a political journalist on the payroll of a weekly magazine that did not overtax his talents which he employed otherwise as an author and translator. He was working on the translation of a biography of Theodore Herzl into Arabic.

Fawzi's office was in a rambling town house located in a side street off Kasr el-Aini in Garden City. It was the requisitioned home of a rich Jewish merchant. As you entered the building you were confronted by a neon sign of Allah in fluorescent green. Doors led off the entrance hall to conference rooms and a dishevelled tickertape spewed unwanted information. The place had the air of a temporary army headquarters. To find Fawzi you had to climb the gracefully wrought spiral staircase to the first floor where he inhabited a room with six others and laid claim to one of its two telephones.

As I poked my head round the door Fawzi jumped from his seat. '*Ahlan wa sahlan. It faddal 'a'od, a'od,*' he said, offering me a seat while embarking on the intricate Arab ritual of welcome, inquiring into states of health and mind, repeating ourselves to ensure we had it absolutely right and that the other was at the peak, the prime, not a whit under or over, liberally interspersing this painstaking investigation with '*il-hamdulillahs*'. Two or three minutes later, having looked ourselves over for the final time, Fawzi asked if I wanted coffee.

'Come on, Alan,' said Fawzi. 'I would like you to meet a dear friend. (Fawzi only had dear friends). Mr. Mohammed runs a textile factory in Mansoura. He does our crossword puzzles.'

Mr. Mohammed had a bullet head and small eyes and at some point had worked in a university in Melbourne, an experience he had not particularly enjoyed. 'No tradition,' he said.

'I think that's no bad thing,' I volunteered. 'I find tradition here a bit heavy sometimes. In a fruit parlour this morning I was asked what religion I was.'

'That has nothing to do with tradition,' he pronounced. 'I happen to be a Moslem. But I am also an Egyptian and above all a human being. There is a *sura* (verse) in the Koran that says so long as you lead a good life and believe in God you will go to heaven. People who make an issue of religion are ignorant.'

'Some people do seem unduly conscious of religion here though,' I interjected, and I told him of Azzam's experience as a Palestinian.

'Yes, but it is easy to make an issue of an individual incident,' he replied. 'You never hear of the millions of Copts and Moslems living together, hardly aware that they are different.

'It was only with the arrival of the imperial powers, the Turks, the French and the British, that people became conscious of religion,' he added. 'It served the interests of the imperialists to use religion as an instrument of government. Religion only began to be institutionalized here about one hundred and fifty years ago, three to four hundred years after Europe if you take the Renaissance as the start of the breakup of medieval society, and it is a process which isn't finished even today. This is because in Islam there's no equivalent to the Church in Christianity. There's just you and God.

'That is true religion and it is still very important to us. You see, it is a way of life, a way of looking at things... a pattern if you like. That is what I mean by tradition.

'We are an old people,' he continued. 'We have experienced invasion and occupation. Often we had nothing except our attachment to the land. But suffering has not affected our love of life. We respect life; friendships mean more to us than possessions.' He became diffident searching for words. 'It does matter that we are polite to one another...'

'Fine,' I interjected again. 'But what happens when the combine harvesters start churning up the Nile Valley and industrialization eats into the available land, when a bit of prosperity makes everyone want more? What of the population explosion, a million more mouths to feed each year?'

'We need the population, we need the productive power. We have the land; it is simply a question of bringing water to it, a problem of organization.'

'Extra mouths to feed make it more difficult to provide the basic requirements of life.'

'You lived in Shobra. You couldn't have more difficult social conditions than Shobra.'

'Well, there's Calcutta. No one's dying on the streets of Shobra. But I take your point. How do you conserve this individuality against all the pressures and the temptations?'

'I don't know,' he conceded. 'All one can say is that up to now it has worked. We still have a balance which you seem to have lost in the West.'

Fawzi looked at his watch. Mr. Mohammed apologized for having taken up so much of our time. As we were about to leave he said: 'It is a pity there is not more trust between Britain and France and the Middle East, (he dismissed America as a country, like Australia, with no tradition). We have very old links with Europe. Remember, Alexandria was a Greek port. We need your culture, but we had bad experiences under your imperialism.'

Fawzi was apologetic when he was gone. 'He talks too much,' he said.

I begged to differ. 'Fascinating,' I said. 'You produce a factory manager from Mansoura who explains how socialism in Egypt works; the individual triumphs over the system. True socialism can't be legislated for,' I continue. 'It's part of a culture. Otherwise it's back to competing elites managed by bureaucrats.'

Fawzi smiled; he knew all about bureaucrats. As the local boy-made-good Fawzi had come to university in Cairo and then gone into journalism. He lived with his widowed mother and numerous brothers and sisters in a small flat in Abbasseya. Now thirty, he had the means to live independently; his family owned a small farm in the Delta and his father had left him a little money. However, he took his obligations as the eldest son and thus the *rab al-bait* (head of the family) seriously, and continued to live at home, forbearing his mother's strictures. He was not allowed girl friends in the house and his mother was constantly on at him to marry and settle down. The thought of a conventional Muslim marriage appalled Fawzi; the emancipation of women he considered Islam's most urgent task. Yet he played along with his mother's foibles; it didn't bother him sufficiently to make an issue of them. Instead, he kept his domestic and his social lives apart.

Fawzi was no longer a practising Muslim. But the same logic that had made him reject conventional Islam had helped him to unclutter his beliefs. Islam had given him the base, for which he was grateful. He no longer had anything to prove; he had moved on, but remained loyal to his roots. For this reason he, like many young Egyptians with left-wing sympathies, had issues with Communism. They found it difficult to reconcile their belief in a 'higher agent' with the Marxist view.

Fawzi took me to the Press Syndicate for a late lunch. Situated in a side street running between Talaat Harb and Sharia Ramses the Press Syndicate, with its spacious, shady garden and comfortable low slung wicker chairs was a popular downtown bolthole for anyone in need of a snack.

'You know,' said Fawzi, 'if we had met three years ago, I wouldn't have kept in contact with you. At that time I was too suspicious of foreigners. It's very complicated and goes back a long way. The English always meant fear. When I was a child and my mother wanted to stop me doing something, she used to threaten to get an English policeman. So when Nasser came he was like a god. He made us feel we were our own masters. Our history books at school were full of Egypt's glorious past. I remember believing when I was sixteen or seventeen that there was absolutely nothing I couldn't do. And there was so much I wanted to do. I thought I only had to raise my little finger and the western powers would run away.

'Then came 1967. Overnight it was all swept away. It is difficult to describe what it felt like, as though I and everything I stood for had been wiped out. For weeks I did nothing. Then I decided I had to start again, to rediscover who I was and what my country was. So I wrote a book, a biography of six of our greatest artists just to find out what they had in common and what they had in common with us all. It did me a lot of good writing the book and it must have struck a chord in people because it sold well.

'I got over 1967. But in 1970 Nasser changed direction again and tried to make friends with the West. For so long he had told us that all our problems were the result of western imperialism, and there he was, making friends with America.

No, if you had met me three years ago, you would have found a very confused and suspicious man. And then ...' he smiled ruefully, 'we were discouraged. It wouldn't have gone well with me to be found mixing with foreign journalists.'

'What has changed?' I knew he was suspicious of Sadat that he might, as he put it, 'sell out Egypt to the West'.

'It's more relaxed.'

We talked of the sackings a little time before of a number of Egyptian journalists. 'What do you expect?' he asked. 'We don't have a free Press here.'

More important than the atmosphere of suspicion and intrigue this engendered was the absence of an environment in which a journalist could test his objectivity and balance.

Leaving Fawzi I headed home. Tahrir Square was a heaving mass of humanity that at times you stepped over and at others queued with. The evening rush hour was always fraught in high summer. The afternoon siesta stopped everything in its tracks. Buses disappeared; taxi drivers, solicitous for their tyres, cleared off the streets as soon as the tar began to melt. If you had to get somewhere in mid afternoon and didn't have your own transport, you tried the Hilton for a hotel taxi or you walked.

When the taxis and buses reappeared around four or five they met a huge, pent-up demand: from those forced to delay their journeys by the afternoon hiatus, and from commuters who had been assiduously conserving their energies for the second big challenge of their day, getting home.

I found a space on a balustrade and waited. The tired fountain in Tahrir Square eructated spasmodically and the patient bus catchers sat on the balding grass and nattered as the sunset proscribed them, a summer sky of lime and yellow and hydrangea blue, thick with dust.

Suddenly there was a commotion. A bus stopped and a man in *galabeya* leapt from it, blood streaming from a head wound. A youth followed. They made for an open space by the fountain. There they stood in the stagy half light, the peasant beside himself, the youth wary, while the bus waited and two policemen and a large crowd looked on. The peasant lunged, the youth side-stepped him. Then the peasant remembered the sacks he had left on the bus. Half way through manhandling two cumbersome bales off the bus his temper got the better of him and he made for the youth again. The youth backed, stripped to the waist, and came forward with a knife in his hand. It looked serious. But the sight of the knife checked the peasant and the moment's pause allowed wiser counsels to prevail. He suddenly thought of his unattended sacks which a bystander had put to one side to let through a long queue of buses. Satisfied that the sacks were intact, the peasant came back for the youth. It was only then the policemen intervened.

After an hour of unavailing waiting, I trudged home. There were always compensations in these evening walks: the caress of the rising breeze from the Nile on the skin, the feeling of coming alive again and this evening a beguiling gibbous moon sandpapered, it seemed, into the grainy sky.

Mr. Sayeed was on his way home and invited me to go with him. I followed him into the slum district behind the hospital. 'This way,' he said, manipulating his bike through a narrow passageway and up some stairs to the roof. 'Here we are.'

It was incredible that Mr. Sayeed who would produced a thick wad of notes when he asked if there was anything I wanted, should live on a roof. 'Home' was three rooms. He and his family had one and shared the kitchen with his sister and brother-in-law who had the other. 'Come and see my palace,' said Mr. Sayeed without the slightest trace of irony. The room was dominated by a huge nuptial bed on which one of his six children slept. There was a narrow couch and little else.

We went back to the porch and sat in the moonlight. Ducks nosed among the disused packing cases.

Sayeed's brother-in-law joined us. He had trained as a lawyer and was now a school teacher. He was very erudite and might have been a little overpowering for the diminutive, not over intellectual Mr. Sayeed. But Mr. Sayeed, it seemed, was used to overpowering people having a wife twice his size.

'Sayeed's wife is always wanting another baby,' said his brother-in-law. 'Sayeed never knows when it's going to stop. He's got six and she still wants more.'

Sayeed was philosophical. 'If she wants another little one, who am I to say, no?' he asked rhetorically. You had to admire his pluck. He approached his wife and his burgeoning family as he did his incorrigible shirtsleeves and his incorrigible bicycle. Energy and good humour were Mr. Sayeed's mainstays.

A few days later I prepared for a visit from the El Gamals. They had been curious to see my flat so I invited them to tea. I bought two large ice creams from Groppis which were packed in ice that made a pool on the floor of the taxi on the way home. I dusted the top of the tallboy and the hat stand, smoothed out the covers on the sofa, made cheese sandwiches and invited my friend, Anais, to join us.

Only Atar and a friend turned up. Am Mohammed was having one of his 'turns', explained Atar who was on his best behaviour. He was direct, spoke when he was spoken to and was disarmingly shy. It was difficult to associate the Atar of Shobra with this quiet, unassuming young man. Anais was enchanted. Atar told us he was going abroad for the summer to earn money. He had given up the idea of Beirut, Kuwait and Abu Dhabi and was now thinking of Rome. Did I know anyone there? He had a friend who was working in a restaurant near Rome who was in Egypt on holiday. They were thinking of going back to Italy together.

'You don't speak Italian, though.'

'Je barle français,' Atar volunteered.

'Oh. Vous parlez français?' Anais was anxious to find a more substantial line of communication than Atar's smile. Two short, crisp sentences, however, disarmed his French.

He had a cup of tea and a cheese sandwich and his friend had the same. They didn't touch the ice cream. Then they left. At the door Atar paused and shuffled uneasily. 'Baba wants the packet of cigarettes you had in your suitcase.' I let him squirm. 'Well, you tell baba I'll think about it.'

Anais thought I was unkind. But she still took me to the Gezira Club. Anais was a temporary member and I wasn't any sort of member, so we had to go through a certain amount of rigmarole to get me in. The Gezira Club, situated in the middle of Gezira Island, is an oasis of urbanity and exclusivity created by the British to give them a sense of home from home. For many an old Cairo hand the Gezira Club and Groppis – and perhaps Shepheard's Hotel and the Turf Club before they were burnt down – *were* Cairo. It was Nasser, bless him, emulating the best traditions of the English National Trust, who opened the doors of the Gezira Club to the nation, enabling the new élite to rub shoulders with the dwindled pool of Europeans and the remnants of 'Le tout Caire.'

Anais, being Armenian, found a table in the Armenian corner of the clubhouse and went round to each table with me in tow to pay her respects. It was inconceivable that she should have done otherwise. Anais Aslanian didn't go a bomb on presentations. 'Hypocrisy,' she complained. 'Me, the niece of the famous architect Rastan Balyan, fine. As the school teacher, that's another matter. Mothers discourage their children from talking to teacher out of school.'

For a girl brought up in White Plains, life took some getting used to in Egypt. Anais fitted uncomfortably into the web of family connections and didn't get on well with the formidable aunt in Alexandria who controlled the family and its fortune. Born in Egypt, she and her mother and father had moved to the US when she was still quite young. She was back to use up a small legacy and she taught at the Armenian school to earn some pocket money.

'It's oriental, this concern with etiquette,' I said. 'Perhaps the Armenians are a little more stuck up. But don't minorities tend to be ... defence mechanisms? And they haven't had life too easy, especially under Nasser. Copts, Armenians being passed over for Muslims, etc. ... and the sequestrations.'

'They've made no effort to assimilate,' she retorted. 'My folk came here for the good life. They all came here for the good life, Armenians, Greeks, Jews, Italians, British, French, the lot of them. They aren't prepared to accept the rough with the smooth. Anyway, it's not that bad here.'

'I must admit I don't get a ghetto feeling with the minorities.'

'Because on the whole the minority groups chose to come here, they came to positions of power or were skilled craftsmen. They were on the whole educated, cultivated people. It wasn't so with minorities in the States. Most first generation immigrants in the States were driven there. They were artisans and labourers and lived in ghettoes. They were the underdogs. And to protect their sense of identity they concocted a romanticized folklore of their homelands that often bore little resemblance to life there. They added a few of the sharp edges of American life, the aggressiveness and the violence, partly out of a self-protective neurosis, partly ignorance. These people lacked culture. You only have to look at the anti-Communist campaigns of the '50s.'

'The Armenians in the States are much more violently anti-Turk than the Armenians here. Why? You would have thought it would be the other way round. After all, the Armenians here are nearer the action. The difference is that the Armenians here have thought it out more. It doesn't mean that they're buddies with the Turks but they realize they can't live in the past.'

'You can't dismiss the Armenian massacres so casually...'

'No. You don't, you can't forget the massacres. Out of curiosity I once started reading about them; I wanted to know where I came from, who I was. But I had to stop, it upset me too much.'

'It must be the same for Jews.'

'Yes, I think it is and more so. Do you know that the Nazis studied the methods used by the Turks in exterminating the Armenians and decided they weren't efficient enough? No, the paranoia is real enough. It's something you always carry inside and it never leaves you. But it's a personal problem now. You can't go on blaming the world for ever.

'What I disliked about some Jews I knew in the States was the way they tended to make you feel personally responsible for what happened to them. Now I accept the trauma of the concentration camps, but the Jews are not the only people to have experienced genocide. No, they have become self-indulgent. They won't grow up so long as they are allowed to get away with it. You can't blame them. In life, you takes what you can get.'

It was dark. The last glimmer of colour had died in the laburnum. The arc lights had come on over the bowling greens. We collected the bill and left, Anais back to town, I to Aguza.

There was a wedding party in progress on the street. The beer was on the house; a rich Libyan was marrying a local girl and they had turned the cul-de-sac by the telephone office into a makeshift theatre. Mr. Badri insisted I stay and found me a chair. The show was very bad; the troupe lacked inspiration and kept repeating their limited repertoire. The audience soon ran out of applause. Eyes wandered to the third floor window where the bridal couple were abed. 'They used to produce the handkerchief,' a bystander observed. 'The Libyans are marrying all our girls,' said another, and sloped off to find another beer.

A few days later, calling round at the Golden for my mail, I met 'doc' Mohammed in a bad way, hobbling and wincing like a dog on three legs from a nasty sore on his heel which he was encouraging with a grubby bandage. 'Bad leg, Meester Elen,' he kept muttering. Susu was talking to Amin. Now there was a turn-up for the books.

Susu and Amin didn't get on. Susu took exception to Amin and Amin, for whom these things were a simple matter of reciprocity, took exception to Susu. It was a long story. Susu was in the habit of requisitioning the telephone for long periods to conduct an affair. So while she whispered sweet nothings and sorted out her love life the hotel was incommunicado. Amin, in whom the fires of natural justice burned strong, thought this a bit much and told her so. Susu took it badly.

Susu was then seventeen. As a second year sociology student at Cairo University and a bit of a bombshell she had much going for her. Susu thought so, and Susu's mother hoped so. Susu's mother worked late into the night on the second floor, designing dresses to provide the wherewithal to send Susu to university, which only encouraged Susu's pretensions.

She had acquired a boyfriend who was not only good looking but rich, a fellow student. The affair flourished over the telephone, in after-lecture meetings and at Groppis. Mother knew nothing about it and, as she wished to observe the proprieties, Susu was anxious it should remain that way. It was therefore essential that Amin not be so antagonized as to spill the beans. Fares, Amin's uncle and the proprietor of the Golden, was called on to adjudicate. Susu agreed to forgo the use of the hotel telephone and queue with the rest of the world for the public phone at the tobacconist round the corner and mother was kept in blissful ignorance.

That morning Susu had urgent business so, swallowing her pride, she had asked Amin nicely if she might use the phone. Amin had graciously acceded. So that was how Susu came to be reunited with the telephone which she was quietly devouring when a man in slacks, bush shirt and dark glasses walked in breezily and produced a bundle of forms which he placed on the counter in front of Fares.

Fares's glasses came off and his welcoming smile evaporated.

'I'm sorry, I'm having difficulty with these forms,' the official informed him pleasantly. They were documents to do with the hotel. 'I need stamps. Sixty piastres should cover it.'

Inadvertently Fares took two pound notes from his pocket. 'Make it one pound sixty while you're about it,' said the man. 'I might need more.' The two pounds were handed over and no change given.

'What can you do?' said Fares, after he had gone. 'It is better to give in than have the tax people on your back, assessing you for too much. With all the bureaucracy and the forms, they have made it virtually impossible to run a hotel anyway. Say your tax assessment is E£600 a year. They can easily raise it to E£2,000. If you take them to court, you pay the E£2,000 first and only get it back when you've won, if you win. On top of that you have the court fees. And it all takes time. A few of them get caught each year. But they make so much that two years in prison is nothing!'

I used to lunch regularly at the Odeon Restaurant, a hole-in-the-wall sort of place situated in a side street off Talaat Harb. It got its name from the Odeon Cinema next door which specialized in showing epic adventures of life in the Soviet Union and turgid Russian war films. The service in the Odeon Restaurant was as brisk as the films in the cinema were slow. This was on account of Ahmed. Ahmed was as graceful as Nureyev and as reliable as a well oiled piston engine. He could take three orders, serve two others, clear a table and make out four bills simultaneously. He made out the bills by shouting them to a bald, kindly greengrocery-looking Greek who sat at a table by the door and took your money, never failing to give you back the right change. His wife, a diminutive woman who looked as though she had once been cracked out of an L-shaped pipe and had never straightened out again, sat across from him and indulged a passion for stray cats by feeding them titbits from the kitchen. Mr. Athenogenes, for that was the kindly greengrocery-looking Greek's name, was running a goldmine. It wasn't all Ahmed's doing, even though he was certainly the engine of the operation. Mr. Athenogenes arranged to make the eating of his food so cramped and uncomfortable that he had people in and out of the restaurant as fast as Ahmed could take, deliver and clear each order.

In the corner, sharing a minuscule table with a gross Egyptian was Dieter, an emaciated, spotty German who frequented the Odeon because it was the cheapest place in which he could find anything remotely resembling his mother's cooking. An import-export agency had placed its fledgling Egyptian business in Dieter's tender hands. It was an act of faith. Dieter was only twenty-four and the furthest east he had been before he boarded the boat for Alexandria was Munich, on a family holiday in 1965. He had arrived with grand designs and had enrolled immediately for lessons in Arabic. But his attempt to master the language had been an abject failure. He blamed the language, complained of the sentence construction and the strange consonants. He strained his vocal chords on glottal stops. To no avail; he would have had more success communicating with a Friesian cow.

He was saved by his Egyptian colleague who neutralized the environment for him and made it manageable, translating Egyptian vibrations into German vibrations and thus allowing Dieter to proceed as if he had never left his beloved Hamburg, seat of his dreams, where one day he hoped, through the fruits of his labours in these foreign parts, to have saved enough to buy a small house and settle down.

Dieter owed much to his corpulent colleague and smiled appreciatively as he made way for him.

'You're going out to the pyramids at five, aren't you?' his minder enquired.

Dieter looked threatened as he always did when asked a direct question. 'I don't know,' he wailed, in a reedy high pitched voice. 'You know I want to but my boss is coming….' Dieter's only interest other than the house in Hamburg, the vagaries of his Simca car and its run-ins with the traffic police, was horse riding at the pyramids. 'What time does the sun set?'

'Around eight.'

'Then six will give us enough time,' Dieter concluded to his satisfaction.

Just before two o'clock Dieter's minder decided it was time to get back to work. Dieter hurried with his rice pudding. As he left he pointed at the headline in the *Egyptian Gazette*. 'Isn't that fantastic,' he squeaked. He had a sense of humour. It read: '[King] Feisal blames international Zionism for Watergate and the Lampton Affair.' The Lampton Affair, involving a government minister caught cavorting with two call girls at the same time created a major scandal in Britain.

After lunch at the Odeon I bought two piastres' worth of peanuts from the little girl on the corner. She always gave me an extra handful which was a touching act of generosity. I steered clear of the other peanut vendor who groused and thieved and made for Café Liberté in Babeluk.

Café Liberté was my spiritual home. It was the one place in the world where I was completely content; the psyche's womb. I spent hours there dreaming, clicking out of thought into the mirrored interiors and back again. There were the people inside and the street outside: reflection and distraction.

It was a place which demanded time as an absolute pre-requisite. The service was appalling. One-eyed Farid and balding, Hitler-moustachioed Abdul, who looked like a prosperous butcher in his white smock and bulging, note stuffed pouch, made an engaging if ineffective team. They were much in evidence walking around. Yet, it was impossible to establish contact with them. If you clapped your hands loudly enough Abdul blinked, but if you wished to be served you had to march one of them to your table. They found collecting money distasteful which made a number of customers neurotic. Bilking was a perfectly honourable activity in the normal scheme of things, but you never left a café without paying.

The hawkers and the mendicants weren't difficult to contact. They liked Liberté and thought, correctly, that its customers were a soft touch. They made a revolving portrait gallery. Standing out from the crowd was the sad ascetic Karikat man who would stop in Liberté on his diurnal and largely fruitless rounds of Cairo's cafés to rest his feet, which were well aired in a pair of shoes with the caps cut off. Before he settled down with a glass of water to work through his grimy notes, he would make a round of Liberté, tapping his frayed satchel and calling out in a mild firm tenor, 'Karikat, karikat,' his jaw set like Lenin, his goatee beard jutting in defiance.

There was a lame boy who regularly tested my compassion and found it wanting. He wore grubby striped pyjamas and always looked as though he had just gone for a wallow in a trash cart. You could see him prepare himself before entering, leaving his trolley by the door, then sliding to each table in turn and pausing. He's doing well. A man with close-cropped grey hair put down a well thumbed book on yachting and delved into his windcheater for a piastre; across to a table where two old men interrupted their conversation to look for change. Then our eyes met. His look was sullen; he embarrassed me. I didn't like to be so brazenly confronted. He wasn't asking, he was demanding, and I resented it. If I was to give, I would do so on my own terms. But I didn't quite say that. No, I cheated. I said: '*Mafish faker*, I have no change.' He knew I was lying. He turned and slunk out to his friend on the pedestrian bridge to count his takings.

****

One morning early in July, a dishevelled morning, a morning like me, still with the sleep in its eyes, I went to the Mugamma for cholera injections. I was going to Yemen.

Ahmed Abdel-Aziz had tried to dissuade me. 'Wouldn't go there unless you want your throat slit,' he muttered. Ahmed, you thought, would have given anything to have been born with eyes in the back of his head. But then he had been involved in espionage in Saudi Arabia. So when Ahmed said: 'Don't go to Yemen,' you weighed it carefully in the balance. However, there were a number of reasons why I wanted to go. It suited me to leave Egypt for the summer and it seemed best to find another Arab country where I could keep up my Arabic, and in an Arab country sufficiently different from Egypt to provide a fresh perspective on the Arab world. North Yemen seemed to fit the bill: a counterpoint to Cairo and untouched by the West or any other external influence for that matter. Moreover Egypt had links with Yemen thanks to Nasser's entanglement in its recent civil war.

I hoped at the same time to visit South Yemen, (Aden and the Protectorates as it used to be known). So after the Mugamma I made for the embassy of the People's Democratic Republic of Yemen (PDRY).

Now I knew that the North and the South had their differences. The North distrusted the South's tight centralized control over everything and Marxist leanings and the South disapproved of the North's fissiparous, reactionary tribalism and swashbuckling individualism. At that time they were talking about unification, though barely on speaking terms, and engaging in time honoured skirmishes across each other's borders.

Lacking connections with an international socialist movement, and a chop for North Yemen already in my passport, I did not rate my chances of obtaining a visa for the PDRY very highly, but I had reckoned without the initial difficulty of finding anyone to process visas.

The Marxist regime in South Yemen has done wonders for Women's Lib, they say, apparently at the expense of men, or so it appeared at the Cairo embassy, where the male staff seemed to be in purdah. Their isolation had been made complete by the embassy being located in the Fellini wastes of Madinit Muhandiseen (Engineers City), as far as it was possible to be from the centre of town, short of establishing a community in the Libyan Desert.

I did finally track down an official who listened sympathetically to my request to visit his beautiful country. He said he would inform Aden and would I mind calling round in a couple of days. Meanwhile I tried to arrange a briefing on Yemen at the Arab League. The man I was told to see was a Mr. Badawi who occupied a third floor office in the League's headquarters in Tahrir Square.

Mr. Badawi greeted me with clasped hands and looked grave. 'The situation in Yemen has deteriorated,' he said. 'It looks as though there is going to be another flare-up. Troops are massing on the borders.'

'Is there anyone I can talk to about it?' I asked.

'I'm afraid not. Mr. Rageb who deals with Yemen is in Damascus and his assistant is in Beirut. But if you care to keep in touch, I will try and find someone else.'

So I did and my remaining days in Cairo were spent trudging to the South Yemen Embassy and to the Arab League. The telegram never arrived from Aden and the experts steered well clear of Cairo.

In some distress I bearded Mr. Badawi on my last Thursday, half an hour before the League closed for the weekend.

'Please, Mr. Badawi,' I enquired. 'Do you know *anyone* who might be able to help me?'

Mr. Badawi's brow creased with concentration, sweat beads started at the rims of his high forehead, the eyes behind his thick glasses went blank. Then he was suddenly galvanized.

'Mr. Mackie, there's one last chance.' He picked up the telephone. 'Mr. Karim Mourad.'

I raced up to the sixth floor. Mr. Mourad was clearing his desk prior to leaving for the weekend. 'Come in, come in,' he said. 'Mr. Badawi tells me you are going to Yemen tomorrow. Of course I know Yemen. I have been dealing with the unity talks for the past eight months and only came back from a tour there a month ago. What can I tell you in twenty minutes? Why on earth didn't you get in touch with me earlier and we could have gone into this thoroughly?'

'Mr. Mourad,' I said, in desperation, 'Nobody told me about you. I have been trying to find someone who knows about

Yemen for the past three weeks.'

Friday arrived and I had to vacate my flat and settle up. The *makwagi* asked 40 piastres to clean and iron a pair of sheets and was hurt when I said he was a robber and produced Mr. Badri to confirm that he was a robber. I left in a welter of unpacked suits. Mr. Badri was especially well disposed towards me; he stood to make an exorbitantly generous tip as I hadn't done my sums correctly and had left him the E£5 deposit on the flat to cover some negligible bills.

I bought my ticket three hours before departure and went to Anais's aunt's place to leave my cases. An hour of peace and reflection sipping ice cold beer and eating steak on her balcony and I was off, for Asmara and the Yemen.

NORTH YEMEN

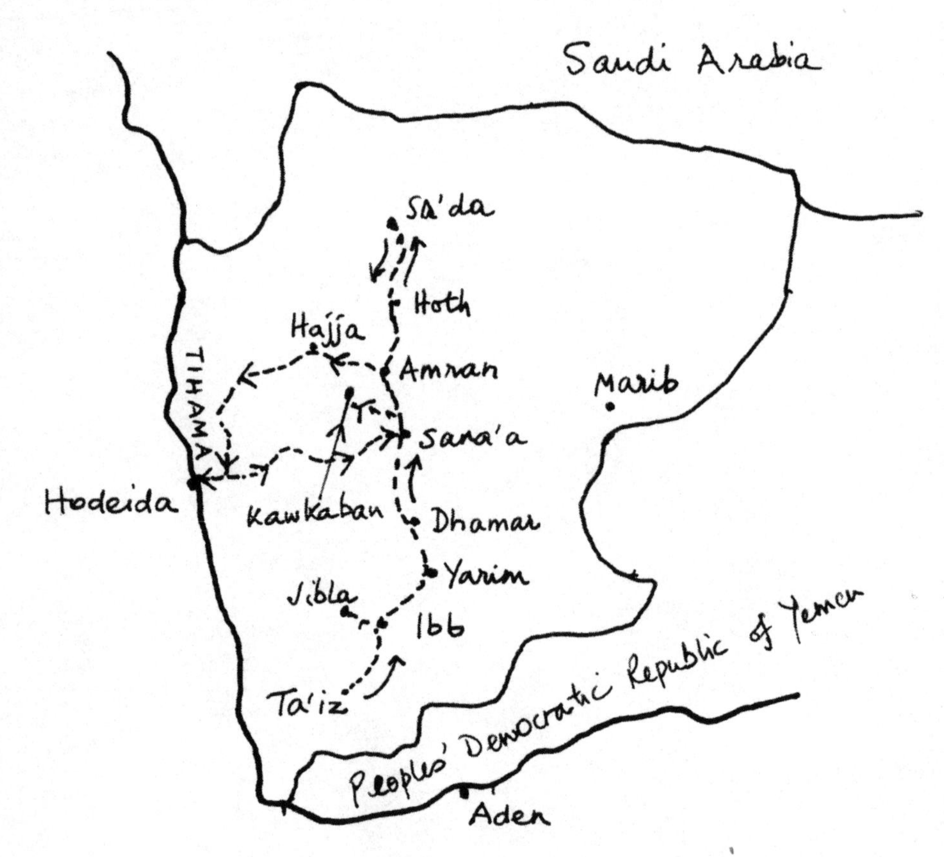

Saudi Arabia
Sa'da
Hoth
Hajja
Amran
TIHAMA
Marib
Sana'a
Hodeida
Kawkaban
Dhamar
Yarim
Jibla
Ibb
Ta'iz
Peoples' Democratic Republic of Yemen
Aden

Chapter Eight

ARABIA FELIX

'Double, double, toil and trouble.' Yemen emerges from the steam bath that is the Red Sea in midsummer as if from the witch's cauldron, ridge upon ridge of arid mountains, conjured up by the sorcerer's spell.

The Romans knew Yemen as Arabia Felix, which is also its Arabic name. Al Yemen means the right or happy place, a name that befits a fertile and isolated mountain kingdom at the end of the incense trail. Unfortunately it hasn't been particularly right or happy in recent years. Less than a decade ago it had been catapulted into the twentieth century by a bloody and brutal civil war. North Yemen has remained, largely because of the civil war, an unbelievably backward country with a per capita income in 1973 of less than $60 per annum, no roads or hospitals to speak of, and electricity in only a handful of the larger towns.

I came to North Yemen via Ethiopia as Ethiopian Airlines had offered an attractive deal to Ta'iz, the country's second city, with a stopover in Asmara in Eritrea.

The short hop across the Red Sea was made in a Dakota which bumped through fierce thermals before coming down heavily on a dusty airstrip overlooked by wild mountains. This was

Ta'iz International Airport. It was linked to Ta'iz by a gravel road built, you were reminded at every kilometre, with American aid. But not by telephone; the line had been cut, I was to learn later, because the utility bill had not been paid.

Little wonder that the town, come upon in a cloud of dust and loose chippings, had an air of impermanence. Modern Ta'iz is, in fact, the product of a trade boom. As the Marxists established themselves in South Yemen thousands of merchants fled Aden, a mere sixty miles to the south, for these virgin commercial pastures where, in the heady atmosphere of the Wild West in its heyday, anything went. They had managed to transform Ta'iz from a makeshift Yemeni Alamo under siege (the walled city bristling with muskets and Republican flags) into a shantytown of one-story cast concrete tenements.

The air of impermanence went with an engaging informality. I arrived at lunchtime. The restaurants reverberated to the twang of the *aud*, (the Arabic lute) on radio tannoys. Kilted tribesmen settled their guns on wooden benches as boiled meat and beans sloshed on enamel plates were thrust in front of them. A goat slept in the policeman's box on the main street across from the Revolutionary Consciousness Library.

In the foyer of the National Hotel, which I found with ease – there were only two in Ta'iz – the portraits above the reception desk of President Al Iriani, Nasser and the proprietor made a curious triumvirate. In Ta'iz, I was told, Nasser was still revered. Ta'iz was the stronghold of the Republican Party. The Republicans had beaten the Royalists on points in the civil war and Nasser had sponsored them.

The rift between Royalists and Republicans was a traditional one between the highlands and lowlands and went way back in history. It crystallized with the Ottoman occupation during which the highlands had remained largely independent under Yemen's traditional rulers, the imams. When the Turks left in 1918 the country settled back into the Middle Ages (whence it had hardly emerged) under the dedicated ministrations of Imam Yahya, who thought of progress as some kind of plague bacilli from which his country must, at all costs, be protected. And there Yemen might well have remained in splendid isolation had Yahya not done something highly controversial: he made the 'imamate' hereditary. Now the whole point of an elected imam was to imbue the central authority with nominal control for the purposes of giving Yemen an identity without unduly fettering the autonomy of the tribal chiefs. When Yahya was assassinated in 1948, to be succeeded after a brief insurrection by his son Ahmed, Yemen had a hereditary ruler for the first time in a thousand years. It did not bode well for this delicate political dispensation. Indeed, it turned out to be the beginning of its end, and it was not helped by Ahmed's unfortunate personality.

Ahmed had large, bulbous eyes, the physique of a bear and made many enemies in a long and eventful reign. He survived three attempts on his life, which he put down with exemplary severity, retiring to an eyrie in his palace in Ta'iz to watch the heads of his assailants come off one by one.

Surprisingly, Ahmed died in his bed in November 1962. When he was gone all hell was let loose. The conservative elements, mostly Zaidis from the hills, rallied to the pretender, Mohammed al-Badr, while the plains people, mostly Shafeis who had no love of the imam as they took no part in his selection, rallied to the progressive cause and Nasser's protégé,

Abdullah al-Sallal. The Saudis, ever fearful of revolution sweeping up on their southern flank, poured gold into the Royalist coffers. It was a classic confrontation: Nasser, the symbol of progress, against the forces of reaction. After the war North Yemen burgeoned with Gamal Abdel Nasser streets and squares while ordinary Egyptians became the butt of ordinary Yemenis' opprobrium.

Two years after the end of the civil war Yemenis still carried guns and *jambias*, the distinctive curved dagger worn as a mark of manhood across the midriff like a sporran. In this undercurrent of violence it was difficult to place the gentle Jain explaining earnestly in the hotel lobby that in his religion, 'We don't eat wegetables from under the ground because we might hurt the animals in the wegetables' who, had he ventured into the town two days earlier, would have encountered a crowd at the Bab el-Kabir inspecting the head of a young man, a neat bullet hole through the right temple, on a plinth, constructed it seemed for such grizzly displays.

The *suq*, which you entered by the same Bab el-Kabir, was a shifting scenario of stalls selling pomegranates, grapes, unripe apricots, prickly pears, small figs, papaya, peanuts and sesame seed. The townswomen were heavily veiled, but the women from the mountains had no such inhibitions. One peasant girl fluttered past in a Mexican hat and what looked like a Fabricci scarf which she wore like a Halloween mask. In the Indian goldsmith stalls on the main street they fingered rings and bangles with expertise. These women were walking banks, dripping sovereigns and gold teeth, born coquettes too, and very beautiful in their striped Regency dresses.

A time-honoured Yemini custom is the eating of *qat*, a mildly narcotic leaf grown throughout Yemen and the Ethiopian Highlands. At midday the *qat* harvest would be brought in from the surrounding hills and the bargaining would begin. It was intense and often led to fights. *Qat* needs two hours of rigorous chewing to have any effect so Yemenis made a meal of it, an afternoon of it, and if they could so arrange it the rest of the day too. *Qat* sessions started after lunch because it was necessary first to take *helba*, a seed boiled to a sticky candyfloss consistency to line the stomach and prevent ulcers. You worked up a good thirst too; chewing *qat* needs lots of water. Then you girded your *furtah* (the Yemeni kilt), filled your thermos with cool water, gathered your water pipe and tootled along.

Thus it was that around two o'clock a transcendent peace descended upon Yemen, broken by the crackle of twigs as *qat* leaves were stripped in the tenebrous gloom of concrete trading stalls, the home or the hedgerow. Peace and hopefully profit, on deals clinched between the slurp of the thermos flasks or an idle thought, accompanied always by silent mastication, regular as clockwork, up and down, up and down, oscillating gobstoppers of the gooey green stuff mellowing the mind. No wonder Yemen was well nigh impossible to govern.

So the authorities thought. *Qat* was a huge business, the biggest in Yemen. Unfortunately its contribution to GNP, like the arts or child welfare, was difficult to quantify. How do you assess the economic benefit of good vibrations? Moreover *qat* wasn't an exportable commodity, it didn't stay fresh long and it wasn't, in any case, the sort of import many countries officially encouraged. The government would have preferred, the World Health Organization would have preferred, the World Bank would have preferred that Yemenis grew coffee. But coffee needed four times the attention of *qat* and a middleman took nearly all the profit; with *qat* the grower took it all.

A hollow-eyed Adeni supervised the hotel dining room. He spoke some English, having worked for a British army family in Aden as a driver. He had earned good money with them, 600 shillings, roughly ¹⁄£30 sterling a month. When the family left with the exodus of the British in 1967 he was offered their car. So he invested his 2,000 shillings savings, bought it and became a taxi driver. When the Marxists took over they expropriated the car and he fled, penniless, to Ta'iz where he now worked as a supervisor in the hotel making 200 ryals (£18 sterling) a month with board for a ninety-eight hour week. Not surprisingly, he detested Marxism and there were plenty like him from the South, ordinary folk who had lost everything – unlike the merchants who had shipped their money out of Aden long before the Marxists could lay their hands on it. And there were plenty of disenchanted immigrant labourers who felt they weren't seeing enough of the easy money floating around. Ta'iz was consequently a hotbed of intrigue offering any number of opportunities for self-styled mavericks. However, it didn't do to underestimate the risks of becoming one.

That summer the authorities had uncovered a highly organized terrorist ring in Ta'iz, with which the head in the square had something to do, and there was much talk of terrorism. Insurgents were hauled in daily and 'encouraged' to confess. A series of show trials were staged in Sana'a, the capital, followed by public executions. There was one such trial taking place during my stay in Ta'iz. The outcome was a foregone conclusion. However, the proceedings were no less punctilious for that. One of the accused attacked the members of the tribunal. It was the indifference and selfishness of their class that made him and others like him take to terrorism, he declared. The defendants were listened to with courtesy. But they had all admitted throwing bombs and planting mines. After ten years of civil war there was little disposition to show mercy.

How strong was this feeling I discovered on an excursion to Wadi Dhabab, some three miles out of Ta'iz. Wadi Dhabab – the valley of mists in Arabic – is locally known as the kissing valley for the gesture the men folk of the valley make when greeting each other. The younger kisses hand and forehead while lowering the head in deference to the older person. In the taxi from Ta'iz I sat next to an ascetic gentleman of around thirty-five who invited me home to his farm. He lived in a stone house two hours up the *wadi* at a point where two streams converged. It was a strenuous climb. On arriving, we clambered through a low door into a reception room. 'Everything lives here,' he said, 'the cows downstairs, the coffee and the grain upstairs.'

Then with exquisite courtesy and sensitivity for my privacy he showed me a guest room and left me with pillows and cool, sweet water, and bade me sleep. This I had no difficulty doing, beguiled by the stark contrast of unforgiving terrain and the delicious comfort and security of this human lair. A Yemeni's home is indeed his castle. When I awoke a huge omelette had been prepared in an earthen bowl with fishmeal and *khubz*, the local bread made from sorghum. Afterwards we drank *bun*, a drink made from the kernel of the coffee bean. The story goes that Al Badr, to save coffee for export during the civil war, ordered everyone to drink *bun* and the habit caught on. The drink is cheap and refreshing.

My host owned land at the head of the valley and made a moderately prosperous living from it. He supplemented his income by working in the Ministry of Agriculture in Ta'iz, which further gave him status and a position in local affairs. He stayed in Ta'iz during the week and came back to the farm every second or third week. The farm was cared for by three unmarried sisters who also looked after his baby son; his wife he kept in Ta'iz. He would like to marry again, he said; he could afford to now.

At dusk he brought out a new lamp. As he dusted it and read the instructions I noted it was made in China. 'We never had anything like this in the civil war,' he said as he primed it, 'we burnt rags.' Over dinner he told me of the changes that had taken place since the revolution. In the time of the imams there were very few schools in Yemen, he said, education was actively discouraged. Now every village had a school and each child received an elementary education in reading, writing and religion.

We talked of *qat* and alcohol. I asked him why Muslims were more tolerant of *qat* and hashish than alcohol. He said the Koran forbade alcohol because it made one aggressive; hashish and *qat*, on the other hand, did not. 'But,' he pointed out, 'the Koran forbids you to take hashish if it is money for food or if your family goes without. If you can afford it, well and good.' And he told me the story of a drunken soldier who had run amok recently in the district and killed several children. 'They killed him,' he said simply, as if talking of a rabid dog that had to be put down. And with the same finality he dismissed the terrorists on trial in Sana'a. 'They will die just as soon as the trial finishes,' he said. He was sick to death with those who argued by the gun. 'What future,' he asked, 'was there for his children with these people?'

My friend from Wadi Dhabab would have approved of the Ta'iz Museum, the imam's old palace, kept as it was to instruct Yemenis in the depraved ways of their erstwhile rulers. The board at the entrance invited you (for $1) to see 'antique and very valuable articles' and to have 'a very extraordinary idea and impression of overthrown Royalist rule'. In fact, the 'very valuable articles' had long since been lifted by looters but enough remained to provide a fascinating peep into what life must have been like in the medieval court of Imam Ahmed.

He had every gadget you would expect to find in an upmarket 1930s emporium and more besides, including wind-up telephones, German field glasses and wireless sets. A machine gun remained trained on the square below just as it had always been. In the imam's bedroom a cine camera was placed prominently beside a rickety wooden-legged screen; at that time, we were reminded, Yemenis went to prison for owning a tape recorder or a cine camera. The surgery was stacked with morphine, opium and bottles of Booth's gin, sanctified as medicine by the simple expedient of writing '*Allah karim*' (God is generous) on each bottle. The bathroom boasted a padded bedpan and a store of Guerlain 'Fleur des Alpes' soap. The harem was a disappointingly austere room, strewn with women's clothes, crude, large-cupped bras bursting out of a number of psychedelically coloured trunks – the same as you could find in any store in Ta'iz. Indeed, the tin trunks were the only point of reference Imam Ahmed's palace had with the outside world.

Then, on a mounted board in the foyer as you left, were sets of photographs of Ahmed's enemies being beheaded. The caption in lyrically deranged English, described 'how the heads of the martyrs flow like sheep'. There was an extraordinary serenity about the condemned. They all turned up in their best clothes. One wrote his last will and testament as the executioner looked on impassively. Then, in another set of photos, in a macabre transposition of roles, the selfsame executioner awaits execution, pointing enquiringly and with trepidation to the spot he must have known so well. A huge crowd assembled for the beheading of this much-hated man who was paying the price for killing a soldier in a brawl. Even Ahrned, who was said to be very fond of his executioner, couldn't save him from the full force of the Sharia law.

****

From Ta'iz I moved on to Sana'a, situated some three hundred miles to the north on the central highland plateau. At that time the road was not fully macadamized so journey times were unpredictable. Ibb was the first stop, a beautiful town set below green mountains at the foot of the central escarpment. Yemenis have a soft spot for Ibb because it is so green during the summer rains. It had electricity and a cinema but these talismans of progress hadn't touched the relaxed rhythm of the *suq* or its narrow cobbled lanes, just as the growth of the new town hadn't blurred the outline of the old.

At dusk the landscape suggested a Chinese painting. And as night fell the city sprang to life, the gorgeous Yemeni houses lighting up like giant Advent cards. Soon after midnight the generator was turned off. The remaining lights dimmed one by one and silence settled, leaving the city on the hillside to the baying dogs and the veiled moon. Later still, much later, after the moon had set and the dogs were sleeping, the *muezzins* set sail, first one, then many, till the valley reverberated with the fruity lilt of the *fajr* prayer, pockets of sound that left a resonance like old music before dying on the shores of the hills.

I travelled next day from Ibb to Sana'a in the local bus with a *bunduqeya* (Yemeni blunderbuss) stuck in my ribs. Spirits were high as we set off, everyone singing a high-pitched Yemeni song that sounded a bit like the finale to Beethoven's Ninth Symphony.

The weather cleared as we climbed the escarpment that divides Yemen. At Yerim you enter Zaidi country. Yerim is set at the end of a long, sweeping, dun coloured plain speckled with green, eight thousand two hundred feet above sea level. Whirlwinds played across the primitive landscape in which people appeared from nowhere and towns lay scattered at random. On every hilltop there seemed to be a castle; it could have been central Spain. And as if this wasn't sufficiently surreal: the surfeit of lorries growing out of the dust, roads rising straight for the sky and camel trains crawling along a low skyline, we came, as we juddered over the worst bit of the road, upon the carcass of a Boeing, the markings still fresh on the stripped fuselage. One wondered how in God's name it was possible to land a passenger jet on a field of cracked granite without anyone being injured or bringing down the telephone lines. The pilot had apparently run out of fuel en route for Sana'a.

We climbed another escarpment and abruptly entered an even bleaker landscape of rock and pumice grey sand. On the last leg of the journey we encountered three roadblocks, a precautionary measure against the executions that had taken place that morning. Sana'a was a city on edge, heady with the smell of blood.

Sana'a is shored up against the side of a wide flat plain, seven thousand two hundred feet above sea level. However, you have very little physical awareness of the height apart from the thin air, the fierce sun and the terrible dryness. Approaching through nondescript suburbs from the south you had no idea of the walled city so discreetly was it hidden. The Egyptians gave the Yemenis concrete but didn't tell them how to build in it. Tahrir Square epitomized the new town's formlessness, an odd-shaped space distinctive for its traffic islands, barrel drums and barbed wire, which guarded a few tired flowers. Around it stood ministries. The notice board outside the Ministry of Education advertised a nuclear seminar in Venice, not yards from the side-alley where they had, that morning, shot seventeen people.

Women flitted by, imprisoned behind *abayas* and *niqabs*, their bright coloured trousers and leggings the only expression of individuality. A glimpse behind the veil was provided by a pair of woman's Polaroid sunglasses just in from Paris, prominently displayed in the window of a chemist with a price tag of 130 ryals.

Food in the *suq* was dear. Yemenis often spent as much on *qat* as they did on food. A bundle of *qat* cost 5 ryals, a meal of *khubz*, meat and boiled beans 2 ryals. They ate few vegetables and little fruit, relying on *qat* for their vitamins.

My first evening in Sana'a was spent with a personable South Yemeni called Selim. In Aden he had edited a newspaper, the outside pages of which he devoted to news, and the inside pages to a local gossip column entitled 'Chewing over the *qat*'. The authorities had taken exception to the 'frivolous' caption, he said, and closed down the paper. He never explained why he was in Sana'a but he dispensed generous hospitality in his hotel room where a very short man lay on the bed, oblivious of all, muttering furiously in sporadic bursts as he composed poetry. About eleven o'clock the whisky ran out and a young man with a pleasant smile and clean cut features which complemented his blazer and grey trousers was dispatched to find more, no easy task in 'dry' Sana'a two hours after curfew. He arrived back with a bottle of Teachers belted in his trousers. The shopkeeper had taken a one-eighth nip as his cut and we tucked into what remained.

The Sunday football match in the city's one stadium was a scrappy game notable for the military police who controlled the crowd by poking rifle butts into the more enthusiastic spectators and waving small twigs to keep the children behind barriers. It looked as though it might rain but never managed to. The thirst for rain in Sana'a is like a craving that each year becomes more acute as the water table falls. Instead, dust chased the players who chased each other in a dispirited game. With the game concluded one faced the bleak prospect of finding anything to do in a family oriented city. Sana'a had a couple of cinemas – for a city of one hundred and twenty thousand inhabitants – Hodeida (Yemen's principal port) had five and Ta'iz three.

That evening I walked through town to the German farm up beyond the Bab el-Shoub to attend a reception. It still promised rain from a sky filled with static, rising dust and menacing silhouettes. It was almost dark by the time I arrived. Lightning flickered and the mountains behind leapt in a jiggery St. Vitus dance. Then the relief as the heavens opened.

After the reception I hitched a lift in the ambassador's sleek new Jaguar. Beside the driver lay a sleek new Bren gun. Another nestled in the lap of a security guard beside me. We purred into Sana'a. 'What brings you to Yemen?' enquired the ambassador. 'Swanning around, eh? Can't be too careful. Keep in touch with us, won't you?' Gruesome tales of random holdups were going the rounds. On one occasion a hapless European returning home from a night out was held up and had a finger hacked off when his wedding ring failed to be dislodged.

It was past curfew and the lights were out in Tahrir Square. It wasn't wise to make jerky actions when stopped at checkpoints as you couldn't be sure how those adolescent conscripts would handle the rifles they poked through the window. The car finally drew up close to where I was staying. I made to open the door. 'Wait,' said the ambassador. 'Let him get to the other side.' The guard extricated himself and his gun from the car and came to open my door. I thanked the ambassador and sank into the anonymity of the Sana'a night.

A few days later I had lunch with a young English couple who organized 'self help' aid programmes. These programmes, which could involve anything from establishing a childcare clinic run by local mothers to a farmers' co-operative, were remarkably successful. The challenge, however, was to sell the idea to innovation resistant local officials and donor countries who were equally suspicious of such a radically new approach to allocating aid which had in it, by definition and disconcertingly, a built-in obsolescence.

Aid workers' ability to adapt counted as much as their skills, they said. Yemen had little need of the distinguished Yemeni specialist, trained in America, who had offered to work in Sana'a so long as he had western facilities; Yemen needed teaching doctors. Similarly, well-trained local orderlies were more use than the fully qualified sister from a London teaching hospital who, it turned out, couldn't adjust to the local conditions. Standards of health and hygiene only made sense, they said, in the context of the local conditions and the ability of the local people to maintain them. Yemenis had to be given a service on which they themselves could build.

They found a cultural divide between the young volunteers in the field and their administrative superiors, most of whom still inhabited a colonial world and ran their aid programmes accordingly. The big agencies, in their view, favoured this old guard and consequently attracted charges of bureaucracy, corruption and inefficiency.

Then there were the experts. I was to meet a young Peace Corps worker, a mild Filipino, very Catholic and placid, who said, almost in passing, that he knew more after ten weeks working as a student assistant about the performance of wheat strains in Yemen than did his boss, an agricultural expert who had been there six months. 'I hardly see the boss. Perhaps he'll pop in for an hour or two each morning,' he said. Where was the boss? The boss liked his tipple and was, in any case, principally concerned with securing an extension to his tax-exempt contract.

The Yemenis were incorrigibly blind when it came to the colour of foreign aid: the more the merrier. And as a 'very backward nation' is, in the eyes of the developed world, rather like an unregenerate tramp in the hands of a zealous social worker, and as North Yemen happens to be on Saudi Arabia's doorstep, there was no lack of callers seeing if they could help 'develop' the country a little and get a foot in the door. But

Saudi Arabia always maintained the whip hand, providing North Yemen with just enough funds to stay afloat, and keeping the philanthropists at bay.

However, there were channels through which foreign benefactors could visibly and productively show their good intentions. They could build roads. The road building programme had a certain cachet and everyone tried to get in on the act: Russians, Americans, British and West Germans; but streets ahead of the field were the Chinese.

The Chinese were prodigious road builders. They built them so fast and efficiently that the Yemenis were worried one day they would wake up to find themselves overrun by Chinese road builders. They not only quoted the lowest prices, their roads were invariably built ahead of schedule and, amazingly, there was sometimes money left over to build more.

How did they do it? Well, the Chinese expected their engineers to work in exactly the same conditions as the Yemenis. They slept rough and ate *khubz* and boiled meat. Yemenis couldn't understand why western engineers had to be pampered when the Chinese could build roads so prolifically and so well without any special perks. They found it hard to grasp the central fact that Western engineers sacrificed a great deal to come and build roads in Yemen, creature comforts essential to their very functioning. There were adaptation costs, hardship allowances, etc. and, of course, price inflation. It was hard to get it across to Yemenis that in western democracies workers had the right to strike, a right they had more and more occasion to use, and this was pushing up the price of the tractors and bulldozers they needed to build the roads. Where was the extra money to come from? The western aid donors couldn't extend their budgets given their straitened circumstances, so the Yemenis often forewent western built roads and road building became a near Chinese monopoly.

On one occasion a West German road building team was attacked in the field. To stop malingering and thefts the German engineers had taken the drastic step of sacking the entire workforce. The Yemenis, who had settled into a routine of skiving and pilfering everything they could lay their hands on, took a dim view of this expedient. And the next morning they attacked the camp from the hills, guns blazing. The incident boosted the upward spiral in insurance premiums and did nothing to help recruitment.

They were a funny, fickle lot, these Yemenis, hospitable individually, xenophobic collectively, and very much their own men. Selim put this distaste for foreign meddling succinctly. 'We, Yemenis dislike and distrust foreign interference,' he told me. 'We won't allow outsiders to make of Yemen an area of experimentation as the Americans did in Vietnam. We will not become the laboratory for other people's ideologies. The quarrel between the North and the South is a family affair.'

On my last night in Sana'a, I walked back from the Bab el-Shoub. It was half an hour before curfew and there was urgent activity. Headlights pierced the clouds of dust raised by the women sweepers. Then suddenly it was very empty and very quiet, just unpaved lanes, the tread of shadows and the jangle of an *aud*. The whitewash on the buildings glowed in the dwindling light and the stained glass windows blossomed as lamps were trimmed behind them. I found myself in an interlacing pattern of alleyways, tall buildings and stars and for the first time felt some of the magic of Sana'a that had so successfully eluded me.

****

To get to Sa'da you catch the communal taxi from the Bab el-Shoub. Sa'da, the provincial capital of North Yemen's most northerly province, is one hundred and sixty miles from Sana'a. The Chinese were half way through building a road there. Meantime only the Toyota Landcruisers could get through.

I arrived early to ensure a seat, paid 30 ryals and two hours later, with liberal bestowals of *bismillah*, we were off. All was fine until we came to the end of the Chinese road. Then, as the track deteriorated, so did the weather. It began to rain, gently at first, then more persistently. The mountains started running with rain, the little trickles turned into bigger trickles which in turn became streams, and everyone said: 'What fun. Look, a waterfall.' They hadn't seen a waterfall before and were most anxious I shouldn't miss the opportunity to record the event on film with them in the foreground to give it context. As it was by then after lunch, they were all chewing *qat* – Salah, the driver, said it helped his driving – and offering it around. Everyone was joining in the spirit of the adventure apart from a grumpy old man seated opposite me, who had bought *qat* that was too young for his teeth, which he was absorbed in trying to cut up and mash in a small pestle with a long knife that he waved dangerously as the Landcruiser lunged.

We had been running up the side of a valley scattering damp, bedraggled chickens which belonged, presumably, to the weird beautiful Yemeni houses stuck with child-like abandon in the middle of nowhere, when we came to a small stream which had become a big stream. Salah stopped, looked at it; and then

Tai'z, bristling with muskets and Republican flags like a makeshift Yemeni Alamo.

Yemenis have a soft spot for Ibb because it is so green during the summer rains.

Jibla, close by Ibb, was an ancient capital of Yemen.

Salah, the driver on the Sa'da run, surveys the flash flood in the cold light of day.

Sa'da: A solitary palm, classic symmetry, just sand and ramparts.

Ahmed (left), met on the road to Hajja, took to the trail like a mountain goat, his ancient musket slung across his back.

Mohammed (centre) collected the heads of Egyptian soldiers for bounty in the civil war, with Hajja behind.

The Tihama: Gone were the stone houses and veils of the mountains and in their place straw hut corrals and bare breasted women.

Kawkaban: Bombardment in the civil war left half the town reduced to mounds of beautiful pink stone.

The *qadi* of Kawkaban (left) who would not let me sleep in the castle

Egyptians keep their flair for display for the barrows and the street stalls.

A display of plaster of Paris busts and plates in Old Cairo.

The back end of a Cairo bus.

Children by a *sabil* near Bab Zuweila.

Making *ful* in the medieval city.

The mirrored interiors of Café Liberté in Babeluk

drove into it at its deepest point. He didn't realize what he was doing until he was in, nose first, rump in the air. And we were out, quick as greased lightning. We threw that Landcruiser on to the bank and collapsed trembling.

A Chinese in a sampan hat appeared. 'What happened?' he enquired.

'An accident,' I said, and pointed. 'Anyone in those houses?'

'No,' he said, cheerfully. 'They're empty.'

The water dripped from his sampan hat and from my nose. We smiled. My Cantonese wasn't up to much, nor was his English, so I continued in Arabic. 'Weather like this in China?'

'No, the weather is not like this in China,' he replied.

There was a shout and a roar as the engine leapt to life. Our prompt action had saved the Toyota's electrical system. Salah was cock-a-hoop. We said our *bismillahs* and, more circumspect this time, with everyone out to lighten the load, Salah nosed the Landcruiser across the stream.

We came across a tea house in the gathering gloom. Over tea we discussed the weather. Salah hadn't seen anything like it in six years on the Sa'da run, and by the time we hit the road again, the arrival time, which had been set on departure at eight o'clock, had slipped back yet another hour to midnight.

A little later we picked up three sodden wanderers. Two went on top, the third, it was suggested, should join us inside. The dour man across the way had other ideas. He had ceased attacking the resilient *qat*, put his murderous knife away and appeased a natural nervousness by periodically taking a revolver from his waistband and putting it in his briefcase and back again. He refused absolutely to move onto the hard shoulder by the door to make room for the dirty, wet stranger. So the dirty, wet stranger joined his companions on the roof.

About nine the headlights illuminated a most unwelcome spectacle. A big stream had found another big stream and had become a torrent. Even Salah, whose reckless optimism had nearly done for us earlier, was beaten. The headlights stared at the rising waters as we took stock.

'There's a workman's camp a little way back,' someone suggested.

'It's Chinese,' said another.

'It's a bit of a cheek us asking them to put us up. Look how many of us there are,' said a third.

'They won't mind if they're decent chaps,' the first rejoined. It was a bit academic, the others thought, discussing whether the Chinese were 'decent chaps' at that juncture. Necessity drove us to the camp and we found they were Yemenis.

Next day we had to wait at the stream again until the water subsided. A tribesman with fine eyes and flashing teeth came and sat next to me. He was a merchant travelling to Najran just north of the Saudi border. He had a couple of lorries bringing goods down from Jeddah to Sana'a.

'Do you want one?' he asked, rolling a joint. 'I don't take this into Saudi. You get thirty years in jail for having this in Saudi,' he volunteered.

'And in Yemen?' I asked.

'Well ... No one minds. But, *qat*, that's quite legal ...'

Arrival time was approaching that flat bit in the exponential curve which signifies eternity when yet another long low wall appeared on the horizon. 'Sa'da,' said Salah. I felt like a pilgrim coming upon the City on the Hill. It was very beautiful: a solitary palm, classic symmetry, just sand and ramparts. We had been on the road for twenty-eight hours.

An evening walk in the town discovered a marvellous tranquillity. Sa'da didn't then have electricity and at night when the gates were closed the city subsided into a magical gloom pierced by feathery lamplight – a setting little changed in a thousand years.

As the Rest House was full I had to share a room with the director. He had a complicated arrangement of wires and coat hangers which extended outside so that his radio could pick up the BBC and Voice of America.

The director's hunger for knowledge was indiscriminate, his reading voracious from week old copies of the *Revolution* (the Sana'a daily newspaper) to books on irrigation. By his bed he kept a pile of well-thumbed novelettes. He had no opinions other than that he was a Republican in a vague sort of way – he owed his job to the fact that his uncle was the local governor – which was curious as Yemenis, in my experience, were never backward in coming forward with their views on the imam, the ecstasies of *qat* and the iniquitous cost of wives. If you asked him why everyone was so forthcoming and he was so reticent he kept his peace until once, goaded beyond endurance, he snarled: 'They're stupid. They're all stupid.'

Any spot north of Sana'a he considered benighted and Sa'da especially so. He deserved better with his cultivated if meagre talents than his present lot, shunted from one dismal outpost to the next as far away from the comforts of Ta'iz and his family as a malign fate could devise. However, the director's habitual dilatoriness evaporated over the question of payment. He charged foreigners 10 ryals a night for the use of his primitive facilities while Yemenis paid five. It was a matter of principle on which he was not prepared to budge, even if I had to share a room with him.

On Sunday the Jews came to market. There weren't many left, most having taken the 'great winged giant of the sky', (DC 3s) from Aden to The Promised Land in 1948. The Jews of Yemen were largely indigenous, remnants of an age-old conversion to Judaism. They were craftsmen of uncommon skill. Most of the stained glass windows in Yemeni houses were their handiwork and they made the most exquisite jewellery. They still did, those who remained, and on Sundays they came down from the hills to sell it in Sa'da.

I returned to the Rest House for my camera to take pictures of them to find the director, a cautious man, had locked his room and taken the key.

'Where's the director?' I thundered. Acolytes scurried to find him.

'He's gone,' they said. Then one wriggled through the hatch where the aerial debouched and came out with my camera.

I met the director leaving. 'What do you mean by locking me out of my room?' I enquired in high dudgeon.

He bristled. 'I didn't mean to.'

'You charge me 10 ryals a night and I can't get into my room. It's disgraceful. I will take it up with the Tourist Office in Sana'a when I return. Meanwhile I will not pay 10 ryals to share a room I don't have access to.'

'You take it up with the Tourist Office, but you pay 10 ryals.'

'No I won't. You see.'

'Yes, you will.'

And of course I did.

Sa'da's timeless tranquillity was living on borrowed time. The only thing which didn't seem to change there was the Maria Theresa dollar. It was worth 1 ryal in 1962 before the civil war, five in 1971, nine in 1973 and heaven knows how many today. But Sa'da now has electricity and the road from Sana'a is complete. Sa'dites viewed with mixed feelings this march of progress and the central government into their lives. In the good old days they used to fight each other, were bought off to keep the peace, and rallied round the imam in times of crisis to repel the external threat. The civil war was marvellous because they could marry principle with interest, fighting for the imam and lining their pockets with Saudi gold. Many made huge fortunes. Some invested wisely in land or shops or started taxi services. The rest squandered their ill-gotten gains and, with the civil war over and the tribal subsidies dried up, were feeling the pinch. If the imam were back, they said, all would be right with their world.

****

To get from Sa'da to Hodeida you either had to return to Sana'a and take the magnificent Chinese road over the mountains or you cut across country from Amran through Kohlan to Hajja. After the most blissful night's sleep of my life in a roadside doss house in Amran I set off for Kohlan. Immune to shocks and having bumped down from the edge of the Yemen escarpment where you gazed into the jaws of precipices two thousand feet deep, the odd lorry or Egyptian personnel carrier dangling from ledges half way down, Kohlan appears quite literally out of the blue. A thousand feet of dead ground before and two thousand feet behind gave it the appearance of floating, a little cluster of Yemeni houses floating in the clouds.

At Kohlan the road gives out and you had to walk the last twelve miles to Hajja. Another passenger was bound for Hajja and said he would accompany me. 'I hope you are looking after Al Badr,' he said. The ex-imam, had settled in England. Satisfied that we were keeping Al Badr in the style his status accorded him Ahmed, who was sixty if he was a day, took to the trail like a mountain goat, his ancient musket slung across the back of his shoulders. We were through the bottom of the *wadi* before the rain overtook us. Ahmed looked up a farmer acquaintance for shelter. He wasn't very pleased to see me. Ahmed did his best to persuade him I was on their side. With exemplary diplomacy he volunteered that I had 'travelled to many places, everywhere. But he prefers Yemen to all other countries, to

Egypt, Saudi, Kuwait, France, even his own country ...'
Six hours out of Kohlan, now a speck high on the mountain wall of central Yemen, Haija was just round the corner. The children came out to escort us to the imam's palace in a damp, miserable dusk. The officials took one look at my pass and said I would have to go to the castle at the top of the hill. 'I'm not moving,' I said. 'I've gone as far as I can today.' They were sympathetic, lent me a greatcoat and told me to go out and get a cup of tea while they sorted things out.

Hajja wasn't what I had imagined. On the map it looked substantial enough, one of a dozen provincial capitals marked on the end of a good bold road. I hadn't been expecting much, the bare essentials of civilization, a clean bed, a smooth, metalled road to Hodeida and a crate of glistening Canada Drys. Now a Canada Dry in Hajia cost 30 buksha (7p). You had to be an aficionado of the road to grasp the grim significance of this. A Canada Dry in Sana'a cost 20 buksha, in Sa'da 30 buksha. That meant a long trail, many mountains.

With a sinking feeling in the pit of my stomach I asked a youth how far Sana'a was. 'Forty miles,' he said. 'Two days across the mountains.' Then he asked how long I was staying.

'I don't rightly know,' I replied. It was probably the most truthful statement I had ever uttered.

'Never mind, the post van leaves on Friday. You can catch the post van,' he said by way of encouragement.

'On Friday? But today's Monday,' I exclaimed, rhetorically. He asked where I was staying the night. I said at a hotel.

'There aren't any hotels,' he informed me. 'You must come and stay with me.' So, reprieved of a trudge up to the castle, I trudged home with Farid.

We climbed and we climbed and it rained. The torch was indispensable on the slippery path. Then Farid said: 'Wait a minute. I have to go and get the key to my room from my mother's place.' He explained that his father had two wives and his mother was the second wife so lived separately.

Lanterns met us at the main door. The room was small with whitewashed walls on which were pictures of busty Indian film stars, inscriptions from the Koran, a picture of the Ka'aba in Mecca and colour photos of Hajja and of his family. His father, a government official, was away from home a good deal and the running of the family of twelve children was shared by the two wives. Lotfi, a younger brother, came in with food. There was shuffling at the door, eyes at the crack, female eyes.

'I'm glad you've come,' said Farid, helping me to some fish omelette. 'Life in Hajia is so dull,' he complained. He was waiting to get married in three weeks' time.

'You're a bit young,' I ventured

'I'm fifteen,' he replied, a bit offended, pointing to his younger brother Lotfi beside him. 'He's nine. He can marry.'

'How old is your fiancée?'

'She's twelve. And there's a problem,' he said. He didn't know what to do with her when he went back to Sana'a. He wanted her to have some education so he would probably enrol her in a school while he finished his studies, he said adding: 'But I don't want her getting too many ideas. I don't want a 'modern' wife.'

'Would you marry again?' I asked.

'No. I don't believe in it for myself,' he replied. 'In any case my father couldn't afford it. But I have a friend in town who has a very rich father. He's twenty-one and he's got three wives and four concubines and is very happy.'

'I'm sure. But are the wives happy?' I wondered.

'I think so. They have enough protection from the law.' he said.

'And the concubines?'

It was tougher for them, he conceded. Anyway, they didn't have to be concubines if they didn't want to be. 'Perhaps they will become wives,' he opined. Then, changing the subject, he asked: 'Do you drink whisky?' He had lost interest in wives.

'Yes,' I admitted.

'I like whisky,' he volunteered. 'I had some in Hodeida. But father doesn't like me drinking. It's *haram* (forbidden), so to please him I don't. It's very expensive,' he added as an afterthought.

When it was time to turn in, Farid said I would have to sleep on the floor next to him because he was expecting his brother to be back late. Around midnight I woke with a raging thirst. The rain pattered against the ill-fitting window panes, the wind moaned. Brother hadn't turned up but Farid was still awake. 'I'm cold,' he murmured. I gave him my blanket.

'No, come and put your arms around me,' he pleaded. 'I had a dream that God wants us to be brothers. He wants us to love each other.'

It wasn't the moment to doubt the word of God nor was it the night to be cast out on a Yemeni mountain.

'We are brothers, Farid. But I don't need to get warm. I'm too warm as it is. Take the blanket.'

He threw the blanket away. 'God is very angry,' he said petulantly. He turned over and went to sleep.

The view next morning took one's breath away. It was as well I hadn't known where I was being taken the night before; the house and the path overhung a two hundred foot drop. And was it beautiful! Calm, as if the storm had never been, as if the world had been born into this dewdrop luminosity. The mountains rose and fell like cadences in a wave that had been held there trembling. It was a morning on which the marrow of the earth was young.

Our conversation of the night before was forgotten. Farid ordered *khubz* and honey and then took me to the local governor's office. The deputy governor was in audience behind the governor's green baize and glass topped desk. I was queue-barged through a long line of assorted supplicants and litigants and told I could stay in Hajja, which was just as well as I couldn't get out of the place until Friday.

The business completed, Farid said he would show me around the imam's palace. In the light of day it seemed more Gilbert and Sullivan than *Macbeth*, which it had decidedly felt the night before. There was a throne room with a very big throne and a bathroom with a large bath, a shower and a flushing toilet.

The water for the royal ablutions came from wells one thousand five hundred feet below Hajja. The water in Hajja itself had to be watched for bilharzia. It was the women's right and privilege, a lifetime's labour of love and servitude, to bring up the water. It was a feature of Hajja, the ant-like processions of women descending and returning from the wells. This daily traffic was the foundation of the town's economy and a woman's social status. There were a select few who could afford the 1 ryal an imperial gallon cost to get others to collect if for them.

We had lunch at Farid's mother's place after Farid had been to the mosque to pray. Farid was particular about his prayers. His elder brother was there, the absentee of the night before. Mohammed resembled a scrawny chicken with bow legs and a clucking Adam's apple which moved in time with the huge wedge of *qat* in his cheek. His long, scraggy neck supported a small, round head which perched on his shoulders as if meant to come off. (Those stories of beheadings; one began to picture every Yemeni head on the end of a pike.) He had a funny way of looking at you too, as if you were avoirdupois, if you know what I mean, meat on a butcher's slab. Farid found him hilariously funny, a judgement I couldn't share so long as he had me transfixed with an inane, unwavering grin.

'Mohammed wants to know if you can find him work in England. There are many Yemenis in England,' Farid declared.

'It's difficult at the moment,' I said. 'There's a lot of unemployment.' The grin clouded, turned a little sour. The wedge in his cheek stopped working, giving him the air of a doe eyed Chihuahua with goitre. 'What's wrong with life here?' I countered.

'Little to do, no money,' said Farid. The grin apparently had lost its voice. Farid was its spokesman.

'Isn't he trained for anything?' I addressed Farid.

'He's a soldier. During the civil war he was an irregular with the imam in the hills.' The grin came out from behind the clouds. 'He killed Egyptians and Republicans and took the heads back to the imam.' The grin nodded in corroboration. 'The imam was so pleased that he gave him one hundred golden sovereigns. With the money he bought a farm and got tenants. But there is no money in farming now. Prices for sorghum are bad. So my brother is broke.'

Farid looked glum, Mohammed looked glum and I shrugged my shoulders in sympathy. 'I see,' I said. There wasn't much more I could say. It wasn't the sort of CV on which to build hopes of preferment in a Republican army.

The Egyptians made Hajja their regional headquarters for a time during the civil war. They were not popular locally and were unkindly accused of having given Hajja bilharzia. Yemen was the last place most Egyptians wanted to be. They were to find too often the salary inducements that lured them there a deadly trap.

In the town were two young missionaries. When Farid left with Mohammed to visit friends in the country, I moved into the surgery beneath their flat. The local girls were in the habit of calling on them for elevenses and afternoon tea. My presence put the cat amongst the pigeons as soon as they discovered a strange male on the premises. They overcame their reservations by pretending I didn't exist and I was consigned to the box room whenever there were female visitors.

They were a lively earthy bunch much given to talk of men and babies, and prospective matches. In this they enjoyed a huge advantage over the boys as the girls could see the boys but the boys couldn't see the girls. There were often very tense bridegrooms on wedding days as marriages were arranged. A Hajja bride cost between 2,000 and 10,000 ryals, a patrician girl from Sana'a as much as 17,000 ryals. Heartrending tales still circulated of little mites of six being betrothed and separated from their mothers, but in practice most girls had a say in whom they married. And the more assertive usually managed to wear the pants. Like the seventeen year-old who used to drag her terrified 'old man', as she called her forty year old spouse, down to the clinic for treatment. Most were married by fifteen which made Nadia the more remarkable. For Nadia was a near-menopausal nineteen, unwed and beautiful; not only beautiful but rich. Nadia didn't have to fetch water. Nadia was very clear in her mind what was right and what was wrong and what she wanted. She had an unashamedly romantic view of love and would not be rushed. Fortunately she was the apple of her father's eye and he did her bidding. He had already turned down a number of offers for her hand as a second wife and was quite adamant that any suitor for his daughter's hand should undertake not to take a second wife.

Nadia disapproved of *qat*, which demanded character. The women were as partial to *qat* as their men folk and had their own *qat* parties. When it came to her father's western pin-up calendar, however, Nadia was uncharacteristically at a loss. She thought it lascivious and therefore reprehensible; but she was mesmerised by the mini dresses.

Once she asked to have her photograph taken but had then backed down. She hadn't thought it through. 'Strange men will see my face,' she said. There had been consternation one day that I might have seen her unveiled. But she concluded that as I was a foreigner passing through it wasn't so bad; if I had been local she would never have lived it down. And that reasoning formed the basis of the compromise: photographs could be taken but they must not be shown to any male in Yemen. She duly turned up with her beauty box to have her picture taken.

At night she read the Koran and exhorted the Prophet to look kindly on her missionary friends who deserved better than eternal hellfire, while the missionaries prayed equally fervently for Nadia's soul.

The missionaries' attitude to Islam, I found disturbing. One evening Cathy let slip, 'It's a dark religion, I can't see anything redeeming in it. Read its history. Mohammed was a frightful man. You only have to look at the way they treat their women.'

'Were we any better even a few generations ago?' I asked. 'Anyway, isn't the way religions actually work on the ground, how they help people cope with the business of living and answer their spiritual needs more important than arguing over whether Christ was perfect or Mohammed imperfect? Surely Islam is just another way.'

'If you are Christian, there can be no other way,' she declared.

'Well, I think there is a fundamental flaw in this reading of Christianity. If God made the roses, the violets and the jasmine, why on earth should He expect us all to be Christians? How boring! It's this damned Hebraic tradition of exceptionalism.'

'The Muslims are part of it.'

'Yes, but thankfully out on a limb, and even more so since the dispute over Palestine. The Christians and the Jews have got to get it out of their heads that they're top dogs. Just because it's written in the Book, they think they can carve up the map...'

'The Bible gave Israel to the Jews,' she rejoined defensively. She was apologetic, would have preferred it otherwise but there we were. 'They are the 'Chosen People'.'

'So does that mean because they are the 'Chosen People' they have the right to turf out anyone who isn't so fortunately 'chosen'?' I enquired.

'If God said so, who are we to argue? God gave the Jews the land from the Nile to the Euphrates. They may not get it today or tomorrow but they will as part of the fulfilment of the prophecy. I believe God meant Jews to lead the world back to Christianity. They will be converted as the Bible says. ...I'd like to play you a tape.'

And she played a tape of a sermon delivered in St Martin-in-the-Fields soon after the end of the Six Day War in 1967. The preacher started by outlining an historical perspective of the survival of the Jews through massacre and persecution. There was much scholarly detail, many references to Biblical and European history. He managed a coy admission of his Church's contribution to this suffering. You almost felt, nevertheless, that it was to 'fulfil God's purpose' that pious Christians had robbed, pillaged and murdered the Jews for, 'wasn't it odd that they should have survived?' Then came the nineteenth century and more liberal attitudes, and the greatest threat to the Jews in their long Diaspora; they were treated like everyone else: assimilation beckoned and with it extinction and disaster.

But God still had a sense of humour, though you wouldn't have guessed it from the sermon. Knowing how human nature, especially western human nature, loves to scourge itself to the great relief of the seers, soothsayers and divines who might otherwise have found themselves out of business, He brought back anti-Semitism, put history on its predetermined path again and saved the Jews. Only the Nazi pogroms were a joke too far and spoilt the Plan. The preacher passed over the pogroms as being peripheral to the story, for in Palestine the seeds had been sown and the prophecy was coming to pass. 'Was it a coincidence?' he kept asking, 'was it coincidence that in all those long years of exile one Jewish village in Upper Galilee should have survived to keep alive the Jews' ancient claim to the Promised Land?' So it was that the first Zionist settlers arrived at the turn of the century to find, not the fertile land of their forefathers, but a wilderness inhabited by a few wandering tribes.

And it continued through the Balfour Declaration and the creation of the Jewish state to the latest, most critical challenge to Israel's existence, the Six Day War. A stunning victory, he said. 'Consider, a little country of three million beset by hostile neighbours many times its size. Now it could just be chance.

But you may think the thread of coincidence too strong...'

I could take no more. 'It's scandalous. It's pure, unadulterated fascism,' I declared.

'I'm sorry you don't like it,' said Cathy, and the matter was dropped. Next day in any case I left.

****

So there I was on a Friday evening leaving Hajja under a rising moon. The post van to Hodeida left in half an hour and there was time to wander. The ancient streets were dead although it was only just past eight. The indigo hulk of the imam's palace paused in its crazy scramble for the stars. In the post office the postmaster was sorting the post bags, gravely licking the dye and softening the wax for the seals while the town elders watched, chewing *qat*.

At eight thirty we hit the road. The seating was more comfortable than on previous journeys. The Landrover had padded seats and it wasn't too crowded. A veiled lady sat in the back, partitioned off. She would have been all but nonexistent but for the champ, champ of her jaws and the occasional rustle of her silks as she surreptitiously raised her *yashmak* to shovel in more *qat*.

The guards made one feel slightly jumpy. There were two of them, one on the roof, one inside, each with Winchester repeaters. The sense of riding the Dodge City stage was not misplaced, having seen the bundles of bank notes carefully counted, stacked and wedged in a steel box that now resided under the driver's seat. Every self-respecting bandit in the vicinity must have known the Hajja mail left at eight on Friday evening.

At midnight we came quite suddenly out of the mountains into the coastal plain of the Tihama. Gone were the stone houses and veils of the mountains and in their place were straw hut corrals and bare breasted women rid of the weight of convention by their African roots and the heat.

We stopped in a clearing. An armada of insects bombarded the lamps; the heat was suppurating. A radio droned in the background about another billion dollar run on the Zurich Stock Exchange. The insects whined, buzzed and flapped against the lamps, drowning the details.

About one in the morning we came to a village, a settlement of large, conical straw huts that might have been a scene from Goya: the *qat* merchants clinching deals in the greenish lamplight. There would be no Hodeida *qat* market report in London or Zurich, but here it was a game played in deadly earnest. The conical huts threw out long chequered shadows; from one sort of Cruella de Vil in Hajja to another, Africa this time. Everyone slept on wicker beds strewn under the stars. They slept in the play of shadow. A child woke from a bad dream. Her mother came to her. A shadow nipple trembled and was swallowed with her shadow as she moved. Then my shadow ate her shadow. This shadow land was the stuff of nightmares but strangely comforting, knowing it would all end well under the open, maternal embrace of the night sky.

Hodeida is not, by any stretch of the imagination, beautiful, and in August must be one of the most unpleasant places on earth. The humidity leaves one feeling like a damp towel wrung out many times, and at night the lamps spring haloes from the moisture and the sweat in the eyes. The salt is ingrained into everything and when it rains, a rare grace, it brings up the brine in a hard-caked crust which looks like frozen slush, as if Hodeida were enjoying an Arctic spring.

A few ramshackle buildings decorated the sea front. They exuded a kind of splendid if slightly louche decadence. The imam's palace was an architectural conundrum: cellular accretion or planned structure, it was impossible to say. In any case with its rotting verandas and peeling hydrangea blue paint, it was long past redemption. The Yemen Bank for Reconstruction and Development nearby was in an even more dilapidated state. 'No Photography' signs plastered its crumbling facade. But the threat from bank robbers paled in comparison with that of falling masonry and the manager had long since removed himself and his staff to the relative safety of the street.

The Egyptians (heaven knows they should have known better) laid out municipal gardens in the centre of Hodeida with decorative lamps, a four-faced clock tower and wandering asphalt paths. The clock had stopped but the wandering asphalt paths provided privacy to defecate and the municipal gardens had become the public lavatory.

****

About twelve miles north east of Sana'a lies the town of Shiban. It nestles at the base of a one thousand five hundred foot cliff and Kawkaban sits atop it. The only way of getting to Kawkaban is by a bridle path that winds up the cliff. Because of its inaccessibility the imam holed up there during the civil war. And because the imam holed up there the Egyptians bombed it. There wasn't much left of Kawkaban by the time they had finished, about half the town was reduced to mounds of beautiful pink stone. And as everything had to come up on donkeys, and as you were fairly away from it all stuck up nine thousand feet in the middle of Yemen, there wasn't much incentive for anyone to come and put Kawkaban together again.

In Kawkaban tourists were housed in the castle, free. It was hardly Buckingham Palace, and it was a bit draughty. But then you couldn't expect much if you weren't paying and the Turks, who had been the last to inhabit it, left sixty years ago. I relished the thought of having a castle to myself for the night… and for free. However, I was thwarted.

Returning to my castle in the gloaming, I lost the way.

'I want the castle, if you please,' I asked a passerby. I couldn't see his face in the half light.

'Are you there alone?' he enquired as he walked beside me.

'Yes,' I said.

'You can't stay in the castle alone,' he said quite shocked. 'You must stay with me.'

He wouldn't listen to my protestations, that I wasn't afraid of the dark, or hobgoblins or foul fiends or any of the other inhabitants of the vasty deep.
'Impossible,' he said, and took my hand. 'Come, we will collect your things.'

So we collected my things and made across the dark town in the silver twilight. At home he showed me up to the *mufraggi* (the living room). It was a lovely room, warm, secure and full of the magic of those who had passed through. A chest expander adorned the wall together with a picture of my host and his father and what looked like a photo of Ava Gardener. Further along there was a beautifully worked *jambia*.

My host was the local *qadi* or judge and worked in Shiban at the bottom of the cliff. He had come to Shiban nine years ago as assistant to the *qadi* and soon after had been made *qadi*. In those days his stipend of 200 ryals a month had given him a very comfortable living. It hadn't changed since and now he had to scrape to make ends meet by settling civil disputes. 'The trouble is, people here are too law abiding,' he said, a trifle ruefully. As a Zaidi and a *qadi* he didn't have much in common with the Republican government. 'The imams were by no means perfect,' he said, 'and certainly there needed to be changes, but at least with the imams there were laws. The Revolution swept that away without putting anything in its place. The present government is too interested in holding onto power than seeing to the many things which need to be done,' he maintained.

'What will become of you?' I asked.

'I'll have to carry on as best I can. I've thought of moving – but where?'

He produced a tape recorder which he had just bought for 250 ryals in Sana'a (he couldn't have been doing that badly) and he ran me through some Yemeni reels.

Then abruptly he said: 'I'm sorry, you must be hungry.'

He called for food. Three snotty-nosed children joined us. They were his. How beautifully tender he was with them! Grave and tender, and they such centred little beings.

I was at peace, luxuriating in the same feeling of security I had experienced in the home of the government official in Wadi Dhabab near Tai'z. Those children would start life with the most extraordinary emotional stability and a little of it had rubbed off on me. I would be leaving Yemen with a strong sense of the romance of the country, its mores and way of life, so little touched by the outside world that they appear surprisingly robust, like a rare species thriving on a cultural Galapagos Islands. Unlike Egypt where external pressures have forced Egyptians to internalize their culture, in Yemen it is in full, extravagant, medieval bloom. It is the innate and exquisite courtesy of the people, however, that leaves the deepest impression, representing the very best of Islam, a chivalry that marries generosity of spirit, bravery and gentleness. Yet it is also a medieval culture, brutal and sometimes barbaric in its external manifestations and it is difficult to reconcile its two faces. Perhaps this is what characterizes the medieval mind: the kernel of civilization conserved under a hard, protective shell against elements that brook no negotiation or compromise. In Egypt, exposed to so many external influences for so long the culture has had to adopt subtler, chameleon like systems of self preservation to survive.

After we had eaten, he settled to talk. There was so much he wanted to discuss, to find out about the places I'd been. The children slept and I felt my eyelids drooping, my heart full with the warmth and tenderness of this haven of civilization on the top of a windswept escarpment in central Yemen. He noticed and said: 'I'll leave you now to sleep. You must be very tired.' He turned down the lamp and took the two boys with him, leaving the girl snoring gently on the floor where sleep had overcome her. At the door he turned and said: 'Do feel this house is yours.'

Later as the lamp swung gently in the wind, rocking the shadows, he returned for the girl and quietly gathered her in his arms.

Chapter Nine

I arrived back in Cairo in mid September. Egypt was still locked in the vice of 'no war, no peace', and beneath the serene drift of Cairo's ordered chaos it was easy to detect a growing desperation, a palpable sense that something had to give. What did give a month later with the start of the Ramadan or Yom Kippur War was totally unexpected and life transforming. The war did not just break the geopolitical and economic logjam of the previous six years; it established Sadat as president in his own right. For the first time in more than a decade Egypt was governed by a leader with strong popular backing. The window this opened for change was to remain open for some four years, until the deadly bread riots of January 1977 put an end to any possibility of a new political dispensation. But it was an enormously exciting time, a time of confusion, hope and empowerment...

11 September

A Calvinistic streak in me fights this sensuality: stepping out of the plane at Cairo to be confronted by that vast sky; to be back in a world of elementals after the brute heat of Yemen; a world of the mind, of light and shade, a Mediterranean world. To be sweating and to feel oneself sweating and to enjoy feeling oneself sweating – as if the perceptual dials had been tuned to a more sensitive register – gently: a kind of autoeroticism. The state of Adam before the Fall.

In the airport concourse I asked some students the way to the 400 bus for the town centre. They were Palestinians. Beneath the easy-going banter it was not difficult to discern a hard edge. They wanted to see me again. I said I didn't think there was much point. There was no middle ground with them. They intended to exact their pound of flesh. No compromise with Israel. All Jews home, or living in an Arab dominated Palestine.

Sadat is making life difficult for Palestinian students like these. They have to get 80 per cent in their examinations in order to stay in Egypt.

September 14

Returning from Yemen, from a direct simplicity of mind that translates seamlessly into action, I am conscious here in Egypt of a certain detachment, a subtlety of thought that feeds a tendency to speculate, and explains the interminable and inconclusive conversations we hold in the Golden on autumnal afternoons.....

Cairo seems a little less shabby – or perhaps the light is kinder. A flowerbed has been planted on the traffic island at the entrance to the Gezira Club; the club itself is a little more 'soigné'. Young girls stare at new faces entering the club with a carefully preened attentiveness; apple hard breasts, manicured hands and mean little mouths.

In the men's changing room, the young bucks groom themselves, immaculately brown and white and slightly flabby in their tennis shorts and sneakers, discussing their latest lays. Not with those angular, bouffant virgin queens, heaven forbid! But with that sad sorority of 'good time girls', usually divorcees fallen through the net of the alimony laws who have few other options to better themselves than to explore the more genteel fringes of the game

Babeluk at ten o'clock: the familiar smells of sweet corn, which has grown to obscene proportions, roasted ground nuts and mangoes. The Mata'm Nasr serves steaming platters of fried liver and rice. Outside, tables propped with empty chairs block the pavement. The air is full of static. For a split second the flash of a tram, its trolley pole broken-backed and sagging like an overloaded coolie's shaft, obliterates the harsh shadows.

The blue smoke from the charcoal fires settles the frenetic activity like dampened dust. Cairo is conscious of autumn.

On the new buses, the ones recently arrived from Spain, they have a 'seating only' rule which has not gone down well with Cairenes who consider it a waste of space.

September 21

Sounds carry with no overlap: the bark of dogs, beaten carpets, braying donkeys, telephones, street cries ripple on the still, cool air. Cairo is undergoing a creaky meteorological adjustment; itchy days of prickly heat and hot flushes, the body at odds with itself, easy to imagine the first feverish symptoms of flu. It will be thus, cool and damp by night, hot and clammy by day, until all the moisture has been extracted from the cooling earth.

At the Press Syndicate last night I found Fawzi and friends eager to know what I thought of the world situation, the Middle East situation, the Egyptian situation, and one of them particularly had much to say. He was angry and bitter at the state of 'no war, no peace' but quickly became tongue-tied. His English failed him and my Arabic was not up to such intense argument.

They wanted to know what I thought of Chile where Salvador Allende had just been ousted and assassinated. Wasn't it the work of the CIA? The Americans were no better than the Russians, worse if anything, worse because of their insufferable hypocrisy. The only option, they concluded, was to take matters into their own hands, to fight with picks and staves if necessary as the North Vietnamese had done. 'If they could do it, so can we.' What sort of life was it anyway, they asked rhetorically, graduating from university into the army, only to kick your heels in a trench for seven years? What sort of career could you plan at thirty? I said I thought trying to shift American public opinion was a more effective course of action. 'Going to war won't achieve anything,' I counselled. They didn't agree.

September 22

I called in at Shobra. Atar starts work as an apprentice engineer soon and the girls go back to school on Monday. The El Gamals went to Alexandria for a couple of weeks in August, renting a flat in Maamoura.

September 26

Waheed owns a penthouse flat on Rue Gezira overlooking the Nile. It is a great place to throw a party which he does regularly when in funds. He has been an actor and a financier in his eventful career and he has also served a spell as an officer in a paratroop regiment. He consequently has an eclectic circle of friends and can be relied on to produce a bevy of beautiful girls. For this evening's party he outdid himself with a sensational piece in a long white skirt with blue brocade and a pink blancmange top, a paler version of her fingernails.

She was immediately requisitioned by a butch lady who fussed around her like a mother hen. 'Vous êtes très jolie,' clucked her self-appointed chaperone, approvingly. 'Comment faîtes-vous les yeux comme ça?'

'Merci,' said the creation.

'C'est une operation sinoise ...' mused the lady, who was Dutch, to an admiring crowd, as the object of her attentions moved my way.

'My name is Hamsa,' she said, sitting on the arm of my chair. 'It means 'whisper'.'

'Very apt,' I said, sitting up, slightly chuffed she should have graced me with her attention.

'I have so much to do,' she confided. 'Term starts on the thirteenth and I haven't done my holiday work.' She was studying Social Science at Cairo University.

The Dutch lady had caught up with us, miffed that her prey had escaped and determined to regain her and the room's attention.

'Egyptian women are so patient,' she proclaimed as a butterfly woven onto the front of her skimpy T-shirt suddenly took flight. 'They all want to get the hell out of it. And can you blame them?'

'The hell out of what?' I asked. It was now my turn to be miffed.

'Out of the home. They have no rights there. They have to get married.' The butterfly was momentarily still.

'And then what?'

The bosom heaved in indignation and the butterfly quivered. 'They get lent around. Egyptians think nothing of lending their wives to their friends. I couldn't take it. We aren't animals. We should be able to choose someone other than our husbands' friends.'

Hamsa might have found the discussion interesting, sociologically speaking, had she been able to follow, and I felt left out, never having been invited into one of these ménages à trois or perhaps quatre.

'How can you say that?' I asked, a trifle petulantly, disconcerted by such an outrageous assertion.

'I was married to an Egyptian,' she replied.

However, both of us might have saved ourselves the effort for Hamsa now made a move to go.

'Don't,' I said. 'It's only nine. You can't work now. Stay a little, the night is young.'

She pointed helplessly to a dried-up walnut of a man, hat in hand, by the door. 'My brother,' she said, and left us, the Dutch lady and me, with a flutter of her pretty hand.

The Dutch lady's assertion I was to discover was not as outrageous as I had initially imagined. In certain echelons of Egyptian society, usually the new power elites in the military, security services and business as well as the party apparatchiks, men can treat their women as chattels. It is the most powerful argument for inscribing women's rights into law.

September 27

Anais had a breakfast rendezvous with a Mrs. Bedreyan in Lappas. Mrs. B. was discommoded at missing her annual trip to London this summer and having to settle for Alexandria where she complained the price of apartments had rocketed. She has spent the last two months searching high and low for batteries for her transistor radio. That morning she had successfully tracked down a set of 5 piastre jobs for which she had to pay an extortionate 50 piastres each. A small tube of Kolynos toothpaste set her back 40 piastres. Where does it end?

In the Odeon at lunchtime a Greek woman from Athens tells me she is returning to inspect what is left of her home in Suez. It is her first time back in Egypt since civilians were evacuated from Suez in 1969. It had been a struggle to get the necessary permissions. She has heard the top floor of the three-storey building has been gutted but she hopes to camp on the ground floor.

Evening and an eerie silence descends ... at the first sighting of the new moon it is the start of Ramadan. The buses skittle round a deserted Tahrir Square in a race to be back at the depot before the cannon at the Citadel is fired. In Shobra everyone was under starter's orders to tuck into the *iftar*, the first orgiastic breakfast supper that heralds the start of the holy month.

At night the streets come alive again, bedecked with flags and streamers and paper lanterns. At the Hussein Mosque they danced the *zikr* to the high wailing chant of the *imam* and the trip of the tambourines. They sleep everywhere: in the mosques, on the road; a workmen's tent is littered with bodies as if hit by a bomb.

September 28

The magic of Ramadan dusks. For half an hour the pulse of the city stills and the traffic lights are turned off. Cairo becomes to all intents and purposes a City of the Dead. On the verandas of the high-rise flats in Heliopolis tables are laid to witness the sun set over the Delta and coming upon Cairo the mosques and minarets seem to be taking off, the Citadel a kind of stellar tracking station.

Anais had for some time been trying to arrange a meeting for me with Hassan Fahmi who had been laid low and bedridden by a heart condition. 'Baba' Hassan, as he is affectionately known is, among his many and multifarious accomplishments, a retired professor from the Faculty of Industrial Engineering of Cairo University. He has earned the sobriquets 'Baba' and Daddy because he is the intellectual father of a generation of Egyptian engineers who revere him. Like many Egyptians sent abroad to study he acquired an English wife during his training at the railway engineering works at Eastleigh near Southampton. He took his young bride May back to Cairo with him at the end of his studies. May never looked back. On arriving in Cairo she renounced her British passport, a course of action the embassy strongly deprecated, and tied her colours irrevocably to her husband's mast. In pre-War Egypt that was a remarkably courageous thing to do. She is as universally loved as her husband and is mother to his extended family of former students to whom she is quite simply 'Mummy'.

Hassan Fahmi is also the father of Farida Fahmi, the star dancer of the Reda Troupe, Egypt's national folk dance company. Mahmoud Reda, her dance partner and the troupe manager and choreographer, had been married to Farida's sister, Nadida. Farida later married Mahmoud's brother Ali, a film producer, in what was to become a powerful dynastic alliance. Tragically, Nadida died young of rheumatic fever contracted as a child. It weighed heavily on Baba Hassan that he was unable to afford to send her abroad for the treatment that could have saved her life. The Reda Troupe was formed in part to keep her engaged when she became an invalid, he later told me.

The Fahmis live in a large second floor flat on Sharia Hassan Sabri in Zamalek. I found him tucked up uncomfortably in bed, looking like a miserable schoolboy recovering from an attack of measles. On no account was he to be agitated, I was told. He is a natural autodidact who enjoys an audience but equally enjoys the exchange of ideas, providing he finds them interesting. He feels intellectually deprived in modern Egypt in a milieu stultified by an increasingly literalist interpretation of religion and the bone headedness that comes with rote learning. He can not be doing with such stupidity and Farida tells me she has to protect him from these numbskulls who come to pay their respects in alarming numbers, for they are bad for his blood pressure.

He perked up when we, or rather he, began talking, and, like a spider with a fly, he wrapped me round with analogies, slowed me down to his rhythm of thinking and cast me under his spell. We talked about painting, about abstract painting, which he does rather well, although he has never been trained.

'Take composition,' he says, shaking his mane of white hair. 'There are any number of criteria you could use for something as elementary as arranging a room and each would be an expression of the person who arranged it. But a painting is not like that. A work of art is a thing in itself, not answering to critical evaluation. In fact critical evaluation detracts from it,' he claims, his moustache bristling. 'That is why a child of six paints better abstracts than I can.'

'Surely you can't dismiss technique as being irrelevant, even in abstract art?' I counter. 'Technique helps you to understand and work with your materials: to make an impression or a point.'

'If you are painting you don't want to 'say' anything.'

'But you must want to communicate, to get something across?'

'Not necessarily. Not in that sense.'

'I can't believe that art is a wholly private matter. You have to establish a rapport, a kind of common language, with the viewer. If art is not an exploration of form and colour, an evocation of resonances, and thus a touchstone to memory and experience, it is no more than a doodle. You are saying abstract painting is a spontaneous outpouring, nothing more?'

'Yes. The music of the eye,' he says, disingenuously.

October 1

Abdel-Razzaq, a friend of Fawzi's, is jubilant about the guerrilla operation in Austria, hijacking a train of Jewish immigrants. 'The best they have done so far,' he says. 'No bloodshed and they got what they wanted.' [The Austrian authorities closed down Schoneau transit camp where Russian Jews were being processed prior to emigrating to Israel.]

Fawzi is fasting, not out of religious conviction, but for the marvellous feeling at the end of the day when he tucks into an *iftar* supper.

Another conversation with Baba Hassan. Religion, he says, developed out of man's need to explain the unknown. If God did not exist it would be necessary to invent Him said Voltaire. We agreed that the internal world manifested itself in our nature, the psyche's forms. If our predisposition is to believe in God, then He exists; although from another point of view it may indeed be invention. But so what? Baba Hassan, as it happens is an atheist.

But by understanding our nature we are better able to deal with reality. In the West we have taken Plato too much to heart. Plato made of his Forms a system of ideas in which logic usurped all other branches of knowledge. We have suffered from an undue emphasis on the dialectic process producing 'concrete' truths… good for rigorous thought and scientific progress – from which we have all benefited hugely – but at the expense of the link between intellect and heart… of the holistic view that provides intimations of the underlying unity of life. Religious faith bridges that divide: for good or ill, especially for ill, if the faith is dogmatic. But in the West we are now so ego driven, so seduced by our own success and the assumption that everyone wants to emulate us, that we find it difficult to absorb anything outside our own cultural experience. We have lost the ability to relax and let things come into us – to go with the flow – to absorb information neutrally. Instead we resort to scepticism to rebut innocence, or anything we don't understand, that is alien to our norms and ideas.

But Baba Hassan was off on another track, ever the provocative gadfly. 'I can't understand,' he mused, his bushy eyebrows furrowing, his deep set eyes staring at me earnestly. 'Why are there different national groups? France, England, Russia, America, Israel. The world belongs to all of us and the natural resources too. We have no right to use oil as a political weapon [as was being discussed in the media].'

'As a scientist I have to say Israel merits the land, she has made it productive. The Arabs are a lot of wandering *bedu*, nothing better than goatherds. Look what they did with the Fertile Crescent. They turned it into a dustbowl. There are too many mouths to feed to have scruples for a culture that doesn't build or conserve.'

I counter that an exclusive emphasis on material wellbeing ignores our emotional and spiritual needs. It can also destroy a sense of community and breed aggression, isolation and loneliness. Materialism drives our ideas of happiness in the West. It may spawn countercultures but these are strictly reactive and don't really change anything.

What other civilization, I continue, could have produced Salamano, the obnoxious, sad old man in Camus' *The Outsider*? Salamono used to maltreat his scabrous dog most terribly until one day the dog disappeared and the old man was lost because he didn't have anything to kick around any more. Only then did he realize how much he missed the dog and how in a strange way he had loved it. 'The West tries to impose its own miserable selfishness on the rest of the world almost as if by doing so it justifies its own inadequacy.'

Said Baba Hassan: 'A man saying his prayers in the mosque got his verses a little muddled. When he had finished, his neighbour pointed out the mistake and was promptly cut down for his trouble. 'What, will you destroy fifty years of prayer?' the supplicant demanded.'

Baba again: 'You know Christians complain that Muslims are preferred over them in Government offices these days. But the Muslims didn't invent job discrimination. Just before the Revolution I was asked to recommend twelve young Egyptian engineers to an oil company for recruitment. There were six places being offered. I was amazed to learn that the six Muslim applicants had been passed over for the six Copts as I knew they had as good if not better qualifications. I advised the British boss that this sort of thing could cause trouble and persuaded him eventually to look into it. The personnel officer was a Copt and had been given full discretion in choosing the recruits.'

October 2

In Shobra (where I had moved back to) Nadia's grandmother died this evening. She had been having fits and was undergoing electric shock treatment. She was taken to the doctor about five with one of her 'turns', having fasted all day; she died under treatment. The news came back from the doctor's clinic around the corner. It swept through the house like a withering wind. Nadia's sister and Malak collapsed howling and beating the ground. Buzeina heard the news and her face crumpled. Fatheya likewise and then Am Mohammed came out to see what was the matter and he too sagged.

'She was an old woman,' he said.

'But she was kind, very kind,' interjected Buzeina, in tears.

Twenty minutes later they brought her back in the doctor's car. The men formed a corridor in the street and as the body was brought in the women began shrieking and beating the walls of the next-door flat.

October 3

The heat droops like a hooded eye. Above the crackle of static, the hoarse voice of the *imam*. They were out on the street this morning, the whole of Nadia's family, sitting in rows on hard upright chairs while a little way along they were preparing the 'tent of remembrance'. This evening the whole neighbourhood was deafened by the *imam* chanting the *'aza'*, the service of mourning.

'Fasting is for God,' says Am Mohammed. 'Take it easy, take it easy.' They all agree that it was foolhardy of Nadia's grandmother to fast. Fatheya with her diabetic condition doesn't fast. The Koran exempts travellers and the ill from fasting.

October 5

Shobra police station was unable to help with my registration until I had first gone to Mugamma in Tahrir Square. 'A new regulation since you were last here,' they said. So I went to the Mugamma where I was shown to the Police Security Department, a room piled to the ceiling with files. 'You will have to go along the corridor, turn to the right, and be registered in the book,' I was told. A friendly officer remarked as he processed my application that I liked moving around.

The joke goes that Khedaffi wanted to declare war on Israel. Sadat stalled. 'We can't declare war on Friday because it is our holy day.'

Said Khedaffi: 'Why not Saturday?'

'It wouldn't be very chic to declare war on the Jewish Sabbath.'

'Well then, Sunday.'

'We can't on Sunday. We have five million Copts and we can't afford to upset them.'

'Then Monday, Tuesday or Wednesday.'

'That's impossible,' said Sadat, shocked. 'There's no meat on those days.'

'That leaves Thursday.'

'That's the night Um Khalsoum sings.'

Sadat chose Saturday....

Chapter Ten

At 14.00 hours on October 6 1973 Egyptian forces crossed the Suez Canal and stormed the formidable defences of the Bar Lev Line. The first the world knew of the outbreak of the fourth Arab Israeli war was a communiqué broadcast by Cairo Radio at 14.15 reporting a fictitious two pronged Israeli attack in the Gulf of Suez. It was some hours, indeed early evening as they made preparations for the *iftar* supper, before Egyptians knew they were at war. Within ten hours the Second Army had established nearly a dozen bridgeheads across the Canal. Over the next week the Egyptians hunkered down in a 15 kilometre wide corridor behind a new air defence system that proved impervious to Israeli counterattacks. At that point, according to the Egyptian plan, diplomacy should have kicked in. But on October 11 Syrian President Hafez al-Assad appealed to Sadat for help to relieve pressure on the Syrian front. In a controversial move Sadat decided to deploy the armoured reserves stationed on the west bank to the Front to bolster an attack on the main Israeli defence lines at the Sinai passes.

October 6

The idiosyncrasies of the flat: the loo chain that needs pulling one and a half times, the telephone dial that has to be held on the last digit... and the smell of stale cigarette ash, mint and *bakhour* (incense). It is good to be back.

Passing by the Golden Hotel around 6 p.m. Amin said matter-of-factly: 'It's happened. An Egyptian force crossed the Canal this afternoon.' It was hard to take in and at the dentist an hour later it was barely mentioned. The lights went out in the middle of my treatment; now one thinks of air raids. It needs the jog of events...

Back in Shobra, Fatheya announced that there had been fighting. 'It's war,' she said. But the Ramadan programmes continued uninterrupted.

October 7

Copies of *Al Ahram* were sold out on Sharia Kholosi by ten this morning. The paper departed from custom to print a banner headline in red announcing the Crossing.

The war has yet to touch Shobra Police Station, however. A duty officer looked at me suspiciously when I presented myself for registration this morning and asked what I wanted, heaving a body aside to get to a cupboard. Then, with book and pen in hand, he demanded officiously. 'What are you doing here?'

Another officer appeared and pushed a sleeping man off his desk. 'Lazy dogs,' he growled.

'Ooh, I'm tired,' replied the offending body, adjusting its arm.

'I was up all night, too,' commiserated a kindly policeman with pixie ears.

The duty officer opened the register. 'Age, occupation, college, address?'

'He's OK' said the pixie. 'I know him.' The duty officer looked at me askance. 'You can't be too careful,' he ventured, lamely.

There weren't many people at the Gezira Club though the schools are closed. A reluctance generally to comment; everyone's in the dark. A young Egyptian with a brother at the Front said a task force went over on Friday evening to prepare the way for the main assault on Saturday. Arrogantly he said: 'We'll show them.'

A mother with two children was more circumspect. 'How many people are going to be killed? It's pointless. War's pointless,' she ventured nervously.

There's disbelief that the Egyptians could have gone over without any ostensible opposition. It makes people suspect a prearranged plan. They don't have enough faith in the government to imagine it could have been done on their own. The Egyptian media says four bridgeheads have been established. According to the BBC the Israelis claim control of the air but are being held up by the Egyptian guided missile system. Some four hundred Egyptian tanks have been isolated in Sinai.

Cairo is now steeling itself for the counterattack. Whatever happens, the army is over on the other side and the Egyptian flag is flying in Sinai. This could be the most significant event of the war. But there is a new factor in the equation: oil, after King Feisal of Saudi Arabia's telegram warning of an embargo if America interferes.

Everyone is still tuned into the BBC and Voice of America as distrust of the Egyptian news service runs deep. Amin says that in 1967 the radio ran up the number of Israeli planes shot down like runs in a cricket match. Then, quite inexplicably, there was a cease-fire. A shaking of heads, no one could make sense of the bland official communiqués that followed, given everything was going so swimmingly....

Queues are forming for petrol and foodstuffs. Rationing begins tomorrow. Gone are the Ramadan meat concessions. However, it is the rationing of tea and sugar that will cause the greatest hardship. There's marginally less traffic on the streets after dark and the street vendors have painted over their hurricane lamps.

October 8

Shaving this morning I caught Am Mohammed coming in from the garden. 'What's the news?' I asked.

'Veery good, veery good,' said Am Mohammed, producing a large egg. 'Chickens good today.'

'No, the war.'

'Ooh, veery good. We have much success.'

Little to add. There's one report that the Egyptians were in Sharm el-Sheikh and had attacked oil installations in Sinai, later another that the Israelis had flattened Port Said. Amin taunts me: 'See, we can do it,' he crows. 'And you said we couldn't, didn't you?' I have become a symbol of western arrogance, my preconceptions humbled.

October 9

America has asked for a ceasefire and a return to the October 5 borders. The Israelis have raided Port Said, inflicting civilian casualties and killing women and children, say the El Gamals. I'm told that if I hear the short pips I'm to take cover, it's an air raid. Nevertheless I go into town.

A strange day, the spirits lurching between depression and elation; I've taken to dreaming in the mirrored interior of Café Liberté, slipping between images and reality. Out of the continuous distraction of Babeluk the outline of shapes and thoughts emerge and become differentiated...

He filled the chair as he filled the universe, holding a small pocket book edition of the Koran up close to him, mouthing the words. He didn't move for nearly half an hour so that his profile against the movement of the Babeluk crowds became fixed. And then he was gone, leaving a void as a felled tree leaves a void, when: pip pip pip pip. The siren sounded.

The *tawlah* players continued with their games. I ran back to the Golden and half way there the all clear went.

'You're not afraid?' Amin needled. 'Just a bit of ack-ack.' And he took me outside to where two small puffs of smoke chasing an elusive Israeli Phantom jet were breaking up in the sky.

At *iftar* you could walk down the middle of Kasr el-Nil from end to end. Not a soul. The tension is mounting.

There is a total blackout now and most of the vendors are off the streets in the city centre. The journey back to Shobra took a lifetime. The night, with a full moon riding high, is menacing. The high-rise buildings look so vulnerable, like butterfly wings offered in supplication to the gods of war. On the bus, I attracted odd looks. Things improved nearer Shobra where, despite the blackout, the street vendors are still trading.

Rumour has it the Israelis have bombed Damascus in retaliation for the Syrians' use of a new forty mile rocket that has targeted kibbutzim. They have also destroyed a radar station in Lebanon and are holding the line on the Golan. The Egyptians say they are five miles into Sinai and have sunk five Israeli vessels for the loss of three of their own. The Israelis do not appear to have established superiority in the air. Radio Monte Carlo states it no longer automatically trusts official Israeli reports. Egyptians quickly pick this up; they now believe their own communiqués – a significant psychological victory for the authorities. The chicken has finally found a head.

October 10

Dusk forms like a film over the eyes. Peace; a peace the more remarkable for being Cairo in the throes of war. At *iftar* the *muezzins* vie with each other, swooping and soaring like gulls in flight. The moon is up; the selfsame moon that only yesterday had threatened retribution. The Israeli counterattack has not materialized and the fear of it has faded like a bad dream; the rituals of *iftar* have taken on the trappings of a feast of thanksgiving. On Sharia Sha'rawy behind the Golden, the radios are tuned to the same prayer, Cairo echoing to the same prayer.

The *iftar* is a symbol of regenerating life and common food. It makes sense of florid generalizations like the 'brotherhood of man', for we are all swept up in the same common experience, asked in by people who have not eaten all day to share their food, to join the circle. 'If you eat alone,' say the Egyptians, 'you die alone.' There is no meat because of the war, a situation in peace which would have come close to toppling the government. Now there are no grumbles.

Up near Khan al-Khalili the Ramadan celebrations are muted; the crowds mill in the darkened streets. A civil defence post has been set up in front of the Hussein Mosque. Walking up to Bab el-Nasr and Bab el-Futouh one is confronted by timeless images of Mu'ezzidin's city: brooding walls and, behind them, the looming priapic mass of the minaret and crenellated ramparts of the Hakim Mosque. He named it Al Qahira, The Victorious which strikes a newfound resonance with the national mood. Sharia Mu'ezzidin Allah is taken up with its prayers.

You cannot help feeling that for Egyptians this is about something bigger than the Crossing. It is about measuring up to themselves. The lack of chauvinism is striking; as is the lack of rancour. For the first time too, for a generation, they are out of the double bind of the West's perception of them: being painted as the aggressors when they have been the victims of aggression. They have made their point now and rest their case. And for that they have to thank Sadat.

Fawzi can't believe what has come to pass. He says that casualties crossing the Canal were less than 25 per cent. 'The pundits were wrong; even friend Heikal can be wrong,' he says, with a touch of irony. Heikal, the editor of *Al Ahram*, had once written that the Egyptians would have to expect 90 per cent casualties if they attempted to storm the Canal. Reflecting how the authorities intended to downplay the Crossing a directive was sent to all journalists instructing them to desist from lionizing Sadat...

On the Syrian front the communiqués are getting vaguer and less space is devoted to them in the papers. Nevertheless, Egyptians appreciate the Syrians have borne the brunt of the fighting. Fawzi's friend says cutting off the Israeli oil refineries in the early days of the war was crucial and Sadat has had to deal with the possibility Egyptian forces might reach the June 1967 borders. How then to hold them back from going further? 'I think [Sadat] hopes it doesn't come to that,' he says.

Amin took me aside in the Golden and said he had to speak to me. He looked grim. Instinctive reflex to check my sins. 'You mustn't ask me any questions about the war,' he said. 'If you do, I won't reply.'

'Does that mean we can't speak to each other?'

'No, I will be correct.'

In the buses and trams posters have gone up asking people to watch their tongues. There are reports of Israeli booby traps, snared pens, radios, trinkets, etc. being dropped on urban areas and pictures in the newspapers. The public is told to beware.

The reporting in *Al Ahram* is sober; its tone and precision a measure of how well the war is going.

Pictures of hospitalized Israeli PoW appear on TV. They are accompanied by friendly interviews, one with a PoW being shown round the pyramids prior to repatriation to Israel. Prisoners are more tangible evidence of success than burnt-out tanks or aircraft. Egyptians realize the longer the war lasts the less it suits Israel. A long war will test the resources of the Zionists in America and mobilize the oil states to use the oil embargo.

Already there are signs of a split in Nato. If the Arabs started applying a squeeze on oil, America could, conceivably, find itself isolated if it came to a confrontation with Europe over landing rights for Israeli transhipments. On the BBC a Cambridge professor said Egyptians wouldn't fight for Sinai. They have no historical attachment to Sinai, he said.

October 11

Each day it is a little more relaxed as news from the Front confirms further Egyptian advances, and the world Press acknowledges that things will never be the same.

At dusk in Ataba Square the Citadel is chalked on the back of Sharia al-Qala'a in crayon whites and dusty mauves, the Hassan Mosque below a wall of shadow. The shielded car lights prick the dark as they nose down the street. Pedestrians hungry for information crowd the cafés. For a piastre you can watch the news on TV without having to buy a drink. The lines of chairs are well patronized, the news a mass of diagrams.

Increasing signs of normality: the second-hand bookstalls in the Ezbekia Gardens are back in business and the peanut and sandwich vendors are reassembled outside the cinemas on Sharia el-Gomhuriya awaiting the end of the second sitting.

October 12

Fatheya emerges from the bathroom in blood spattered head kerchief, knife in hand: the muted cackle of condemned birds as she despatches them.

The war is at a difficult phase. The Israelis are making progress in their drive to Damascus but the Egyptians still seem to be making ground, or so the papers say. The Jordanians have now entered the fray. The war is costing Israel £100 million sterling a day....

American aid is arriving in Israel. The Egyptians and Syrians are receiving Russian arms but the Egyptians are concerned by Russia's Foreign Minster Andrei Gromyko's less than categorical support for a 'just' peace. The pressure on King Feisal to use the oil embargo grows. It is said he has already halved America's oil supply.

October 13

Fatheya has a headache. And the war goes on.

In Liberté a school teacher with a slight squint and bad breath came over and asked if I needed help with my newspaper. He himself was reading an old copy of the *Daily Mirror* which he buys occasionally to brush up his English. He has read most of the novels of Walter Scott and got half way through *David Copperfield*, he says. They have left traces in his English.

'What does 'Pull your socks up' mean?' he enquires, pointing at the paper. 'Ho, ho,' he chortles.

He buys the Friday edition of *Al Ahram* for Heikal. 'He writes very well,' he informs me. *Al Ahram* is the Government's mouthpiece and Heikal, its editor, consequently enjoys quasi official status. However, Heikal is a political force in his own right, having served as Minister of Information under Nasser and as his long time confidante is seen as the keeper of his legacy. He is one of the few people in Egypt able to question the received wisdom, which adds piquancy to his weekly column.

My friend teaches Arabic in a secondary school in Giza near the Botanical Gardens. He loves the gardens and in his spare time goes there to paint. They are a bolthole from the constrictions of his small two roomed apartment up near Ataba Square. The block is crowded, 'too many children, too much noise.' When he can't get to the park he comes to Liberté. 'You have a bit of privacy here and you can hear yourself think,' he says.

His other love is animals. It makes him mad when people mistreat animals. It makes him especially mad when people say that dogs are unclean. 'There's nothing in the Koran that says dogs are unclean. It is just down to a few ignorant *sheikhs*,' he claims. 'I'm constantly quarrelling with cart owners. I tell them if they didn't overload their carts, their donkeys would work better. They shout at me, tell me to mind my own business. Sometimes I bribe them with a cigarette. That works.'

October 14

At Daddy's I met someone who blamed Nasser for pretty much all of Egypt's ills.

Much of Nasser's political energies, at least latterly he said, had been taken up with neutralizing his domestic opposition and this had disastrous consequences for the country. Field Marshal Abdel-Hakim Amr (the popular and increasingly erratic head of the armed forces in the run-up to the June war) to whom he had once been very close was a particular thorn in his side. So he determined in early 1967 to cut the army and Amr down to size by raising tensions on the Sinai front. He didn't for a moment expect the Israelis to take his manoeuvres seriously...

Equally he had difficulties after June 1967 in quelling the growing power of Vice-President Ali Sabri and the Communist Party. Nasser tried to neutralize Sabri, who brazenly flaunted his allegiance to Moscow, by appointing three more vice-presidents. However, he was soon reduced to the comedic expedient of gating each of his vice-presidents in turn to maintain control of his increasingly ungovernable country.

By contrast Sadat showed guile in neutralizing Sabri and the Moscow clique by mounting a coup months after he came to power that had them all safely under lock and key within twenty-four hours. This broke the back of the million strong Communist Party and Moscow's hold over Egypt.

Sadat should never have been underestimated after his 'Corrective' Revolution of May 1971. Expelling the Russians in August 1972 consolidated his hold on power and gave him room to manoeuvre. It might have seemed an impulsive move, but it did force Egyptian engineers and mechanics to familiarize themselves with Russian equipment without recourse to Russian help. All repairs and modifications are now done by Egyptians. When it came to the Crossing the infantry and sappers were fighting with arms the Russians left (and it should be noted supplemented) but adapted to their needs. [Sadat was later to make quite a lot of this.]

There have been fundamental changes in the army (completing reforms initiated by Nasser). Officers live more with their men and fewer *fellaheen* are recruited into the ranks. 'The troops who crossed the Canal and the soldiers manning the Sam 6 missile systems are nearly all students and graduates. That is the big difference this time,' he said. To confuse the Israelis Sadat apparently called up the reserves five times before the Crossing.

King Feisal has joined the war. The Syrians appear to be holding the Golan front and there are reports that the Egyptians are at the Mitla pass. In London there were demonstrations against American aid for Israel *Al Ahram* reported.

On October 15, a day after Israel had blunted the main Egyptian advance into Sinai in the biggest tank battle since the Second World War, Ariel Sharon mounted a daring counterattack across the Canal adjacent to Ismailia in a district known as the Chinese Farm, near Deversoir. In the ensuing days the Egyptians tried desperately to nip the incursion in the bud by cutting its supply lines. They failed and the bulge grew and a second bridgehead was established, enabling Israeli tanks to range freely behind Egyptian lines, wreaking havoc with missile defence systems left vulnerable by the decision to deploy the armoured reserves in Sinai. Sadat resisted calls to withdraw the reserves, fearing it would damage morale, and this enabled the Israelis, having gained air superiority, to drive a wedge between the Egyptian Second Army in the north and the Third Army in the south, eventually opening the Third Army up to encirclement and cutting off the port of Suez.

October 15

In Liberté my school teacher friend was downcast. His cat has caught flu and is going blind. 'When I'm there he's fine,' he says. 'He knows my smell and the sound of my voice and comes running to me. But when I leave he hides in the corner and stays there until I return. He's so helpless I have to take him to the lavatory and show him his food. Without me he would starve but with exams coming up I have less and less time. It is better that he dies.'

War has made a man of Dieter. He is less spotty, more solid somehow, more flamboyant and less threatened. He is amazed at how Egyptians responded to the showing of PoW on TV. 'They were embarrassed,' he says. The Ministry of Information has apparently scrapped these parades as being counterproductive: exciting too much sympathy for the prisoners.

According to Dieter, Egyptian commandos deactivated the napalm sluices on the Bar Lev line on the night before the main forces went over. The bridges were made and held and the main part of the army was over the other side within six hours.

October 16

Amal is a Socialist intellectual and a poet. According to Madame R, the Golden's artist in residence who pays her rent in paintings, he is Egypt's answer to Rimbaud. Amal has no visible means of support, having been expelled from the journalist union in one of its periodic purges and consequently has to rely on the goodwill of family and friends to keep body and soul together. He can usually be found at Café Riche, a block down from the Golden Hotel on Talaat Harb, or in the Atelier des Beaux Arts off Sharia Mohammed Bassiouni. Neither a Communist nor a Muslim – he finds the Koran poor in ideas – he seeks his Creator through science and art and puts down his ecumenism in religious affairs to the fact that he had a Christian wet nurse and his parents would call in the Coptic priest to bless him when he fell ill. Amal has a good mind but little to occupy it and his view of the world tends therefore to be very elaborate and conspiratorial.

He claims a sandstorm was raging in Sinai at the time of the crossing. This threw out complicated electronic equipment which would have automatically activated the petrol and napalm defences. The Egyptians only suffered two hundred casualties where they had been expecting fifteen thousand. Amal is too sceptical to believe in miracles but an impressionable group of *sheikhs* at the highest level are investigating reports that angels were seen at the Front. [This sighting was later the subject of literary and theological review.]

October 17

The *makwagi* made eyes at a girl in the street and got clumped on the head with her shoe, to Am Mohammed's glee and the *makwagi's* mortification.

In the Golden there was a farmer just back from burying two relatives who had been killed when Israeli Phantoms scuttled their bombs over Banha. The *fellaheen* watch these dog fights with relish, totally disregarding their own safety, and retrieve pilots who bale out. They are not kind to them. Am Mohammed says one fair-haired Egyptian pilot who bailed out and was mistaken for an Israeli was almost beaten to death or was beaten to death (the story varied) by *fellaheen*.

The Israelis claim to have put a bridgehead across the Canal

October 18

Moshe Dayan is reported to have given a Press conference on the west bank of the Canal. The Egyptians are warier. The tank battle in the Sinai Desert [at the Chinese Farm] that the papers have been saying will determine the outcome of the war drags on interminably and the reports get vaguer. There is a feeling that someone, somewhere, is not coming clean.

Life has been made difficult for me ever since *Al Ahram* published a photo of a smiling Egyptian squaddie and a tall blond Israeli PoW. This morning on the bus I was asked for my passport. Foolishly I didn't have it with me. I was taken off the bus at the intersection of Twenty-sixth of July Street and Sharia al-Galaa before a sea of staring faces, handed over to a patrol jeep and taken to Bulaq Police Station where I was taken to a reception room. The officer in charge snapped at the sergeant and then rang Am Mohammed. 'He is coming,' he said. 'If he has your passport you can go.' He motioned to a chair in the corner and returned to picking his teeth and reading the paper. A shoeshine boy came to clean the officer's shoes; you wouldn't have known the feet belonged to him.

Am Mohammed was an unconscionable time. But the wait was worth it. He paused as he entered then, with the full authority vested in him by his walking stick, he moved slowly and purposively up the hall. The irascible officer showed him deference. Am Mohammed removed his dark glasses (I was touched, all his fly buttons were in order), and with a theatrical gesture slapped the passport on the table. Then he walked me out to a taxi.

'Must have passport .... always,' he said gravely. 'Veery dangerous.'

He had rung a friend in the *muhafiza* (the governorate) who had rung the police station to find out what I had done wrong. Said Am Mohammed: 'He told me Elen done nothing wrong, just must have passport.'

I thanked Am Mohammed and went to bed with a migraine.

October 19

The irony of Abba Eban's remark in response to Sadat's speech of two days ago, that it was arrogant in tone and that Israel would never be dictated to from a position of Arab strength, is not lost here.

The war is becoming unreal; the reports losing credibility. People are beginning to suspend judgement. They can't see anything more than a diversionary value in the west bank incursion but the BBC keeps harping on about it while the Egyptian papers and radio remain silent.

October 20

The Israelis claim to have strengthened their bridgehead across the Canal. Am Mohammed is asking me to listen to the BBC reports to see if they say anything more than the Voice of America and the BBC Arabic services. He is becoming concerned.

Fatheya's nephew, Hussein, has returned from the Front with his company commander, a great good-natured bear of a man. We steer clear of the war as they are on thirty-six hours' leave and want to enjoy themselves. The company commander says he is going to England next year for training.

October 21

The tension is mounting. The interminable battle in Sinai drags on and not a word about the Israeli thrust into the west bank; it is not deemed worthy of comment. I retreat to Liberté.

It was about ten in the evening when I made tracks back to Shobra. I try not to arouse suspicion on the buses for it only needs one person to ask for my papers… But just before the railway underpass the tram broke down. Nothing for it but to walk. Groping my way out the other side I was stopped by a couple of students. They made nothing of my passport – it was too dark to read – and requested my presence at a police station. The nearest was on Sharia al-Galaa where they took me.

I was taken to a first floor office which was a hive of activity, very different from Shobra Police Station. An officer seated behind the desk looked at my passport, notebook and newspaper.

'You read Arabic?' he asked, and then we went through my movements for the past eighteen months. He was particularly interested in my chop for North Yemen. Then he rang Am Mohammed. He had finished.

'Take him next door,' he told the orderly. I was taken next door with my notebook and the offending copy of *Al Ahram*. Here there were three officers seated at a table, and a made-up bed in the corner. I repeated my life story in steadily improving Arabic. Then one of the officers turned coolly to my notebook.

I anticipated the question. 'Yes, I record all the words I don't know. Look at the paper, the words I have underlined. Then I write them down with the meaning.'

'They are all to do with war.'

'There does happen to be a war going on. Find an article in the newspaper that isn't to do with the war.'

He smiled. 'OK,' he said. The ice was broken. 'I'm sorry about all this.'

Twenty minutes later, having signed a statement in Arabic I didn't fully understand, I was released.

'We must find you a taxi unless you want to come back here,' said the policeman accompanying me.

The taxi driver was amused. 'Not the night to be out on the town,' he quipped.

Sharia Shobra was deserted. It was almost as though Cairo was battening down. A few vigilantes patrolled the streets. It was all quite orderly: tense but controlled. They seemed to be spoiling for a fight.

I was dropped on Sharia Kholosi, a stone's throw from the flat. As I stepped from the taxi there was a hand on my arm. The cabbie explained I had just come from the police station. I asked the cabbie if he would wait until I had reached the door and I walked the few yards home. It was just after midnight.

Chapter Eleven

In view of the US airlift to Israel that got under way on October 14 and Israel's steadily strengthening position on the west bank of the Canal, Sadat asked the Soviet Union to negotiate a ceasefire. On October 20 Henry Kissinger flew to Moscow and the following day the UN Security Council unanimously passed Resolution 338. The ceasefire came into effect on October 22 but almost immediately broke down, provoking the Soviets to threaten intervention, which in turn prompted the US to put its forces on peak nuclear alert. The Israelis, meanwhile, used the breakdown of the ceasefire to seize the main Suez to Cairo highway, thereby cutting off Suez and the Third Army. A new ceasefire sanctioned by the Security Council, Resolution 339, came into force on October 24 and took hold the following day.

October 22

And there is peace – or supposedly so. People hang on foreign news bulletins having deserted their own. There was some doubt whether the Egyptians would accept the ceasefire, but at 5.52 p.m. it came into effect.

The whole situation is obscured by the constitutional crisis in the US following the sacking of the Watergate special prosecutor, Archibald Cox.

The ceasefire is buying time. At one point the credibility gap would have widened until one or other version snapped. It was getting dangerously close to that point.

Am Mohammed says the Egyptians have caught two Americans and a large number of Dutch volunteers in the Israeli forces. Khedaffi, he says, has offered $4 million for an Israeli pilot to fly a Phantom or a Skyhawk to Libya.

It is *leila al-qadr*, the night when the Prophet Mohammed had a revelatory dream in which he was transported from Mecca to Jerusalem in the twinkling of an eye. If you see a comet in the sky tonight your dream will come true, says Buzeina.

October 23

Last night I slept through an air raid alert. The whole building assembled on the ground floor, in accordance with the air raid drill, but no one thought to wake me.

The fighting continues despite the ceasefire as both sides strive to consolidate their positions. There is very little more the Israelis can hope to gain apart from wiping out the missile systems but to open the way to bombing the Egyptian heartland. The further they move into Egypt, the longer their supply lines.

The *Fight* newspaper, which was published to report the war, is being wound up. However, the Arab League remains barricaded and security at newspaper offices is stricter than ever. I had to produce a pass to get in to see Fawzi who is unhappy. He smells a rat. 'Why the ceasefire now? Unless the situation is very bad. Talks can be extended into *bukra fil mish mish*.' Fawzi would have preferred the Israelis invaded Cairo. 'How are we going to change things in this country unless we all know what war means?' he wanted to know.

Al Ahram is already talking about Geneva as the venue for the peace talks. The Arabs refused New York, the Israelis Paris.

Tempers fray on the trams but people are making a conscious effort to keep the temperature down. Difficult, as it is sticky weather. Lappas is temporarily without sugar and the fruit parlours have stopped serving *a'sir lamoun* (fresh lime juice).

October 24

The second ceasefire is turning out to be as fragile as the first. There's been heavy fighting west of the Canal and BBC reports that the Israelis have cut off the Suez road are causing alarm.

At the Hilton I met a Belgian photographer just back from the Front. 'It was amazing,' he said. 'They'd removed every trace of wrecked Egyptian tanks before taking journalists around the battlefield. No wonder de Borchgrave (*Newsweek's* veteran Middle East correspondent) said that in a dozen campaigns he had never seen a tidier battlefield.' Back in Cairo he can't get a squeak out of anyone. 'The Israelis are going to announce that the Egyptians have won the war,' he observed laconically.

'Funny,' he added. 'Coming from a small country I can't see how holding land in depth will guarantee security. At some point the Israelis will have to think of security differently or there will never be peace.'

Life at Shobra has become monotonous: There's little to say and it's better kept that way. We don't talk much about the war apart from translating the news bulletins. The schools are still closed so the girls are at home. But they would be anyway because of the Bairam feast.

It's difficult to concentrate… we seem to be living in suspended animation, tuning into the hourly radio bulletins. They might as well be discussing the weather. What the hell is happening on the Suez road?

October 25

The weather has broken. I went with Anais to the Gezira Club. It was almost too cold to swim in the big pool. We watched Russian Antonov transporters crawl across the sky, their distant drone interspersed with the percussive thud of shellfire. In Heliopolis houses shook with the blasts. But, unlike '56 and '67, the inhabitants stayed put, despite rumours that the Israelis were almost at the outskirts of the city. On the other hand, they say the ceasefire is at last beginning to hold.

There's talk of treason when the Israelis broke through at Deversoir, and that a general and two high ranking officers were court-martialled and shot. According to one account one was a Copt. Daddy says the Israelis came into Deversoir in captured Egyptian tanks disguised as a returning Kuwaiti force. 'There wasn't a shot fired.'

October 25

The first day of the lesser Bairam, the *'eid el-fitr*, was spent at Shobra. The El Gamals were inundated with visitors, each with the traditional *'eideya*, the money gift distributed at the feast. In the morning a teenage cousin called by. She's a student at the Faculty of Commerce at Cairo University and is a student volunteer working in a hospital. She's disturbed by the ceasefire – as are all her friends. Like Fawzi she would see Cairo flattened before a ceasefire. 'We need to know what we are fighting for. Otherwise everything will be the same after the war,' she says.

Am Mohammed appeared in some agitation. A tanker had been sunk in the Gulf of Suez; the prelude to more fighting? It transpired it had hit a mine and was an isolated incident.

In the evening Madame Malak called with Tariq and her hollow cheeked, toothless maid. Tariq is Maher's son, though Madame Malak speaks of him as her own. Then more brothers turned up with their children. The children were sent out to the balcony while the grown-ups talked about the war with a newfound confidence in themselves and their nation. The old maid listens; she only moves to make tea. Am Mohammed dispenses 5 piastre *'eideya* to each of the children, mentally checking how much this is going to set him back.

October 26

This morning over breakfast Am Mohammed confronted me with wild eyes. '*Khalas*,' he said, 'finished.' After the tanker incident yesterday Am Mohammed is very jumpy, building up any action on the front into a critical situation. A couple of nights previously the Egyptians had surrounded the Israeli pocket encamped in orchards in Deversoir and exterminated it using tanks and rockets, he informed me. They had also wiped out three small towns in the process. 'Must be, must be,' he said in distress. '*Fellaheen* and civilians killed. Many, many. Israelis lost eight hundred men.' The *fellaheen* had been told to move but not all could do so in time.

Am Mohammed then picked up *Al Ahram* and underlined the headline which referred to the Deversoir operation. I said there had been nothing about it on the English news; it seemed incredible the Israelis had made no mention of it. Fatheya asks half joking, '*inta yehudi*, Are you Jewish?'

I am bruiting the idea of returning to the Golden. 'I can't spend half my time at the police station,' I tell Am Mohammed and he understands.

Waheed is throwing another party. He hesitated initially, wondering whether it was appropriate with so many of his former comrades still at the front, but decided it was.

Before joining the army Waheed, like many enterprising young Egyptians, had set off for Blighty to broaden his horizons. In London he had found work as a window cleaner in Golders Green. However, this avenue of employment was abruptly closed after he pasted a picture of Nasser in the window of a Jewish outfitter. The window attracted a brick and he judged it prudent to move on. It in no way altered his affection for Jewish women whom he described as 'very warm'.

I stayed over after the party as it was too late to return to Shobra, and was awoken in the middle of the night by Waheed, drunk as a lord, fiddling with the bathroom door. He was yelling, 'Who's in there?' and when the door refused to give he called on the 'spy' to come out.... such is the paranoia gripping Cairo.

October 28

The third and last day of the Little Bairam. The children should be out on picnics visiting the tombs of their ancestors in the City of the Dead, but as it's war they are all cooped up in the city with nothing better to do than look for Israeli spies. I fit the bill, emerging unshaven from Waheed's flat at ten in the morning.

The city is alive with spy rumours and it is no longer safe for Egyptians speaking foreign languages, let alone foreigners, to be on the streets, even in the city centre.

At the Golden, Fares says spies have indeed been picked up in Kasr el-Aini. Anais reported a hair-raising incident just behind Kasr el-Nil where three Egyptian youths with long hair and wearing jeans, were set upon by a hostile crowd who had to be constrained by the police.

Tense times on the tram out to Shobra; nearing Sharia Kholosi a passenger suggested I go to the police station. I said I was just going. He accompanied me to make quite sure I did.

Shobra Police Station was not the place I knew from past acquaintanceship; it was a hive of directed activity, the very antithesis of panic. While I joked with two young officers I espied Walim, who seemed anxious not to catch my eye. I told them I was moving back into the city centre. They then rang Am Mohammed and packed me off in a taxi.

'It's impossible, I can't move. I must go back to the hotel,' I told Am Mohammed when I got home.

'Very well, as you like,' said Am Mohammed. 'Very dangerous for you in the streets now.'

Fatheya added, 'You know you always have a bed here.'

'Better you go before sunset,' said Am Mohammed and Atar was sent to find a taxi.

'Very dangerous,' Am Mohammed reiterated. 'Someone killed yesterday. One man found with bomb near the *nafaq* (the railway underpass). Israel has sent three hundred spies.' This last, he said, was official.

'Look,' he said, pointing at a diagram of the Deversoir operation in *Al Ahram*. 'That is what happened.' Then, 'Here, look about this picture of Sadat. He is smiling because of Deversoir.'

They were all on the balcony to see me go. The taxi driver said: 'You are much loved.' I was grateful for his goodwill.

He took me the long way round, down Rod el-Farag to the Corniche. It had the advantage that once on the Corniche there would be fewer traffic holdups but the first mile through the congested back streets seemed to take a lifetime. I arrived at the Golden Hotel, frazzled and a little frightened.

October 29

It's all over. Amazingly the tension has eased. I went with Fares to the central police station on Kasr el-Aini to find out what I needed to do about registering. Nothing, as it turned out, as I had gone through all the formalities in Shobra.

The mail has started again and the UN is moving in troops. The latest article by Heikal in *Al Ahram* claims the Canal crossing achieved its two principal aims: uniting the Arabs and isolating the Israelis. The Egyptian papers are insisting the Third Army was never cut off on the east bank of the Canal, as western press reports maintained.

Internationally the Atlantic Alliance appears under strain; only Portugal is willing to grant America landing rights for its massive airlift to resupply Israel. Meanwhile, Washington's decision to declare a full-scale nuclear alert has antagonized its allies who are upset that they were not consulted, as well as the Russians. More African countries are breaking diplomatic relations with Israel; there are calls for Dayan to resign.

October 30

I'm still lying low. But the airport reopened today and there are more lights on in the centre of town.

October 31

Hoardings are going up in Tahrir Square telling people what to do in the event of napalm attacks.

I watched Sadat's speech to the nation on a television in Fawzi's office. The room was packed. The crude TV images of Sadat – uncannily like Groucho Marx – missed the subtleties of his features. He started by thanking his fellow Arabs, the Third World and the Russians. 'The Russians have fulfilled and are fulfilling their obligations to us,' he declared, deadpan. He accepted the ceasefire because he didn't feel he could call on Egyptians to fight America. The Israelis had got hold of some fearful weapons in the last few days of the war. If it hadn't been for America's intervention, Israel would have been defeated in three days, he claimed. The Arabs had made their point; now was the time to talk.

But no one should imagine that Egypt was suing for peace from a position of weakness, he added. A segment of the Third Army had been encircled by the Israelis who in turn were encircled. He was having great difficulty restraining his army commanders from wiping out this pocket. There could be no negotiations, no talk of prisoner exchanges, until the Israelis had retreated to the October 22 ceasefire line. But as a gesture of good faith he said he would add another ten miles in depth to the area claimed by Tel Aviv that day.

He apologized for the misreporting on Deversoir. The Israeli breakthrough had not been reported earlier because, according to the information available at the time, it wasn't considered noteworthy. When the full facts were known no one took the initiative to rectify the situation and the two day delay enabled the Israelis to consolidate their foothold.

Speaking on the broader perspective, he said there had to be changes in attitudes and added these couldn't come about overnight. 'It will take us generations to change,' he added, presciently.

Fawzi and his colleagues were happy with the speech. Sadat had redeemed himself somewhat in Fawzi's eyes. Others noted that when Sadat referred to '*yehudi*', he quickly corrected himself to 'Israeli', and he referred to 'Mrs.' Meir. Egyptians like to observe the niceties. Natural courtesy didn't always obtain under the late 'immortal leader' Nasser, some noted caustically.

This new spirit of self-appraisal is illustrated in the joke going the rounds that the Israelis were down on their hands and knees imploring God, 'Where is Nasser? Where is Nasser?'

Sadat lost a brother on the first day of the war. He had dive-bombed his stricken plane into a radio installation in Sinai rather than be captured. Sadat is going to his village this weekend to attend a memorial service for his brother.

November 1

An event which may indeed herald the dawn of a new era; the new bus station in Tahrir Square, at least eight years in the making, was officially opened today.

November 2

At Daddy's an ex-minister (who also had little love for Nasser) said there would be a big debunking after the war. Sadat couldn't do it before the war for fear of damaging Arab unity. Sadat's problem was to explain away the defeat of '67. He couldn't have done it without something like '73. Another guest, an army officer just back from the Front said the Israelis were on the outskirts of Suez for forty-eight hours and then retreated. All the roads bar one are now open and operating. He is adamant that the Third Army was never cut off.

Daddy told of one of his students who had won a scholarship to study in an East Bloc country. Immensely devout, he had made intricate calculations to determine how the Prophet during the *leila el-qadr* had got from Mecca to Jerusalem 'in the twinkling of an eye'. He concluded the Prophet would have had to travel faster than the speed of light. Faced with this conflict of faith and science, he chose faith and his Communist hosts sent him home.

November 3

During my séances in Liberté I have befriended a young scientist called Farouk and a company director called Ali Amin. Long ago Dr. Amin had studied accountancy in Leeds and married an English girl. They parted at the time of Suez in 1956; her parents had been dead set against her returning to Egypt with him. He had never quite got over it and had never remarried.

Farouk and Dr. Amin were trying to help a mutual friend. He is a divorcee and wants to remarry but his intended comes from a poor family who won't settle for anything less than an E£800-E£1,000 *shabka*, which he can't afford. She's needed to supplement the family income. The whole project consequently has to hold fire until the girl's brother returns from the war.

Fares Sarofim is just back from his family estates in Minya. He says the *fellaheen* are anxious for news of their sons at the front. Information is trickling through but there have been no official notifications yet of deaths or casualties.

November 4

My friend at the Arab League says the spy scare was real. A number had been picked up; they were looking for information on Israeli PoW. The Israelis are having difficulty recruiting Arabic speaking spies, he said. It has never been a problem in the past. But now the younger generation in Israel no longer speak colloquial Arabic. He fears the Israelis may be tempted to do a 'clean shave', to relieve the Deversoir pocket. He was against the cover-up. 'Why not say the Israelis had mounted a massive attack with new arms. You don't have to go into details,' he said.

I met Helmi passing by the Golden. How the war has made men of us.... He is ebullient, having joined the Civil Defence and learnt to cook, tie bandages and smother napalm fires.

Dieter too has changed. He is to be seen in the Odeon on occasions without his minder and is notable for his sardonic comments on the war. He awaits the resumption of hostilities and, contradictorily, the mail. It is now over two months since he had word from Hamburg.

November 5

Ahmed, the ex-spy, is also a little more relaxed, giving you his undivided attention for minutes at a time. He says there were court martials and sackings as a result of the Deversoir operation but no executions and reports of a Copt major-general being involved in treason were simply not true. An American spy plane spotted the chink between the two armies and the Israelis attacked there. He adds that there was rivalry between the two army commanders who refused to take responsibility for covering the gap. There was hesitation for two days because the Israelis were lodged in orchards and, if the Egyptians had attacked, there would have been civilian casualties. The Israelis used the civilians as a shield while they consolidated their positions and removed scores of *fellaheen* who now constitute a large number of the Egyptian prisoners they hold. Finally, the order came to bomb. The Israelis were never in Suez although they cut off the road for a time. There was no value for the Israelis in taking Suez. Now they are entrenched in the orchards unable to move from their vehicles for fear of sniper fire.

There is a big change in the climate, he concedes 'But Sadat is still walking a tightrope. He hasn't much room for manoeuvre and can't afford to make a wrong move. If he had done nothing he would have been ousted within a year. 'But,' he adds, 'at least now the police are beginning to take a grip on the situation. After '67 the traffic police didn't care. The driving has improved.'

November 6

Intimations of winter: Venus glimmers with preternatural brilliance, striped winter *galabeyas* billow like felucca sails and shabby greatcoats are resurrected against the evening chill. The cold tones up the sky as well as the skin; it creates space between men again.

November 7

Outside the Mohammed Ali Club on ShariaTalaat Harb a crowd collects for Secretary of State Henry Kissinger, who is in Cairo as part of the US mediation effort. The police attempt to move it on. [This was Kissinger's first visit to Egypt and heralded a fundamental shift in Egypt's diplomacy to using US intermediation].

I met Farouk in Liberté. There is an agonizing lack of detail about casualties and people are getting very concerned, he says. A few deaths have been notified unofficially and those not too badly injured can be visited in hospital. Meanwhile the Post

Office, which was working a mere three hours a day during the war, is working sixteen to cope with the backload of mail.

Farouk says the Israelis destroyed a number of Sam 2 and Sam 3 missile sites (used against high flying aircraft) but didn't manage to capture a mobile Sam 6 missile system.

The war hasn't upset the work routine of his laboratory; only four out of the one hundred and seventy strong workforce were called up. As a research scientist he is exempt from military service but he has enrolled in Civil Defence. He enthuses about the encouragement Sadat is giving research and believes it will be given a high priority in the reconstruction programme. He mentions with approval Khedaffi's promise to establish a nuclear centre to attract back Egyptian and other Arab scientists working in the US and Europe.

November 8

America and Egypt are resuming diplomatic relations.

I returned to Shobra to collect the remainder of my belongings. Am Mohammed is more relaxed, full of theories about the war. He says they showed a young Israeli on TV who ejected from his Phantom when he saw a Sam 6 missile on his tail. He said he had only had four months' training with Phantoms before being sent up in one. 'Not good for the Israelis,' maintains Am Mohammed. He adds that the Israelis were so short of reserves before the ceasefire that they were putting untrained men in tanks. 'It was nearly the end,' he avers.

Having settled the national and international situation, Am Mohammed then told me Atar had finally started work in

Helwan. 'First job, long way. Hard for some months but it will make him a man,' he says, solicitously. Fatheya complains that tea and sugar are almost impossible to find.

Rummaging in the bottom of the wardrobe in the front room I noticed my newspapers had disappeared. I asked Am Mohammed what had happened to them.

'The man from the *mukhabarat* took them,' he said, looking intense. 'He came after you left. He said, 'Is there a foreign man living here?' 'Yes', I say 'he is now living at Golden Hotel.' Then he went away. Two days later he comes back. He asks in the street: 'Is this man a spy? Does he have radio?' Then he comes to see me. He asks: 'Is there special radio here?' Am Mohammed mimed a high-powered walkie-talkie. 'Has Elen special radio, camera, or any of these things?' I said, 'Elen has camera, but no radio. Elen is no spy.'

'Thank you, Am Mohammed. I'm very grateful. But why did he take away my papers?'

'He asked if Elen left anything. I said, 'Yes. He left slippers and these newspapers.'

Am Mohammed mimed the sleuth from the *mukhabarat* with my newspapers. Up went an eyebrow after the requisite pause. 'Then what is this?' pointing at the underlined words.

Am Mohammed became concentrated and spoke softly as if trying to get into the man from the *mukhabarat's* bone head. 'No, no, no. Elen leerns Arabic. Must remember the words that way. Must do.'

'Must take them,' said the man.

'With all pleasure,' said Am Mohammed.

Discreet enquiries at the Golden when I returned revealed that no men in mackintoshes had been asking for me (if indeed the men from the *mukhabarat* wear mackintoshes), and if they searched my room at the Golden they did so with scrupulous care. I took a perverse delight in the thought that some computer in the bowels of the Intelligence Directorate had broken down deciphering my attempts to improve my Arabic vocabulary.

November 10

King Feisal has sent a congratulatory letter to the Soviet Union on the anniversary of the Revolution. That has put the cat amongst the pigeons.

Farouk's friend's wedding is off because he refused to provide his fiancée with a sufficiently expensive *shabka*. This she read to mean that he didn't love her very much. Farouk says the reasons lie deeper. He is tactless and didn't show sufficient consideration for her family's problems. She had a secure secretarial job and it would have been another two to three years before the next member of the family was old enough to replace her as a bread winner. She didn't feel she could leave her family in the lurch.

On November 11 at Kilometre 101 on the Cairo Suez Road Egypt and Israel consolidated the ceasefire by allowing the UN to supervise the provision of supplies to Suez and the beleaguered Third Army. It was the first agreement

signed between the two countries since the 1949 Armistice Agreement.

November 11

A day spent at the pyramids with friends. We found ourselves a mini pyramid, watched out for snakes and listened to Debussy. Flares lit the gathering dusk as we prepared to leave, the silence broken by the distant thud of artillery. The new ceasefire, the definitive ceasefire, the ceasefire to end all ceasefires, was barely thirty minutes old. We had survived to the cessation of hostilities only to take our lives into our hands negotiating the Pyramid Road in the blackout on the way back to Cairo. It was the most terrifying experience of my war.

At the Sheraton we caught the moon coming up behind the Muqattem, a big cheesy moon, and shortly after we were ensconced on the balcony of Marie-Christine's flat on Gezira Island, watching the reflection of the selfsame moon, now shrunk to a compact disc of beaten silver trying to wriggle into still water. Six thirty on a mid-November evening. So calm and warm!

We set off to visit the renowned architect, Hassan Fathi, at his exquisite Fatamid house under the Citadel. No sooner arrived and seated than we were treated to a discourse on modern architecture. 'The architecture of the square rule,' as he calls it. 'Nowadays we sacrifice everything to function. Life is slowly reverting to a kind of protozoan slime, totally uniform, totally determined, crushed by huge pressures, without light. Ugh. What a future,' he exclaims.

'I have something here which I think will amuse you,' he

chuckles. 'It has a certain topicality in the light of Watergate.'

He produced a 1952 edition of *Al Mussawa* (how beautifully they printed magazines before the Revolution), thumbed through to an article and began a free translation of the Arabic.

'The pharaoh's foolproof method of selecting honest politicians! Professor Fathi has discovered a papyrus which he thinks was commissioned by a pharaoh for the screening and selection of honest and competent ministers. The papyrus is in the form of a diagram showing a series of chambers through which candidates passed during selection. Having been thoroughly vetted, they came to the main chamber where a jury of ordinary citizens assessed their common sense and overall competence. If they were still thought ministerial material they were then sent next door to an inner chamber of fools and idiots who tested their sincerity. Only then were they considered fit to govern.

'There is no mention of the papyrus in existing records nor do we know the pharaoh for the papyrus is in too poor a condition to date it accurately.

'The article (which came with fine colour photos) was dynamite. The Government was on its knees, charges of corruption rife, Farouk's reputation was at rock bottom.

'I therefore held my breath after publication. Sure enough, a few days later there was a summons to the Palace. The king had read the article and wasn't sure whether he liked it. In any case he wanted to discuss it with me. But when I saw him he chose to take a favourable view, congratulated me on the find and asked if he might see the papyrus. I said that was difficult because the papyrus was in very bad condition and was still being restored. Fortunately for me, he let the matter drop there for, of course, there never was a papyrus.

'But the most bizarre point in the story came two years later. You may or may not have been aware that Nasser dabbled in the occult. One day soon after he came to power, I was contacted by an intermediary who said Nasser had read my article with great interest and wanted to know if there were any other details on the papyrus I hadn't published. He also wanted to know if any other papyrus existed.'

Dr Fathi is a small wizened man like Baba Hassan a polymath of a kind rarely found now in the West. 'Human intelligence,' he said, 'has evolved out of our capacity to differentiate, but everything in modern life seems aimed at destroying harmony, destroying the natural rhythms in our lives. Yet art is only strong insofar as it feels those natural rhythms. How can art be strong when we put function in place of space? Culture primarily has nothing to do with politics, philosophy or economics. It has to do with the intelligent adaptation of man to his environment.'

He showed us photos of Mali textiles with distinctive patterns that eerily matched aerial photos of the topography of the local landscape. 'How on earth did they manage that?' he asked.

November 15

Prominence is given to a leader in the *New York Times* demanding why four Arab oil *sheikhs* should be able to decide whether New Yorkers go cold this winter. The cheek!

Waheed maintains petrol rationing is a farce. 'If you know your petrol pump attendant there is no problem,' he says. Certainly the traffic doesn't seem to have diminished.

A friend of Daddy's had a brother helping to remove the injured when the Israelis mounted their breakthrough in Deversoir. 'They were so used to seeing captured Israeli tanks trundling back from the Front that they didn't think twice about it – until four or five started opening fire.' He said the Israelis opened the bridgehead with massive air support and latterly the Russian built Egyptian tanks were no match for the new M60 tanks airlifted to Israel by the Americans. The task force did an immense amount of damage to the fixed Sam 2 and Sam 3 missile sites and mounted a massive attack on the Third Army's HQ. At that point the army was very sorely pressed and there was some panic. The ceasefire followed.

November 21

As soon as the security situation eased I initiated an assiduous if ultimately fruitless courtship of the telephonist at the South Yemen embassy, hoping to pin down the elusive Mr. Mawgoud, my contact there. It needs a week to contact anyone at the South Yemen embassy. One has to telephone between nine and ten in the morning as after that lines are permanently engaged. But first you have to get a line. Having dialled and finally got through I asked for Mr. Mawgoud, trying to keep my cool as it had taken me days to get this far. In place of Mr. Mawgoud I find a charming secretary on the line who unravels my story in English, my Arabic by then having totally disintegrated, and tells me Mr. Mawgoud is out but that she personally will ensure he gets the message. However, she omits to tell me that Mr. Mawgoud apparently has an aversion to telephones, for he never returns my call.

So when Karim Mourad at the Arab League said he could arrange a meeting with a South Yemeni minister passing through Cairo I dropped everything for three days while he tried to fix a meeting.

I had thought of giving Mr. Mourad a call to jog his memory but thought it discourteous, casting aspersions on his competence. Then, yesterday morning, Mr. Mourad came on the line to say he had made an appointment for me to see the minister the day before but had forgotten to tell me. Still, he had arranged another meeting at ten o'clock today at the Hilton. 'Don't be late,' he said. So I go to the Hilton. Reception tells me the minister is out but will be back at eleven. I return at eleven and see an aide. 'Ah, you are the man who was supposed to be here at ten yesterday,' he said icily. 'I don't know when the minister will be back. You will just have to call.' So I called regularly and at five I am told he checked out at three for Algiers.

November 27

The police have been busy interdicting contraband. According to the papers they have impounded a lorry containing five tons of contraband tea, and confiscated two hundred kilos of sugar, one hundred and eighty radio batteries and one thousand eight hundred cartons of matches from an Alexandrian grocer. A lady in Muharram Bey has been caught with ninety-nine kilos of tea in bags, fifty-five kilos of loose tea and nine kilos of black pepper, all destined for the black market.

I'm told the smuggling of proprietary drugs out of Egypt has almost dried up. Normally it pays to smuggle drugs manufactured under licence in Egypt to Beirut, where they fetch higher prices.

November 30

A fifteen minute documentary has been made of the Crossing. It is a mild, low key propaganda film taken up mostly with ground and air units preparing for battle, a few scenes of the storming of the Canal and a few shots of burnt out bunker stations and charred bodies. The audience clapped occasionally during the showing and at the end rose to its feet and applauded. No catcalls, no cheers.

December 10

The Greeks are still waiting in the Golden for a letter from Australia. The police have been informed of a potential missing person. Meanwhile poor Mrs. Christoforedes has been in an altercation with a motor bike. She shows me the bruises, her upper lip quivering on the brink of tears, and then the swelling on the leg. 'La nuit dernière j'ai crié, j'ai plaigné à Dieu,' she simpers. There is no pain there now but it has gone to the chest. Her husband explains the difficulty she has with breathing; her medicines don't seem to help. The only thing that does is Stella, he says, producing a bottle wrapped in newspaper.

December 12

The Press Centre was milling with foreign journalists this morning. One, a fortyish, chain-smoking woman, enquires my business and admits it is her first time in Egypt. 'Still finding my feet,' she volunteers. When she discovers I've been in Cairo throughout the war she says she'd like my story for the *Daily Express*. Finished at the Press Centre, she suggests a cup of coffee somewhere. I can't make it so she counters with, 'I'll see you tomorrow, then. You're coming on the trip to the Canal, I take it? You're not? Well, do you know anything about the trip to the village? Mike is trying to arrange a trip to an Egyptian village.' She flags down Mike. 'This young man was here during the war,' she continues. 'I've been trying to persuade him to have a coffee with us. Where are you staying, the Hilton? I'm at the Hilton.' Drawing a blank there she concludes, 'Oh well, I'm bound to see you around… Cairo isn't a very big place. I'm going to be here at least another month. I'm researching a book on Egypt.'

Says Anais: 'We were taught three cardinal rules when I was a kid: not to cry, not to tittle-tattle and always to play fair. Here they cry incessantly, are forever telling on each other and they never, ever play fair. Yet they're larger than life and so tactile. None of the children in the Armenian school touch each other...'

December 14

It was the first time I had been back to Aguza since May and I was full of trepidation. Funny how I find it difficult to revisit my past, like Bark the slave, the eternal outsider never able to put down roots, never able to belong….

Unsure of myself I kept going, looking straight ahead, never smiling, despite the looks of recognition. How do you deal with the past when you've moved on and closed the door? Sharia Mohammed Shaheen looked as jaded as its jacaranda trees. The fruit vendors had disappeared to be replaced by nondescript tinkers. The only reminder of that old exuberant vitality and colour, that archaic splendour, were the oranges. There were Mr. Badri and Hussein – Hussein leaves soon for

Libya – so calm on the bench sipping tea. '*Kullu kwaiss*, all's well,' says Hussein, to the afternoon flowing past, and we discuss the sugar situation and the war, picking up the threads of yesterday's conversation when I wasn't there. I didn't stay; it was too upsetting.

Back on the street again the cries echoed through a film of dust and shafts of sunlight gleaming on the oranges. The ache was heartbreaking. When suddenly, click: that I could have been so blinkered! And the response was instantaneous, smiles and more smiles and more smiles still and I was back again asking after Mr. Sayeed, for Mr. Sayeed incredibly was not there.

Along by the Nile an officer passed with a little girl. 'Say something to him in English,' said the officer in Arabic as the girl backed away. 'Come on, don't be shy.' I smiled and found myself close to tears. That I could have forgotten.

Chapter Twelve

So Cairo drifted into peace. The street lights were turned on gradually and then turned off again for fear, it seemed, of lulling people into a false sense of security, but more probably so as not to overload the power grid. The crime page of *Akbar al-Youm* picked up as the criminal classes ended a tacit moratorium, their mark of solidarity with the war. And life was back to normal.

But things had changed. The city was a little more orderly, the traffic more restrained. We heard the police were using new stratagems, taking the names of traffic offenders and serving up the fines when driving licences came to be renewed, removing a potent source of street incidents. A series of short, humorous films exhorted the public to be more considerate, to observe lane discipline on the roads, to wait for the lights to change at intersections, to refrain from spitting and smoking in buses and from throwing rubbish out of windows. With the shortages there were scrimmages but they were more sedate, and occasionally there were queues.

It was coming up to the New Year festival season. People could not remember the street kiosks being so choc-a-bloc with goodies: three, four bottles of whisky where there had only been one; stacks of soap, cigarettes and tobacco. Christmas Eve and Groppis was running out of chocolates. Soliman Pasha Square sprouted with Christmas trees, gift shops with silver balls, tinsel and bottles of 'Old Spice'. In Maison Thomas, the old-fashioned grocer on Sharia Sarawat, the tills tinkled and it was almost, you felt, as old times must have been before Nasser and the tiresome complications of the 'isms'.

But on Christmas Day you realized that the city was just paying a courtesy to its foreign community; and pocketing its cash: December 25 was just another day; the Copts had their Christmas and the Greek Orthodox and the Armenians theirs. You could take your choice for celebrations; during the first week of January Cairo was closed.

I was invited to Shobra for the *'eid el-kabir*, the big feast or Kurban Bairam in Turkish, to distinguish it from the *'eid el-fitr* or Little Bairam that marks the end of Ramadan, which fell in Christmas week that year. Cairo is turned into a giant farmyard for the *'eid el-kabir*. Bales of straw confront you in Babeluk and copulating sheep trip you up on Kasr el-Aini. For a couple of days the butchers sharpen their knives and the prayer tents go up around their establishments, to lend the full weight of religion to the ritual slaughter of livestock for those Muslims unable or unwilling to perform the sacrifice in their homes, the sacrifice that commemorates Abraham and Ismail's heart stopping encounter with Allah on Mount Marwah in Mecca.

No animal was slaughtered at the El Gamals but we ate red meat. It was the first time I had eaten red meat in Shobra. For some inexplicable reason the El Gamals' financial situation had taken a turn for the better. Fatheya had gone to Beirut to purchase a television and all the children had new outfits for the feast. Fathheya complained at the E£7.50 she had had to fork out for Malak's orange and brown sweater and white pants with violet stars. She had bought Atar a pair of black flared trousers and a mauve slim line shirt which had put her back E£8 and he still wasn't satisfied. Now he wanted a new pair of shoes. He had no idea of the value of money, she said.

The uncles and aunts arrived from Dokki and Falaki in the familiar convoy of foreign cars, little cousins scrubbed and shining in navy blue and white. They were sent to buy postcards and when they returned with a random selection of views of the pyramids, cats in baskets, girls, boys, pin-ups, views of Tahrir Square by day, by night, they all sat down together and sent them to friends and relatives in the farthest corners of the Arab world with greetings for the feast. When it was time for the distribution of the *'eideya* Am Mohammed winced less visibly at the 5 piastre pieces he distributed. There was no lack of goodwill or prosperity at the El Gamals.

But it was not so for everyone. For many there was no meat at the feast, no *'eideya*. Sugar, admittedly, was no longer rationed; supplies had improved, which was a great relief for the very poor who relied on it for their energy. Government stores now sold it at 25 piastres a kilo (as against 15 piastres for the old ration and 50 piastres on the black market). But for other things shortages were as chronic as ever; cooking oil, soap and medicines were almost impossible to find. The shortages hit everyone, even the small entrepreneurs. The partial ban on serving meat meant the street grills had to close down and the attendants at the Al Ahram food stores, who used to put aside a few subsidized chickens to resell to the street grill operators, were out of pocket too.

The *ta'riffa*, or half-piastre piece, was gradually losing currency. It still bought a pat of *baladi* bread, thanks to massive Government subsidies, as well as a pencil made in China. You could travel first class on the trams for one and a half piastres but the cost of a *ful* or *ta'meya* sandwich had been raised by half a piastre to 2 piastres. Newspapers were going up by a similar amount. It seemed that the whole price structure that had held up more or less intact for ten to fifteen years was slowly crumbling and you didn't know where it was going to end for those on fixed or low salaries, the casual labourers on E£10 to E£15 a month, or the government employees on E£25 to E£30 a month.

One evening, walking by the Nile, a young man brushed past me and as he did so something fell from his hand. He gave me a dark look as he picked it up; I apologized. A moment later he tapped me on the shoulder.

'*Khalas* ,' he said, and thrust the packet at me.

'So what,' I thought, but looked inside the packet. A 240-volt tungsten bulb. No doubt about it, the lamp was smashed.

'*Khalas* ,' he said again, and tried to grab it from me.

'Wait a minute, wait a minute. How much did you say?'

'Twenty-four piastres,' he mumbled. 'Never mind, it's broken. I will go home and mother will thrash me.'

And he burst into tears; a soft, blubbery adolescent of sixteen or so burst into tears on me outside the Semiramis Hotel.

'What does your father do?' I enquired, stalling.

'He's an official.' That meant E£30 a month at the most,

brothers, sisters; mother would have something to beat him for.

'Have you change for one pound? You did say 24 piastres?'

He gave me an odd look. 'No,' he wailed, '124 piastres. This bulb cost 124 piastres. Look, I was getting a bottle of oil too. Here's the oil.' And he held up the bottle of oil wrapped in newspaper.

We looked at each other. Then he turned, crying still, and said, '*malesh*, mother is going to beat me.' And he shook my hand, repeating '*malesh*' as though this act of friendship would atone for the beating. I gave him the pound.

It was harder, if anything, in the country, for it was the country which took the brunt of the casualties and where the shortages hurt most. The question of casualties seemed to be officially avoided, no figures of the dead were given and in Cairo you could have been forgiven for thinking hardly anyone had died. The only way of knowing was the swollen obituary columns in the papers, but no mention was allowed of the fact that these young men had died in war. Egypt paid the price in dead but it was a price which had already been discounted over six years of military mobilization and economic hardship. It was a small price, relatively speaking, compared with the price of the *karitha*, the catastrophe of '67.

Then the weather broke, after a day of false spring, when a mild east wind sprang Cairo out of its winter trance and you thought you would go mad with the movement and the colour. It came after the Epiphany storm, discreetly, a thin film of drizzle blurring further the steamed windows of Lappas, imbuing colour into the crumbling limestone facades to the buildings across the narrow side street. And when it was gone, leaving dark clouds massing behind the Antikhana, (Cairo Museum), it left the city softer, the air moistened, and the shishing of the car tyres, printing tracks in the tarmac, deadened sound.

The next day there was more rain, heavy this time. The crowds scattered for cover like crabs on the sea shore; spattered nylons. The rain left large puddles which proscribed pedestrians, bunched on the narrow ground between the pools, to pick their way carefully by circuitous paths. The roads were death traps of oil churned to slushy ruts. Cars crawled, tyres slithered. At dusk the mass of blue clouds over the Antikhana, rolled back at the edge to let in the sun, the far buildings of Dokki were floodlit by it, and over the Omar Makram Mosque the crinkled cloud was tipped with crimson like the folds of a cardinal's cape painted by Raphael.

Still it rained and the damp began to eat into you so that at night you were cold with three blankets and you waited in the Golden for the hot water in the evening and the chance to get warm by soaking under a steaming shower. Whether there was hot water or not became a matter of vital importance and, when there wasn't any, there was an inquest. Amin talked of sabotage and personally supervised the lighting of the antiquated boiler. Then the trouble was diagnosed. The Greeks – it had to be the Greek couple. Amin swore that they were running off the water before it had a chance to get really hot; the Greeks swore blind that they weren't. Then Amin hit on the idea of putting in a water cock to cut the Greeks out of the hot water system while it was heating. And that was when the fun started.

One morning I came down to find Fares in heated discussion with the Greeks, who were demanding exemplary action and preferably Amin's head, given that Amin had knowingly and with malicious aforethought denied them hot water. The management was in a cleft stick because in a sense this was precisely what Amin was doing. That night, and it was cold that night, it was the third night without hot water, the boiler was lit and Amin turned off the water supply to the Greeks' flat. Monsieur heard the boilers being lit, turned on the hot tap; found it dry and shot downstairs. Madame remained to check developments. Soon she was down.

'Why is the water off?' she thundered.

Amin had a way of half lowering his eyes, pursing his moustache into a circumflex and cocking his head when he wished to be particularly officious. He did so now to great effect.

'But, madame, it is off for the whole hotel. We told you, we cut it off while it is heating.'

Madame was prepared to do many things but balked at calling Amin a brazenfaced liar in the foyer of the hotel.

'You're sure?' she asked fiercely, and swept out, leaving Monsieur implacably erect in his usual seat.

Thereafter there was piping hot water: for everyone. And the Greeks, whose obsessive fear that others might run it off before them, were mollified.

But the hot showers were only a temporary respite. The cold

left you with a kind of dull numbness. You felt it even as a pampered European. There were simply not enough calories to go round from the Odeon's fishcakes, boiled veg and rice pudding to offset the drop in temperature. The circulation became sluggish, so did the mind and after a time a kind of grey haze encircled your field of vision. You found yourself shivering involuntarily and discovered how hunger breaks down your logic.

Then one morning the rain was gone, leaving only the cold. The sun shone and the breath was sharp in the sunlight. Everyone was muffled; the newsagent on Soliman Pasha Square was so wound round with scarves that all you could see were his spectacles. The cobbler, a few doors up from the Golden, was still shuttered at ten in the morning. He had difficulty getting up on these cold mornings and it was tough on his assistant, a small man, furry from scalp to jaw with the same grey stubble, who was left shivering on the street. Periodically the assistant took shelter in the Golden, driven out of the confines of shining shoes to exclaim that it was: 'Too bad.' He had been waiting since seven thirty, he told us, with a consumptive wheeze accentuated by a marked lisp, for he had no palate. He was so cold that he was vibrating gently like an electric generator under the grubby night shirt which was all he had to wear. It was the first time I had seen him away from the shoes which he polished with such dedication, the first time I had seen his eyes or heard him speak or protest or had known that he was anything other than the shoeshine man in the cobblers next door.

And the cold stripped Cairo of its magic, reduced it to a wasteland, a stage set for a 'cinema verité' of New York copland. Sharia Talaat Harb seen from a car at nine in the evening was cold bright with blurring neon, electric without warmth, and you realized that the cold was another kind of war.

The best place to escape the cold was Lappas; if not Lappas, then Restaurant Riche. Restaurant Riche was the lugubrious haunt of intellectuals and the Karikat man; in general people who were far too otherworldly to notice the reek of stale vegetable soup or the recent attempt at redecoration which had somehow misfired and made Riche look even more like a morgue. They didn't notice the gingham tablecloths or the greasy plastic plates on which macaroni caked with cold sauce and limp salad was served. If you were fool enough or so reduced as to eat Riche's 8 piastre macaroni that was your look out. You went to Riche for other things, for the conversation, for the sense of history – the Revolution was reputed to have been plotted at these selfsame tables – and the coffee, which wasn't bad.

The waiters at Riche were as sweet and cheerful as well trained dormice. They had their allotted corners where they fell fast asleep. It left the customers free to let off steam without upsetting anyone; which was important if you were intellectual and out of work, especially if it was the government which had put you out of work for having too many of the wrong ideas.

Towards the end of January the lights went on to celebrate the start of the Israeli withdrawal. Amal was full of premonitions (he went to Riche because he was an intellectual and because he was out of work). He said the peace plan was an American plot to reassert control over the region and to get the Arabs to buy European rather than Russian arms. The Americans had decided it was time for peace; the arms build-up threatened a confrontation with Russia. European arms in

Arab hands would help stabilize the area. America, he added, had engineered the war to get Israel to withdraw – and had succeeded, dividing the Arabs at the same time. The ceasefire had almost caused a split between the Syrians and the Egyptians with the Syrian Baath party accusing Ismail Fahmi, the Egyptian foreign minister, of colluding with the Americans.

Amal was also concerned about Heikal's sacking as editor of *Al Ahram*. Heikal had disapproved of Sadat's overreliance, as he saw it, on Kissinger's mediation. Despite his foibles and his political ambitions, Heikal had been a civilizing influence, said Amal. Almost singlehanded he had educated Egyptians to see their situation in a world perspective; he had been particularly effective during the war. 'We don't have many men of culture and we can't afford to throw them away,' he asserted.

Not everyone agreed. Heikal had not been forgiven by some for being such an uncritical mouthpiece of Nasser. They said he was an opportunist and had used his position at *Al Ahram* for empire building. He was loyal to his staff, many of whom could attest to his kindness and consideration – *Al Ahram* looked after its own – but they were virtues which didn't necessarily extend to the world outside. No one could work out who was the essential Heikal. He seemed to have a chameleon capacity to adapt. Even Fawzi, who recognized his talents, was at a loss to relate the Heikal of five years ago with the Heikal writing during the October War.

Heikal's enemies said that while he was around there was no possibility of laying Nasser's ghost. There were the niggling anomalies like the fact that Heikal was the only journalist who didn't have to submit his copy to the censor. So when eventually Sadat sacked him (ostensibly for casting doubts on the wisdom of his unqualified support for Kissinger's 'step by step' peace plan) he made a point of abolishing the censor.

Egyptians still find it difficult to be objective about Nasser. He had the good and the bad in huge measure which, coupled with the pressure of world events, meant they have never had the chance to stand back and take stock. In an oblique way, this was what October '73 was about: a symbolic war to enable Egyptians to find their feet.

Waheed, with his penthouse flat on Gezira Island and family estates, was an ardent supporter of Nasser. 'His job was made impossible by western meddling,' he contends, adding: 'At least he made Egyptians proud to be Egyptians. He threw out the foreigners, distributed land to the peasants and gave industrial workers the semblance of a deal. He also laid the foundations of the socialist state. And that was no bad thing.'

What can be said with certainty is that few leaders have ever come to power on such a massive wave of popularity and with such a sweeping mandate for change. But something went wrong, badly wrong, and whether you blame that on America's imperial machinations, Israel, Nasser himself or Egyptians is really up to you. They talked about it endlessly, of course, at Riche.

One of the most cogent explanations of the Nasser phenomenon was provided by a diplomat friend of Baba's. 'Nasser was a military officer by training; you should never forget that, and he had a good grasp of tactics and military strategy,' he contended.

'Then why did he leave his army in Sinai almost completely

defenceless in '67?' I asked.

'He had a promise from [President] Johnson that the Israelis wouldn't attack.'

'But do you pin the security of a nation on a verbal promise?'

'He was politically naive. Remember he was a sub postmaster's son with a military training catapulted into a struggle between the superpowers. He had no real political education and was never allowed to find his bearings even if he'd been able to. Consequently he had little sense of the forces he was riding and came to rely on the strength of his personality. The temptation to cut corners was irresistible... Voilà. ... the bureaucracy and the secret police.'

'What about Sadat?' I asked.

'Ah, Sadat. You can't say much about Sadat other than that he survived – no mean feat! He kept his eyes open all those years and he was prepared to learn from mistakes. He also knows what it is to go hungry, really hungry. Sadat is an Egyptian in a way Nasser never was. Nasser was caught up in his aspirations to lead the Arab world. There is no such conflict in Sadat.'

Poverty was purifying another rising star in the Arab firmament. Helmi, my Kuwaiti Palestinian friend and resident Lothario, was not his normal self. Over coffee in Lappas to which I treated him because, he said, he could no longer afford such luxuries, he confided that perhaps his latest conquest didn't love him any more.

Helmi had just spent three idyllic weeks with an American girl who had come over to share an apartment he had rented at vast expense in Garden City. It had to be in Garden City otherwise people would have talked and it was for this reason he was now out of pocket. They had parted, Helmi assured me, very much in love – a state of affairs the girl's father had apparently done his utmost to discourage – and he was now wretched that he hadn't heard from her in two weeks.

They intended getting married, perhaps in the summer. But where to live? Not in America. He was too proud for that. Europe would do but Karen couldn't work there. Kuwait or Beirut would be the best solution, he said. 'In Kuwait and Beirut you can do what you want and no one bothers you.'

'There is another thing,' he added. 'If I get married I'll have to earn a living. While I'm studying and single my mother will support me. But who's going to support us if I get married and I'm studying? It wouldn't be fair on Karen.'

A couple of weeks later I bumped into him again. He was dazed like a man who has won the pools. As I had suggested, the whimsical Egyptian mail had been hoarding her letters. They had arrived in one fell swoop, a plethoric outpouring of passion.

'She is paying for me to go to Washington,' he pronounced waving a desultory hand in response to deep emotion. 'I can't believe it. Usually I have to work so hard for everything I get,' he said without the slightest trace of irony, 'but Karen....she has just fallen into my lap.'

But Helmi never went to Washington. The next time we met Karen's stock had fallen. He didn't explain why but intimated she was 'too possessive', adding 'She is going out of my heart.' Instead of the States he had promised himself a holiday in Europe and had written to Karen declaring it would be his 'great happiness' if she decided to join him but if she had other things to do or didn't want to come he 'wouldn't mind'. It was a curiously ungracious defence of his super inflated ego. But there was no harm meant and as with most of Helmi's liaisons it was probably a case of ships passing in the night.

The last person I expected to see in Lappas was Maher. For some reason I thought he was out of the country. He was thinner, more wiry, laden with cakes and couldn't stop. We arranged to meet next day. Rumour had it that he had brought home a beautiful Swedish pop star from his latest European sortie. Maria turned out to be a university dropout he had picked up in a Rome youth hostel. She looked sad and pallid, as if deprived of sun, which indeed she probably was, as Maher kept late hours. If Maria had followed Maher in search of adventure, glamour and a touch of the exotic she had drawn the short straw. Hers was an introduction to a side of Cairo that didn't feature in the tourist brochures. Life with Maher had its moments but they were interspersed with spells of excruciating boredom, enduring interminable meetings with Maher's friends who spoke little or no English. She regretted having 'run away' as she put it, and admitted to feeling lonely and homesick. She missed girl talk, letters from home and a kind of consideration Linda Kanelous could have told her is rarely afforded women in the Arab world.

That night, however, Maher unwittingly engineered a piece of theatre that provided an insight into the latent tensions still simmering beneath the surface of Egyptian urban life and the lengths the authorities would go to play them down and foster reconciliation.

He took us to a café in a side alley behind Sharia al-Qala'a and ordered tea and grilled kidneys. Suddenly and quite imperceptibly there was a heightening tension on the street – absolutely nothing you could put your finger on. The trams rolled past, the smoke from the charcoal fires curled alluringly in amongst the neon lights and the tea and grilled kidneys arrived. A police jeep passed, then another with wailing sirens. Maher announced there had been a fight down the road at Muski Police Station in Ataba Square and went off to find out more. He returned to tell us there had been an incident on a bus involving a security policeman and a soldier. The soldier had insulted the policeman's girl friend. The policeman had tried to arrest him. Two other soldiers on the bus had come to their comrade's aid and the policeman called for reinforcements. At that point the crowds intervened.

The news got back to the soldier's barracks at Bab el-Hadid near the railway station and reinforcements marched up to Muski Police Station where a fight ensued in which a soldier was killed – or so rumour had it.

Maher said such incidents weren't uncommon. There had been an altercation that summer in which a number of people had been killed in Sayidda Zeinab after a security policeman stumbled on a hashish den.

By the time I made my way home around eleven the tension had eased, though a crowd still lingered outside Muski Police Station. I asked an agitated peanut vendor what had happened. 'There was a fight inside the police station. A soldier's dead. Dead!' he shrieked.

'What are you doing here?' A man in a raincoat had overheard the exchange.

'I was passing, saw the crowd and stopped to find out what was going on,' I replied.

'Nothing to worry about,' he said firmly. 'A small incident. It's all over now. You'd better move on.'

The next day the papers reported a 'regrettable' incident at Muski Police Station involving a soldier and a security policeman. The Minister of the Interior and the Minister for War intervened to settle the dispute. Fortunately no one was seriously injured, the papers claimed. But after the incident the Security Police ceased carrying firearms and a few days later it was announced the Governor of Giza had held a tea party for the soldier and the policeman to meet and bury the hatchet.

The Security Police are not popular. Nasser created the *amn al-dawla* to counter corruption. They are better paid than the regular force and are of a higher calibre. However, they are often young men with little practical experience and they could be arrogant. This arrogance was resented. The incident at Muski Police Station gave the public the opportunity to vent their spleen at the *amn al-dawla* – and to stand foursquare behind the army.

Egyptians have an inordinate pride in their army for restoring their self respect – although they could be disarmingly casual in showing it. I was in Alexandria to witness the homecoming of the Third Army. The procession seemed to happen almost accidentally. From the Café Délice in Zaghloul Square it looked at first like a trade union demonstration. Subdued crowds came into the square chanting the '*Bismillah*' and other war tunes, songs of vigilance and sombre patriotism. They were followed by convoys of tanks and armoured cars bedecked with palm and laurel leaf, with the more exuberant riffraff edging their way up the sidewalks of Sharia Sofia Zaghloul to keep up with the procession. At the intersection with Rue Fouad the traffic tried to nip across between the tanks and armoured cars. Then as the second wave of the convoy turned into Sharia Sofia Zaghloul a deep throated roar drowned the ululations of the shop girls. The roar swept up the street to where the first trucks were turning left at the Eastman Company building.

Almost before it had begun it was over, like a passing shower. The banners with 'Welcome to the fighting heroes', 'Egypt salutes and thanks the heroes of the Third Army' were folded up and the crowds drifted away.

In the Sultan Hussein Café on the corner of Rue Fouad the old man clutched his temple, sucked in his hollow cheeks and prepared to reply to the Queen's pawn opening in his game of chess, the parade forgotten.

I was in Shobra for the TV sequel to this national rite of thanksgiving and remembrance: the award of campaign medals in the People's Assembly. There was Sadat, granite faced, drowned under a huge peaked cap that engulfed everything but his radiant smile. He seemed overwhelmed and fragile; and close to tears when he received the award for his dead brother. But his voice was strong, the same ponderous de Gaullian cadences that Egyptians used to love to mimic before the war. 'We'll go into the future without bitterness,' he told the nation.

Ahmed Ismael, the Commander-in-chief, was made a full field marshal, the first since the hapless Amr, and Khedaffi and President Mobutu of Zaire, who were attending as distinguished guests, took it in turns with Sadat to distribute the medals. Khedaffi then made a speech without notes in short, clipped sentences at the end of which he produced a written speech he said he had been too shy to read in front of the television cameras he hadn't been expecting.

'Look about Sadat,' Am Mohammed chortled. 'He takes Khedaffi by the ear. Khedaffi leetle boy, too much money.'

Thus Egypt ceremoniously laid their martial ghosts to rest and I returned to Shobra.

Chapter Thirteen

The arrival of the television was greeted with aplomb. It was watched, but not avidly. The El Gamals liked the old movies best and there were plenty of them. There was a comforting substance about these pre-war films, a touch of Hollywood in *galabeyas*, Gloria Swanson hairstyles, book lined libraries and solid Lagondas, such total contrast with modern Egyptian films with their tinny rundown Chevrolets, cardboard film sets and purple sunsets by the Nile. Programmes were interrupted indiscriminately, brutally, for prayers; advertisements were sandwiched in as best they could be. Sadat's appearances got top billing and were always repeated unexpurgated, and once there was a big star-studded charity performance for the Palestinian resistance.

The television didn't interfere with the homework, nor with the solemn processions of the tutor into the guest room on Tuesday and Thursday evenings, the same tutor who had left such fallow tracts in Atar's French. There was a special ritual to his leaving. Buzeina showed him to the bathroom and waited. A half-hearted pull on the chain, (the chain now required to be pulled one and three quarter times to flush properly and only Am Mohammed had the knack), and an apologetic cough let Buzeina know that he was done. Buzeina turned on the outside light and stood to attention as he exited silently, hands at side, bowing from the waist.

I woke my first morning back into the hour of grace between seven and eight when a somnolent hush descends and the little street is left to the rumble of carts, the cries of the honey seller, the bird song and the crowing cocks. Through the door to the balcony I could see Am Mohammed in his Selfridges dressing gown, swaddled in scarves like an oversized Billy Bunter, dragging on a cigarette held between thumb and forefinger as he leant over the parapet. Buzeina had developed the infuriating habit of taking to the loo with the paper just when breakfast was about to be served which meant I had nothing between me and an uncommunicative Am Mohammed.

A slight distance had come between us. It wasn't anything I could put my finger on, but there was a reserve which there hadn't been before. He knew I resented his constant cadging but he was also out of sorts, his back troubled him and he had nothing constructive to do, which sapped his morale. Yet he wanted to talk for he leapt at any opportunity to tell a tale.

Once I came back indignant that a taxi driver had tried to charge me double.

'Bravo, bravo,' he cried, when he heard that I had sent the cabbie packing with no tip. 'Egyptian taxi drivers not good men.'

'There are good ones and bad ones, like taxi drivers everywhere.'

'No,' said Am Mohammed sagely. 'Egyptian taxi drivers not good. In London taxi drivers very good. I know.' There was no one to contradict him. 'They open the door and then, 'Can I help you with this thing and this thing?' But Egyptian taxi drivers. Aha.' He shook his head and rolled his eyes. 'One man asked 40 piastres, 40 piastres from here to my sister's home in Falaki.' He looked at me hard. 'Twenty, twenty-one, twenty-two, must be, no more..' He paused and then drew himself up with magisterial calm, 'I told him, then take me to the police station.' He spoke ever so softly with the same wide eyes.

His histrionic tales were, in fact, our only point of contact. As he sensed my resentment he drew into himself, became moody, taking to long silences; and the more estranged we became, the harder it was to break out of them. It was then I became aware of his depth and a range of feelings he hid well under his bonhomie. It had never occurred to me, for instance, that his having me as a lodger was anything more than the curiosity of having a European in the house and a meal ticket. But then one day, talking of his school days in Port Said, he said, 'The last time I spoke English before you came was 1938.' His eyes misted. For the first time I was aware that Am Mohammed was old. His age had seemed something he had come to terms with, like his bad back or the chronic lack of cash; he had never shown that the struggle to accept had hurt and left its mark on him.

It gave him nobility now to speak with intensity of an old romance. She had been English, a nurse. They met in Cairo. He had loved her with all the insouciance of his twenty-five years. 'I was rich man. Yes. I earned E£8 a month. Before the war, veery good money.'

He took her on holiday to Luxor and Aswan; they visited Abu Simbel. When they got back to Cairo, Am Mohammed asked her to marry him. She accepted. But she had to return to England; her assignment had come to an end.

'Couldn't she stay?' I asked.

'No,' said Am Mohammed, 'must return to England. In the contract must go home. I went to the British Embassy to look about this thing. I had new suit, very smart: tie, hair, very nice. I asked the *bowab* at the door, Englishman. 'Please, I want to see someone to marry my English girl.' He said: 'impossible.' Yes, he didn't ask if someone can help me. He said: 'impossible'...'

'Am Mohammed, that is scandalous.'

'Never mind. I asked another English friend to look about this thing. He said: 'Impossible. Must go to England and marry there.' My family said: 'Delighted that you marry Mary, with all pleasure; but must live in Egypt.'

'She went back to England. She wrote and asked me to come. She said if you don't come there is nothing. She wrote four times. Last time she said she will become a nun. Then, nothing. I kept the letters for many years. But when I married Fatheya she said I must throw the letters away.' I had never seen him so grave or so sad.

'You must write about that thing, Elen. Must.'

It was about this time that Am Mohammed was given increasingly to 'turns'. Once I arrived home to find him ill in bed. He emerged from the bedclothes like an old, gnarled hippopotamus. His age showed in his skin which was usually so supple and smooth. From then on the family lived in the shadow of Am Mohammed's heart trouble. He went to hospitals and was advised to cut down on cigarettes. He recovered. He was sent away to the country to recuperate and then afterwards to Beirut. Malak said: 'Home without Baba is nothing' but in fact Fatheya managed better on her own.

She too resembled a hippo, a good-natured hippo, as she bumbled and chortled through her chores, bursting into tuneless song, grunting as she manhandled the curtains and the washing. There was a kind of inertial drag in Fatheya between the stimulus and the response which gave an exaggerated flourish to everything she did. Like a flywheel it took her time to get going. A superego told Fatheya she was slow-witted. Her face was a screen for her cunning or her bluffing or, when these failed and the shouting failed, for the blind panic which overcame her when she felt the ground give way. The children teased her. She was still prone to her headaches and her vile moods but she was chirpy in-between and, as communication between us improved, she emerged as a formidable person.

It was not often Fatheya was bettered in the market. Once she thought she was very clever to have got some American flour that had just come in at 8 piastres a kilo – until she took it home and found it liberally adulterated with local flour which she could have bought for 3½ piastres a kilo round the corner. Fatheya was not amused. She cursed Egyptians in all manner, shapes and forms and asked how stupid I could be to waste my time with such shiftless, unprincipled people.

The feckless *fellah* who brought the rabbit food tried to double-cross her. He started at a disadvantage because he looked dishonest.

'What's this you are giving me, dry rabbit food? And you want me to pay 5 piastres. For that?' screeched Fatheya. 'Robber,' she seethed. 'I'll pay you tomorrow and you won't get a *ta'riffa* over

3 piastres.'

'Ouch,' he yelped, as the door slammed on his foot.

There's no knowing the stupidity of some people. He was back next day with the same story, rising prices, no food, the same dry rabbit food and the same guilty look. It wasn't good for Fatheya's blood pressure but it did, at least, give her an excuse for not paying him again.

It was strange weather; odd days of dust presaged the *khamaseen*. But then one day a freak hailstorm hit Cairo out of a livid sky and turned the streets white. It was winter again; long spasms of shivering, neon light refraction, the violet flash of trams, tramps stooping for the stubs of foreign cigarettes, fly swat sellers with bloated stocks. Then, as if we had gone from positive to negative, it was summer, the city stark with the autumn flurry of acacia leaves, hot in the middle of winter.

At dusk by the Nile, in the little garden by the Long Distance Swimming Association, the *baladi* women sat under the bare trees and the toddlers played in the gloaming. Everything was black and vermilion, lovers caught against the swaying reeds on black marble, a black palm dancing against vermilion water, the glittery black of the women's gowns.

The spell of Liberté hadn't weakened. It took about twenty minutes to settle down, get over the restlessness and tap the vein, to get into the other place where no time was, behind the crusty mirrors with their bric-a-brac of faces, up, up to where the conversation flowed between the smoke and the sunlight, filling the space where the fans stirred with its echoes. You were in a strange duality then and each seller of Nefertiti handbags,

Revelation suitcases or penknives became a massive study in concentration.

A young boy selling Turkish Delight, rebuffed by me and then recalled in a fit of conscience to be given a piastre, moves on to an old man, horn rimmed spectacles, trim moustache, white hair, clean shirt, pressed suit, his knobbly walking stick laid neatly on the table. He looks at the flyblown fare, chooses the choicest morsel with delicacy, pays 5 piastres, adjusts his tie and nibbles with pursed lips.

Being able to give graciously so that the recipient is not made to feel the recipient of charity is surely the mark of a superior human being. Admitting it is a state I have yet to attain there were nevertheless others swimming in the shark infested waters of Liberté who thought me, perhaps with good reason, fair game.

He was having his shoes cleaned at an adjoining table. Dishevelled and garrulous, he announced himself, as he quaffed his beer, by saying he had studied engineering in London in the mid '60s. He was now an oil engineer working at Alamein, or so he claimed.

Did I know Mr. Silcox, the Cultural Attaché at the British Embassy, he enquired? 'He's an old friend of my father's,' he continued, in excellent English. 'He was very kind to me when I was in London and I try to do the same for strangers here. Perhaps you'd like to meet him. Why don't we meet here tomorrow and arrange something?'

He was punctual, too punctual in retrospect. On the dot of two he materialized, breathless and haggard, and concerned lest I might have been and gone.

'It's all arranged,' he said. 'It's my wife's birthday. I've told her about you and she'd like you to come to her birthday party tonight. Mr. Silcox will be there and we can arrange to see him in his office on Saturday morning.' That should have got alarm bells ringing.

His wife, a history teacher; was due back from a school outing to Suez that afternoon. She was constantly on his back, he complained. 'She says I forgot her birthday and hadn't bought her a present. And she wants to know why I wasn't in last night when she phoned.' He felt this unreasonable, given he had just got back from Alamein and she was in Suez. 'She doesn't like me staying out and we've had rows in the past. But I don't often spend nights out now,' he confided. 'Still, she's a remarkable woman,' he added graciously, 'but difficult to live with. You'll see.' Then, ordering another beer, he said: 'I'll have to leave you shortly, I'm afraid, and get things ready. She's told me to get cakes and flowers. I'd better or my life won't be worth living. By the way you couldn't lend me a fiver, could you? I have to get the cakes in Cairo. It'll save me going all the way out to Heliopolis to get money and come in again.'

I gave him a pound. 'I really need more than that,' he said, uncomfortably. So I gave him two.

'Do you want an IOU?' he asked. I said: 'No.' There was an awkward silence. Then he said: 'I'd like to show you round the Coptic churches in Shobra, perhaps next week. There are some very fine ones there.'

I was slightly disconcerted by this turn in the conversation.

'You know about Coptic churches?' I asked.

'Of course. I'm a Copt.... It's not easy for Copts. We're thinking of emigrating. There are no opportunities here.,.' he muttered darkly.

'Why not?'

'Problems, between Copts and Muslims.' He looked around.

'What do you mean?'

'I can't talk about it here. When we get home we can talk more freely. Look, have you eaten? I must get something to eat.'

'Go ahead. I've eaten.'

'OK. Stay here. I'll get a couple of sandwiches and I'll be right back.'

Minutes later the shoeshine man came over and smiled. 'He made you pay for the beer?'

'Yes, and that's not all. He got E£2 out of me.'

'You should have asked me first. I would have told you not to lend him money.'

'But he seemed so chummy with you when you were shining his shoes. I thought you knew him well.'

'I never saw him before, and you won't see him again.' And he was right.

Yes, it was the *khamaseen*. They began pulling down the fruit parlour on the corner of Rod el-Farag and Sharia Shobra. At first the pall of dust seemed to emanate from the rubble, until there was nothing but a hole in the ground where the fruit parlour had been and the dust persisted.

The *khamaseen* made the buses impossible: interminable waits at traffic lights, dirty fingernails: and the fleas. The trams broke down too and sometimes you would see a flotilla of them stretched the length of Sharia Shobra like a fishing fleet in port.

New buses were being introduced on some routes and fares were being raised. The 100 still cost 5 piastres but the 200 was being upgraded and the fare increased to 3 piastres. I took to slumming it on the 176 for half the price. The 176 ran from Midan Kholosi parallel with Sharia Shobra along the Sharia Tara'a al-Bulaqeya to Ataba Square. The 176 had panache. Cruising down Sharia Tara'a al-Bulaqeya on the 176 on a fine spring morning, building up steam with a full complement of passengers, was one of the experiences of life. However, the 176 buses were old and decrepit and prone to break down, and the service being cheap was many times oversubscribed.

It was therefore with some self-congratulation one morning that I found a seat in the 176 after a mere ten-minute wait. The bus filled quickly and the conductor took our fares. At that point the driver announced the bus was out of service and returning to the depot. The passengers were upset; some had been waiting nearly two hours. So we all accompanied the bus back to the depot. At the depot the driver said it was the end of the line, the protest had been fun but could we get off now? When we didn't, he became angry. A young man, a typical young man with thick, sweptback hair, short shirtsleeves, exercise books and plastic briefcase, politely informed the driver that this wouldn't do. The driver said it would have to do.

'Then I'm going to find the depot manager,' said the young man.

A minute or two later he came out with the depot manager. The depot manager was impeccably courteous, heard our case and pressed another bus into service. The young man was modest. 'It was a team job,' he said, and we left the depot to cheers and honking.

One day, despairing of buses, I walked back to Shobra from the medieval city by way of Abbasseya and Clot Bey. It was a day when the *khamaseen* was particularly oppressive, when the heat brought out the flies and the liquorice sellers, and the smell of damp dust with the play of hoses. It was also the day Zaire beat Egypt at football in the African Cup and Am Mohammed arrived back from Beirut.

Clot Bey is one of the few relics of the Raj left, an Angkor Wat come upon in the middle of the urban jungle, crumbling and overrun, with some of the magic still of a lost civilization, prosaic, for the British were prosaic, its arcades hung with travel bags like pennants in a Gothic cathedral. You picked your way through puddles, peered into smoke blackened interiors, stumbled over impromptu restaurants on the pavement, and everywhere the grime was inches thick. Clot Bey was all trams and commerce vying for space. Fried fish hung with sandals on smoke black racks, putty green sheep's heads next to brains stacked in piles, like monstrous Dali creations of plasticized electric circuits. Here too the trams matched the multiplicity of life, tram makes, tram lines, Washington '43, Brussels '35, a living museum to the genesis and evolution of the tram.

The tram lines from Clot Bey took you to many places. They took you up Sharia Sidki Pasha quickly losing you in the accumulated silt and rubbish of the *ta'maya* grinders and the coopers' yards. Back in Ramses Square the road running parallel to Ramses Street led to the undertakers' quarter where upended coffins lined the pavements outside the Coptic Hospital, a sobering reminder to those venturing therein. Hearses of pre-war French design (black, of course, with purple trimmings and many cherubim and seraphim) waited in the wings. Death for the Copts was a serious business; Muslims shuffle off this mortal coil more casually.

In Ramses Square the peddlers welcomed the soldiers spilling out of a troop train with trays of badges, emblems of their war: red for Suez, green for Ismailia; the shoeshine boys had strips of old tyres laid out to sole their boots. Nothing was wasted. Likewise with the caravansary located on the other side of the railway bridge outside the Shobra entrance to the station. Here you could buy replacement straps for your flip-flop sandals or refills for 2 piastre biros.

Wending up Sharia Tara'a al-Bulaqeya across from Midan Shobra past the Weight Lifting Association you entered authentic Shobra, a world of boutiques displaying photos of grotesquely touched up couples on their wedding day, pictures of Christ risen, on the cross, with a lamb, Madonnas spangle cheeked and haloed, the Virgin with Child.

If you persevered, continuing way beyond Sharia Kholosi, and followed the road down to its roots in a mouldering compost of rotting vegetables, horse dung and human excrement, in the outer reaches of Shobra el-Kheima, you came to another Shobra. This Shobra was breathless for space. Here people walked in tens not twos and the jerry-built apartment blocks formed an unbroken facade. Shobra el-Kheima was the *batn* or stomach of Nasser's city, where Cairo generated its stupendous vitality.

I was late arriving back at Shobra but Am Mohammed had still not returned. He had been held up, first in Beirut where his steel brace had done funny things to the metal detector and the security guards had pounced on him and taken him to pieces, and again in Cairo, by a plane load of *fedayeen* en route for Algiers.

Once home 'Baba' wasted no time. Out of his suit into his pyjamas and settled comfortably with his cigarettes, matches and the telephone to hand, he began dialling. For the next hour the house echoed with *al-hamdu assalaamah* as the network was reactivated and the word got out that Am Mohammed was back in town. Then, having put down the receiver for the last time and extricated Atar's false *jeton*, he told us about Beirut and the cost of things.

'Bad, very bad,' he said, pursing his lips. 'One sandwich, small, like this,' he picked up pieces of bread, 'two lira. Hotel, not good hotel, deerty. Must pay ½E£1 for one night, one night.' Then, continuing his consumer's guide and searching round the table, he said, 'Beans like this, 2 lira a kilo, here in Egypt must pay 7 piastres. At the airport,' he groped for the words with his hands, 'must pay 1 lira for this bag, 1 lira for this one. Pay 6 lira for one bag to the aeroplane.'

He was warming to it. 'Cloth-es. One jacket in Beirut ½E£45. In

England must pay 1/£40 Sterling for one suit... You are going?' Am Mohammed looked up, alarmed. I was. I excused myself and went to bed.

Next day as I left he asked for a couple of pounds.

So, gradually, it came to a head. My biros had a way of disappearing. Fatheya was concerned for this poltergeist. So did a dozen other things. Then, one day soon after he arrived back from Beirut, Am Mohammed asked for 25 piastres for my washing.

'What do you mean, Am Mohammed?' I exploded. 'I paid 15 piastres a week for my washing in the hotel, washed and ironed. Here I pay extra for the ironing.'

'Take it easy, take it easy.' He tried to humour me but the lid was off.

'You know I pay too much for this room. I have a friend who pays 50 piastres a night for a room in a hotel; that's as much as I'm paying here. Before I went to Yemen I paid more because I had money and because you needed money but I said then that when I came back, I wouldn't be able to pay so much. But I'm paying the same. My things disappear. I asked you for a table and still there is no table.'

'Take it easy, take it easy,' said Am Mohammed in some agitation. 'I have said 20 piastres. What is 5 piastres? Why the fuss?'

'You know, Am Mohammed, it's more than the 5 piastres. It's this constant cadging. I don't like living like that.'

'It's only money. You know if you needed anything we would give it to you.'

'I know you would, Am Mohammed, but this constant cadging upsets me.'

So we agreed on Am Mohammed's magnanimous concession of bringing the laundry bill down 5 piastres and we were ostensibly friends.

When I came back that night there was a table in my room. And the next morning Fatheya put in a rare appearance at breakfast.

'Where were you last night?' she asked, giving me a sly look. 'Out on the tiles? You didn't telephone, did you? You should have telephoned.'

'I'm sorry, Fatheya, I should have telephoned but I'm not often out after midnight.'

'It doesn't matter so long as you let us know. Otherwise we go to bed and then you wake us up.'

I said it wouldn't happen again and thanked her for my slippers which had reappeared.

Then she said: 'Do you like the table?'

'Thank you very much. It's made life much easier.'

'We had to wait a long time for the carpenter. He's very busy these days and wood is difficult to get, very difficult. You know, he now charges ˡE£1 a day.'

Then as a further act of friendship she showed me the kilo of Lipton's tea Am Mohammed had brought back from Beirut.

On the bus that evening I met Ibrahim the Palestinian who had been living with the El Gamals when I first moved in the previous May.

'They're sharp ones,' he said when I told him what had happened. 'You need to watch them. They wanted ˡE£18 a month from me for full board. I said, no, I wanted the room only. Finally I got it for ˡE£8 a month. They didn't like it.

'Twenty-five piastres for your washing. That's what they pay the washerwoman. They're getting the family wash *baksheesh*. They pay for the soap, you pay for the washing. They're onto a good thing.'

When I got back, there were two tables in my room!

Next morning Malak found me at the washbasin cleaning my teeth. 'Tariq is dead,' she announced, wide-eyed. 'You know, Tariq, Madame Malak's son. He was killed yesterday playing on his bicycle.'

Little Tariq! Of course I remembered. Madame Malak doted on him. He had been round only three days before dressed in a blue sailor suit and looking solemn.

'How did it happen?' I asked. But Malak knew no more than that Tariq had died and that Am Mohammed and Fatheya had gone to help with the arrangements.

Am Mohammed arrived back late that evening very tired and dejected. 'What's the use, what's the use?' he sighed, stamping his cane. 'I fear for Malak. She loved that boy. God help her now.'

The boy had been knocked down and left in a secluded side street that runs off Sharia Mohammed Mazhar by the Nile at the northern tip of Gezira Island. It was three quarters of an hour before anyone noticed him and another half hour before he was taken to hospital. Madame Malak's maid told her when she returned at two o'clock that Tariq had been taken to hospital but she didn't know which one. Madame Malak had frantically rung round all the hospitals of Cairo trying to locate the boy. None had any trace of him for he had no identification. In despair Madame Malak had then rung an influential cousin who had got the wheels turning and Tariq was traced to Bulaq Hospital. She had arrived at the hospital at four o'clock to find the boy unwashed and unattended in a side room while the doctors watched a football match next door. She went berserk. Telephones rang in high places, the hospital stirred. Tariq was given transfusions and oxygen but at one in the morning he was pronounced dead.

'It was terrible,' said Am Mohammed, 'blood coming from ears, eyes, nose. The boy was dying, hit on the back of the head, nothing to do. But must try. Must do everything. Not leave the boy like that.'

The rest of the family were less charitable. 'That's the trouble with this country,' said Mohammed, a cousin who used to help Buzeina with her homework. 'No one cares. There he was, left to die. The doctors didn't lift a finger. They don't get paid properly, so they don't bother. Look at me. I work to go to night school to become an engineer. But for what? It won't get me anywhere. They're no opportunities, here. Why? There's no money.'

'Money gives you choices; it doesn't change attitudes,' I interjected. But they were unreceptive to such philosophical niceties.

'It's fine for you to talk like that,' he retorted. 'You can go away whenever you want to.' And, of course, I could. 'We can't. We're stuck here,' he continued. 'We need choice, we need opportunities. Only then will people care.'

They held the condolences in Madame Malak's flat in Falaki in the dingy sitting room with the bare electric wires sprouting from the walls and the faded photographs of schools and military academies. There they were: Fatheya, plump in her black party dress of sequins; Zizi, another sister crying gently; the old maid, her face shrunk into a mask of mute suffering, a stoical anodyne to pain which seemed sublimated into an all embracing sorrow; and grandmother, detached, inscrutable. It was to her they turned.

Zizi asked me how my Arabic was getting on. Fatheya mentioned the difficulty she had in getting spare sequins. Then Zizi asked how Am Mohammed had got on at the hospital. Fatheya replied that he had been told to give up smoking. Zizi said that wouldn't do him any harm.

'Oh, what does it matter?' whispered Madame Malak in tears.

'I'll go and see Maher now,' I said.

Maher stirred as I entered his room and groped for his glasses. 'It was God's will,' he said, 'but it wasn't kind.'

'Have you found the person who did it?' I asked.

'Yes, yesterday. I took him to the police station. I couldn't sleep until I had found him.' Maher had aged.

That evening Am Mohammed told me the whole story in an English that surprised me for its eloquence. At one o'clock in the morning they had rung him to say the boy was dead.

'I didn't sleep. I smoked one cigarette, then another. What to do? At six o'clock I went out to buy more cigarettes. Must do something. Then at seven o'clock I went with Fatheya to the cemetery to tell the *bowab* to open the tomb. Fatheya's family have a tomb at Abbasseya. Must get the keys to open the tomb.

'Then I went to Khan al-Khalili, near the Al Ghouri to buy incense and rosewater and a special soap for washing the body. Then I bought shrouds, seven for a man, five for a boy, blue for a man, red for a child. Every Muslim must have seven shrouds. If he is poor then five, but never less than five.

'I found a bier and went to the hospital. At the hospital I laid out the soap and the rosewater and the shrouds and helped the two women who washed the little boy. One person from the family must help.

'At ten o'clock we went to the cemetery. The *sheikh* said a few prayers. Then Maher and another uncle took the body into the tomb, not me because of my back. Inside there are two rooms, one for men on the right, the other for the women. They must put the boy in the men's room and then tear open the shrouds. Must do that because the belly swells quickly. Must open the shrouds.'

Then he described how the worms break out in the body within hours and how within a day the body is bloated and barely recognizable and how, in three, it is consumed, the worms eating the worms until there is nothing but the bones and the hair and the shrouds which after a few months come away in your hands. 'It is God's way,' he ended.

And after Am Mohammed's magnificent peroration there seemed nothing more to say. The climactic worm feast no longer seemed obscene but the right way by which life regenerated and consumed itself, fed itself back into its elements and was quiet.

For a time I caught myself playing with notions of what might have been; broke down time into days and weeks. But gradually Tariq lost his hold on me and slipped into the ever rolling stream.

It was not long after Tariq's death that Claudette held a party. Claudette, of mixed European and Egyptian blood, had invited some school friends and a few Europeans. It was strange to be in these new and confusing crosscurrents, the beat music and the angst. An Armenian girl fretted about her culture and the disintegration of civilized values. And there was Anne-Marie, Bernard's secretary, dreaming of Greece or Italy; she would have given anything to be out of this God-forsaken hole.

And they danced in each other's arms, minorities fighting for identity, imprisoned in concepts of themselves, bound in alliances of interest not nature. A girl with puffy eyes smooched and was smooched over and a plain girl watched them, fingering the tassels of her chair in grim, passive helplessness at being denied a place in the dance which was no dance. Nana Miskouri sang of roses, Moustaki of the sun. But they had but one thought, for the time slipping through their fingers and that other place, somewhere north, where the planes took them in the summer; offering beaches, romance and the luxury of culture, great buildings, clean pavements and fine soap.

Squirts of rain. The paper boys were on the streets with the first editions. Their cries danced with the swirling litter, the rain damped down the dust. By the time I had walked as far as the midan at Shobra the rain had turned to heavy squalls moving the length of Sharia Shobra like wind in corn; the *kosheri* stalls scattered for cover as the shutters closed. And when it was gone, leaving the street aglitter, there was an unfamiliar desolation; the huddled pedestrians picked their way under the dripping eves in silence. It was good after the party to be in the rain.

But they were not all like that. There was one girl who offered, in her gentle humour and her acceptance of the lonely way, hope of an alternative to weaving cocoons and closing the blinds. I met her at Marie-Claire's farewell party out at the pyramids in the most inauspicious circumstances, dumped on each other after cursory introductions and nothing to say. She was plump and pink, very fair for an Arab girl and she wore glasses. She had just returned from the States where she had won a scholarship to study sociology. It was her first trip back for three years. I asked her what it was like returning after that time.

'Much as I expected,' she said. 'I left to get away from the family and I'm back because of my father's heart trouble, though really it's because my mother is afraid I'm getting too independent.'

She didn't get on with the family, an offshoot of an old Syrian tribe which settled in Egypt several generations ago.

'Don't think all colonialists had white faces. The amazing thing about us Shawamis,' she continued, 'is that we carry on as though time has stood still these past twenty years. Yes, believe it or not, there are still people in Egypt who behave as though Nasser never existed! I was at the hairdressers within twelve hours of arriving, before I had even had time to see my father. I'd come from jeans and woolly hair to hairdressers!'

'How fantastic. I'd never thought of blue rinses and pink poodles in Cairo. And you coming from the land of blue rinses and pink poodles. It's delicious.'

'Not if you have to live with it. The terrible part of it is that I love Egypt but I can't live here with my family.' She giggled. 'The most hilarious thing was when they held a family conference to discuss the inheritance – father has something like a hundred Shell Egypt shares rotting in the bank. During Nasser's time, of course, they weren't worth the paper they were printed on. Then one day my mother thought, 'Aha, Sadat is going to open up the economy. They will be worth something. We must set up a family trust.' I mean they can't be worth more than 1/E£5 even now, yet they wanted to start a family trust! They were terribly upset when I couldn't take them seriously. Then it started, 'Your father has worked himself into a heart condition and this is all the gratitude...

'Yet when I want to go on the roof, I can't. As a child I used to love going on the roof and talking to the servants. The other day my mother caught me up there and suggested it wasn't such a good idea.

'It's all so wrong. There's my mother prospering off the goodwill she despises. It's only because the Egyptians are who they are that they have got away with it so long. In any other country they would have been disposed of long ago. How Egypt has suffered!'

'And yet this marvellous softness... Their art is in their lives.'

'Where, of course, it should be!'

'Yes. And their humour. There's this nihilistic streak in their humour. You know, the film '*Oh What a Lovely War*' created havoc in Cairo when it was shown after the '67 war. There is a line in it somewhere that goes, 'And what did you do in the Great War, Daddy?' And they all got up chanting: 'We ran, we ran."

We moved outside, out of the lamplight into the starlight.

'Have you ever slept under the stars?' she asked. 'We used to at Petra in Jordan. There is nothing like the night skies of the Middle East.' Then, 'Do you know Lebanon?'

'Only Beirut, and I didn't like it.'

'No, I mean the mountains. They're quite different. I used to go to the mountains to paint. You get a really powerful combination of colours in the mountains, blue sky, green trees, red earth. I have never seen so blue a sky as you get in the mountains of Lebanon.'

'Not even in Egypt?'

'Not even in Egypt.'

We seemed adrift on the sands. Above us the Milky Way hung like a spray of blossom you could reach for with your hand. As we turned she said, 'I used to write poetry too.'

'In English?'

'No, no, in Arabic. Arabic for the feelings... I swear in French for the benefit of my mother, Arabic is better but too rich in associations, too hurtful. And I think in English. Perhaps that's what I missed most in America, not speaking Arabic or wanting to.'

'Will you go back?'

'What alternative have I? Come, I have been talking about myself too much. How did you come to be in Egypt? You haven't told me.'

'Funnily enough it all started here at the feet of the Sphinx.'

And I told her about my cyclonic stopover with Linda. 'You know, I came here with this belief in magic, but Egypt's better.'

We were called back into the circle.

Chapter Fourteen

At Agami the figs were coming into leaf. With the last of the winter storms the sun was established in its sway again, the weather settling. A year past, or nearly, and I had forgotten, or never properly remembered, the stooping *bedu* girls and the shimmering haze, or the strength of the light. There never seemed to be a past at Agami, just a recurrence of the same long, slow day, held up, as it were, to the sun and turned through the seasons.

I had forgotten or never really remembered the different consistencies of the sands, speckled where the scummy tide had licked and smoothed them. There was no evidence of the storms, except the wind barriers and the dunes piled high on the patio of the Hannoville Hotel.

Someone called across the rubble of the builder's yard and the rubble of the sea.

'Come,' he said. So I went to him, slowly. 'What are you doing here?'

'Walking.' There was a silence.

'Enjoying yourself?'

'Yes, enjoying myself.'

At the bus stop I met a gnome with bad teeth who complained that he was having to knock off early because there wasn't any wood. 'So much to do but since the war it has been difficult to get materials.' On the bus he offered to pay my fare.

We passed by the aerodrome and the desert fringe, honeycombed with mines, the perfect habitation for troglodytes, for the gnome. At the fish restaurant he was joined by others like him, workers coming off the afternoon shifts in the quarries who brought in with them the limestone dust as well as their laughter. Here, the trams started and the noise and the bustle of the city. The sea was no longer blue but a dirty pea green from the port, and the sky smudged with the smoke from the oil refineries and the cement factory.

We rumbled past the dockyards, glimpsed Lake Mareotis through the jumble of railway sidings, and at the Mahmoudia Canal ran into the congestion of the town along Sharia Osman Pasha, finally debouching at Rue des Soeurs. Here, the passengers disgorged and the bus, relieved of the weight, shot round Mohamed Ali Square and at the Naval War Memorial turned right for Zaghloul Square along the Corniche, where the evening sky was gathering in the gaunt windows of the cafés.

By April the threat of storms had passed and the ragged iodine haze out to sea that used to presage foul weather had cleared. It was the most perfect time, still with the brittle stillness of winter, the colours settled, fresh and warm with the warmth of the warming sun.

There was no one at Agami which made the clarity more breathtaking. You woke to white light and if the north wind was blowing, to sea colours which made you gasp, sapphires, emeralds and peacock blues running to violet at the edges of the sky. And, further in amongst the rollers, water the colour of galaxies, of shredded ice, in which you dissolved to the tingle shriek of the surf. It was the time of the roses, the oleander, and the first of the honeysuckle, of nights redolent with scents which matched the damascene of the stars.

And each day at midday the shadow was a little lower on the wall. You had to be quiet and patient to notice it, or the significance of it, this allegory of life, the struggle of the sun with the unstable elements. But with the storms gone you had a new faith in the sun. And in the spreading warmth love found a new meaning, just as in a ray of sunlight the dance of life is given colour and depth.

With this faith in the sun you saw from a different perspective; the correspondence between things, how the light changed with the wind and the sea with the wind and the sea with the light. Sometimes you would wake to white fluffy clouds which seemed forever to be moving away from you, till the sun burned them off, or the wind would veer to the south and still the rollers, throwing the mosquitoes off course from their breeding grounds on Lake Mareotis, while the dry air brought out the scents and the cicadas. Once at dawn a mist gathered colour with the light and the sea heaved under the tug and pull of the currents. Narouz Island was barely visible, a yacht flapped out to sea, eviscerated.

Days of stillness. And if you were still long enough, and it needed days, so that your heartbeat became the world's heartbeat, then the sun's fight to control its unstable elements became a mirror of your own, and in the slow settling was a way through to seeing your nature. So much was new to you.

You could discern what were your struggles and the struggles of others and the struggles imposed on you to keep you in line.

You found, for instance, there was a world out there that didn't threaten as we in the West had been led to believe; on the contrary, it welcomed you, so long as you could surmount your fears and accept it on its own terms. And having found the way through to seeing this other world it really was quite simple: you had to keep faith with the efficacy of goodwill, or the stabilizing power of the sun, or something like it. For how else did you find the coherence to make sense of form or light or even darkness, or the drudgery of the daily round; or the germination out of the winter silences, the storms and the prismatic light of this Agami spring?

And as Agami became my life so, slowly, I disengaged. April turned to May. There were more windless days now as the wind began to lose its edge, and the nights were softer, filled with warm glimmering stars. On the windless days the ships at anchor slept on mercury and the striations of the currents, the seaweed stains on the sea floor and the ships' smoke were all patterns on the same breathlessness. With the heat the silences were different too, burnt out of the calx-white glare, the slither of lizards on bare stone, the shimmering pinks and mauves of rocks burnt to spirit colours.

But it was never more than a couple of days and then the north winds would come rolling in again with the white horses, and the evening walks by the sea would be a kind of perfection you had no right to but took with gratitude; the flesh in the hazy foam left no trace of sensation on the mind but, instead, a kind of creepy exhilaration, golden skin moving through ultra violet spray.

Then it was June and I was ready to go. Agami was changing. There were people, and the tranquillity was gone.

The goodbyes were casual. The light was hurting, so was the laughter. The bus was the perennial bus, the exuberance the same. It was slaughter day at the abattoir, and along the Route de Mex the sun smiled on the graffiti. At the docks the Customs man was circumspect and afterwards a young man in white nylon shirt and tight trousers approached and said, 'Is that all?'

'Yes, thank you.'

'And is there nothing for me?'

'For you?'

'Yes, for the Customs man.'

'What do you mean, for the Customs man?'

'*Baksheesh*, for the Customs man,'

'There's no *baksheesh* for the Customs man,' I yelled.

The ship's hold was clean. An immaculate steward harangued us in Turkish about tidiness and smoking. The Egyptians, who didn't understand, continued to flick cigarette ash on the floor. The cards came out. The talk was of Naples, London and Paris. A garage owner from Embaba asked how to get to Hendon. Another asked about the market for stuffed camels in Naples; he had them stacked outside in the gangway. 'Perhaps I'll go on to Marseilles,' he said. They were full of hopes and expectations.

We were late leaving. A light mist had come down over the port and it was calm. The Naval Academy seemed to be floating, the whole of Alexandria suspended with it, anchored on calm waters. Soon after seven the gharries, the spindly gharries of Alexandria with their painted axle wheels, turned tail and fled and we might have been at any port saying goodbye.

The bowlines stacked, we moved away. The tugs hooted and the city echoed to the farewell salutations. Slowly we slipped past the Naval Academy into the main channel by rows of coasters, their Arabic names painted clearly without embellishment: Tanta, Banha, Mersa Matruh, a glossary of Egypt's trading and commercial centres, little coal stacks which run the coast route along the Delta, or to Libya, Lebanon and Cyprus. We came up close to the fish restaurant; we could see the Agami bus crawling along the coast road, its windows glinting in the late sun. Over beyond the point appeared Narouz Island, Agami hidden by the fort.

With the sun gone we were in the open sea. And as the coast receded, it opened up, the Alexandrian skyline sinking away in a jumble of cranes and high buildings, the dome of the Naval Academy last of all. Then, when the coast had quite gone, a thin white line emerged as if from the maws of the sea. For a minute or two it hovered.

Then Narouz Island disappeared and the beaches.

Envoi

I next returned to Egypt in June 1976. Shobra had changed little in the interim: a few more shops, a little less shambolic. But there had been big changes in the ground floor flat at 12 Hara Hadad.

Fatheya opened the door to me and told me when I enquired after Am Mohammed that he had died four months previously. After all those years of treatment for his heart it turned out he had cancer. He had died in terrible pain, Fatheya said, and it cast a long shadow over Buzeina's wedding, pictures of which she showed me with pride. Buzi had married an engineer and moved to Kuwait shortly before Am Mohammed died. Atar was in Milan working in a bar. He had rung after the earthquake to let her know he was alright. Malak was still at home and proving a handful. 'She's never satisfied,' Fatheya complained. Maher was married to a German girl and living in Zamalek. His mother's goodwill finally exhausted, his foreign jaunts are history.

Cousins arrived and we discussed Fatheya's imminent departure for Kuwait to stay with Buzi. The lane reverberated to the '*aza*' for a neighbour who had recently died. The dining room seemed empty and bare without Am Mohammed. Fatheya proudly showed me the new lavatory she'd had installed and as we moved to the sitting room, which had been my room, she remembered how I used to let Am Mohammed use it when he needed to entertain. The flat seemed haunted by his ghost. As I left I felt him behind me on the balcony waving goodbye, as he always used to, and like Orpheus grieving for his phantom Eurydice I dared not turn to destroy the illusion.

I saw the family again nine months later. Fatheya's problems with her children had not eased. Unlike Buzi, as Fatheya was fond of pointing out, Malak and Atar were incorrigible spendthrifts. Atar had returned from Milan and was shortly off to Kuwait where Buzi's husband was finding work for him. He seemed a shadow of his former self.

Malak suffered from nerves and was putting on weight. She was proving to be a headache in her own right. An Iraqi lodger had fallen madly for her, a totally inappropriate match which put paid to any idea Fatheya might have had of continuing to supplement her income by taking in paying guests.

Attempts to find a more suitable mate had not borne fruit. The previous summer a cousin working in Medina as a doctor had secured an introduction to a Saudi boy with a personal fortune of three million ryals (about $1 million). The young man had come to Cairo to meet the family and rented an apartment for $200 a week. He had treated the family royally, inviting thirteen of them to dinner at the Shalimar Restaurant at the Pyramids which had put him back well over [1]E£200, Fatheya told me. However, it hadn't worked out with Malak. He was coming back in the summer to give it another try but Fatheya didn't hold out much hope for the match.

I caught up with Buzeina in Kuwait on the next leg of my journey. Dear Buzeina was as button bright and sunny as she had always been, the mistress of an 80 Kuwaiti dinar (about

1/£160 sterling) a month apartment in Rumeitheya and proud mother of twins.

And there the trail with the El Gamals goes cold.

I was to work in Cairo throughout the latter Sadat years as a journalist and returned periodically through the 1980s and early 1990s. There followed a gap of some ten years when I didn't visit Egypt at all.

I next returned in March 2002 and revisited many of my old haunts. The time had long since past when Cairo cabbies coddled their brakes and conserved their fuel. That era of easeful leisure disappeared for ever in the first heady days of *infitah*. With it went the beautiful old Semiramis Hotel, pulled down in the mid '70s on the specious grounds it was too vermin infested to save. Over the ensuing years Cairo was transmogrified by a network of overhead freeways that kept the traffic moving but somehow scarred the face of the city and homogenized its personality. Completing this concrete nexus was a ring road built in the 1990s that exposed the ugly underbelly of a megalopolis bursting at the seams, rashes of informal housing spilling out onto the agricultural lands like the intestines of a bloated carcass.

Worst still was the vandalism wrought on Alexandria by an overenthusiastic governor who thought to relieve the city's chronic traffic congestion by driving a six lane highway the length of the Corniche, effectively cutting off the intimate coves around Stanley Bay – and indeed large swathes of the city – from the sea. A number of its more evocative landmarks had disappeared, notably the billiard hall round the corner from his flat in Rue Lepsis (now a museum) which Constantin Cavafy used to frequent in search of rent boys. The mood of the city had changed too, become even more hard-edged; uncovered women on public transport met with undisguised hostility.

The biggest shock of all came on taking the No. 11 bus to Agami. A kindly passenger alerted me to the Agami stop which I would otherwise have missed. A steelworks had been built nearby and completely changed the terrain. But that was not all. The half mile walk to the beach through what used to be walled lanes and fig orchards was now more reminiscent of Gaza, a slum of crumbling, algae stained tenements, pools of fetid groundwater between them. The remains of the old bus shelter come upon in the rubble like an archaeological find, was the sole heartbreaking touchstone to my lost Apollonian paradise.

The march of progress had been kinder on Shobra. A spanking new Metro line to Shobra el-Kheima worked as a subterranean magic carpet effortlessly transporting me from Sadat subway station in Midan Tahrir to Rod el-Farag in what seemed the twinkling of an eye compared with the long trek home I used to make on the 100 bus. The open-air cinema had made way for apartment blocks and Sharia Kholosi sported several prosperous looking shops, a Sainsbury's supermarket – one of a handful opened in Egypt in an ill begotten venture abandoned soon after – and Cairo's most exclusive fish restaurant. Gentrification, however, had left Hara Hadad endearingly unscathed. I asked a stranger lounging on the balcony of No. 12 what had become of the El Gamals. They had long gone, he said: Fatheya to her native Mansoura some ten years ago; he had no idea what had happened to the rest of the family.

As for the other protagonists in this story, Amin Simaika

received his papers and emigrated to Brazil in 1974 and Anais Aslanian returned to the suburban comforts of White Plains in upstate New York. Most have passed away: Baba Hassan in 1982 after a routine operation went tragically wrong. Fares Sarofim died in 1992 having battled Alzheimer's for many years. He was taken to the cleaners by a crooked manager he brought in latterly to run the Golden who purloined the hotel in cahoots with the family solicitor. After protracted litigation it was closed in the early '80s.

Fawzi Wafei – who was to go on to an illustrious career with *Al Ahram* – and the youngsters who used to congregate in the flat in Shobra had to wait for their children to grow to adulthood and into early middle age to witness the 'blooding' they had so earnestly desired for Egypt in those intoxicating days at the start of the October War.

It was of course to end in bitter disappointment. Disillusionment set in during the war when the *ma'araka hasima* (decisive battle) in Sinai petered out so inexplicably and inconclusively signalling to Egyptians they could no longer trust their media and were on their own again. However, they came out of the war knowing they had it in themselves to change their circumstances and for that they thanked Anwar Sadat.

There were several reasons why they were unable to build on the massive symbolic achievement of the *ubour* or Crossing. In 1974 Egypt, like Prometheus, had only partially been unbound.

True, the *ubour* sundered the shackles of 'no war, no peace' and purged the stigma of belligerence and bellicosity that hung so heavily over Egypt after 1967. Sadat had finessed the

Israelis in presenting the war as the continuation of politics by other means, to paraphrase von Clausewitz. This time it was tacitly accepted Egypt had been pushed to war – the first war, ironically, the Arabs had indisputably started.

There were other gains. The quadrupling of oil prices gave the Arab oil states, and particularly Saudi Arabia, newfound leverage in international affairs while the oil boom opened up work opportunities abroad for Egyptians they could barely have dreamed of before the war. And most importantly Egyptians still had confidence in Sadat.

The opportunity to make a fresh start was lost partly due to Sadat's temperament, partly because society was not ready for the challenges of participatory government and partly because the geopolitics were working against Egypt, pushing it inexorably into a separate peace with Israel.

Sadat was a visionary. And his vision for his fellow countrymen had them waking from their economic nightmare to rows of low cost housing stretching to the horizon with a gleaming new car before each door. 'At a stroke' featured prominently in his political lexicon. However, he lacked the intellectual stamina to realize the vision. By his own admission he had little time for pettifogging detail and economics made his eyes glaze over.

The war may have broken the deadlock but it did not ultimately change the status quo and where cracks appeared, the new dynamics did not work for Egypt. The Americans hardly allowed Sadat time to draw breath before demanding he follow through on his promise to open up to the West and consolidate the ceasefire with Israel.

Within months of hostilities ending Sadat launched *infitah*, his flagship Open Door Policy, the purpose of which was to attract foreign investment to kick start economic development and seal Egypt's transition into the western camp.

One of his first initiatives was to invite a select group of chief executives from America's *Fortune* 500 companies to visit Egypt and see at first hand its exciting potential. Being Egypt and Sadat being Sadat too many unfortunately accepted. The tour was a shambles and did more harm than good to the country's investment prospects as exhausted tycoons returned home with stories of logistical snarl-ups and malfunctioning taps and phones.

The new policy was ill-starred in other ways. No proper regulatory framework had been put in place which meant *infitah* quickly became seen as a licence to print money for those with the connections to tie up lucrative import deals. Egyptians, long deprived of consumer goods, gorged themselves (at least those with the means) on foreign imports giving little heed as to how those imports were to be paid for. By early 1976 warning lights were flashing: the country was running an alarming balance of payments deficit and inflation was soaring. Then the cotton workers of Mahalla al-Kobra (the caged canary of Egypt's industrial relations) went on strike.

Sadat's response was to sack his reform minded Prime Minister, Abdel-Aziz Hegazi, and replace him with a policeman, Mamdouh Salem. He was losing his nerve, reverting to type; the way Egypt had been governed for centuries, as a pressure cooker which on all accounts had to be prevented from blowing apart.

But that is precisely what happened in January 1977 when Sadat, in desperate need of IMF assistance, petulantly bowed to its demands to reduce subsidies by doubling the price of a *baladi* pat of bread. The streets of Cairo and other cities erupted with marching crowds chanting '*ya batal al-ubour, feyn al-futur*' (Oh Hero of the Crossing, where's the breakfast?). By the time the order had been rescinded, seventy-nine people had been killed and several night clubs on the Pyramids Road reduced to smouldering ruins.

The bread riots destroyed Sadat's presidency. The connection to the people he had won through the October War was irrevocably broken. Thenceforth he was too afraid to test that invisible red line and it put paid to any hopes of engaging popular support for the difficult political and economic decisions that had to be made if Egypt were ever to be lifted out of poverty.

Feeling rejected Sadat turned his back on his domestic problems and concentrated on foreign affairs, aware that securing a Middle East peace was now the only way he could salvage his presidency.

Getting nowhere with the Israelis and gaining little traction with other Arab leaders who distrusted his unilateral approach Sadat, in a typically bold initiative, took up an invitation by Israeli Premier Menachem Begin to go to Jerusalem. There on November 20 1977 he addressed the Knesset in what arguably was his noblest hour. Nothing became him so well as that speech in which he offered to bury the hatchet with Israel and extended the hand of friendship. However, he warned Israelis there could be no permanent peace unless it was a comprehensive one. Within days Begin had welcomed the prospect of peace talks but insouciantly declared 'Judea and Samaria' (the Occupied West Bank) were not on the agenda. It signalled that Israel had no intention of abiding by UN Security Council Resolution 242, the internationally accepted basis of a peace settlement, and intended to leave the Palestinians out in the cold. It signed Sadat's death warrant.

Sadat was snookered yet irrevocably committed to a separate peace with Israel, which was duly enshrined in the Camp David accords of September 1978 and signed into treaty in November the following year.

Isolation from the rest of the Arab world followed, as did an economic boycott that further undermined the Open Door Policy. Egypt, having failed to attract sufficient western investment, had pinned its hopes on marrying Arab petrodollars with western technological expertise to establish the joint ventures that would kick-start economic development.

The Peace Treaty compensated for the loss of Arab financial support with a $2 billion a year package of American aid which Egyptians viewed as a bribe to keep them out of any future Middle East conflict. It evoked Khedive Ismail, a bankrupt Egypt beholden to American largesse much as it had been to Great Britain and France in 1875, with the field laid open for the fat cats (*qotat siman*) and foreign carpetbaggers to move in and plunder: not so much *infitah* (open door) as *infighrar* (open legs) as wits were fond of noting. Female shop assistants, bank staff and state employees began wearing the *hijab* or headscarf as a way of disavowing Egypt's ever deepening embrace of the West and all things western.

The more Sadat was lionized in the US, the more he was

reviled at home. He played up to his new patrons, basking in the applause of Congress, and pandered to their democratic predilections with his own quixotic version of democracy. After his May 1971 Corrective Revolution, in which he ditched Nasser's Arab Socialist Union for his own creature, the National Democratic Party, he had encouraged the formation of 'platforms' which later graduated to parties and became his 'loyal' opposition. However, the liberal mask slipped as the opposition became ever more fractious and unruly.

The most potent source of opposition, however, was the banned Muslim Brotherhood (still maintaining a low profile after its bruising persecution at the hands of Nasser) and its shadowy fellow travellers, Al Jihad (Holy War) and the Gamaat Islamiya (Islamic Groups). Sadat's early cultivation of the Brotherhood (to which he had been affiliated as a young Free Officer) now came back to haunt him.

Religious extremism first emerged in Sadat's Egypt in June 1977 when a group called Takfir wal Hijra (Atonement and Flight from Sin) kidnapped and murdered an education minister. Takfir advocated recreating Islamic society at the time of the Prophet in the seventh century and for this purpose had set up a commune in Yemen.

The rise of Islamic radicalism was part of a pan-Arab trend that grew out of a combination of increased social mobility and the failure of military style nationalism to deliver the prototype of a modern, economically strong Arab state able to hold its own against western cultural imperialism and Israel's regional dominance. The disaffected started to dig deeper into their Islamic roots for a more authentic identity. By contrast, in Saudi Arabia the Wahhabis, a deeply fundamentalist sect, had long advocated an extreme, austere form of Islam that made virtually no concessions to modernity and castigated the sybaritic excesses that came with oil wealth. More generally traditional Arab societies failed to develop the modern urban equivalent of the *majlis*, the tribal forum where the views of ordinary people could be heard. These two trends were to make for a toxic combination in Al Qaeda.

By the autumn of 1981 Egyptian society was in turmoil over *infitah* and the *mubadara* as the peace initiative was known and the economy was overheating. In early September Sadat snapped and arrested one thousand five hundred of his critics from across the political spectrum, including Mohammed Hassanein Heikal, his Nasserist nemesis. Even the Americans balked at such a draconian measure. In the uneasy calm that followed it became evident that Sadat had lost his way. Like the pharaohs of ancient Egypt he had been raised up and isolated by his court, the modern equivalent of the *kahane*, the pharaonic priestly sect, and the adulation of his foreign admirers.

Less than a month later on October 6 the last act in his tragedy unfolded on the military parade ground in Nasr City. Taking the salute on the eighth anniversary of the *ubour*, his supreme triumph, Sadat was gunned down by a renegade cell of his own soldiers proclaiming: 'Death to the Pharaoh!' He died unmourned by his own people but honoured by the international community who accorded him the funeral of a world statesman.

The transition to Hosni Mubarak was remarkably smooth. After the pyrotechnics of Sadat he was a dose of normality and judged a safe pair of hands.

Before becoming vice president in 1975 he had been a highly decorated air force marshal, a genuine war hero, and he initially ran the country as he had the air force. If he had had his way he would have mounted spot checks on industrial plants at 4 a.m. as he was wont to do with his air bases and for a time he was given to subjecting Egyptians to evening harangues on TV on good citizenship.

Mubarak was not bad, but he had a mulish streak and a vain one: he dyed his hair in a quest for eternal youth and had an acute dislike of being beaten at squash. His main fault, however, was a lack of political imagination. He was a military man who inherited a military regime, essentially the one created by Nasser in the mid 1950s. Sadat had tried to depoliticize the military in the late 1970s but failed; Mubarak showed no such inclination, at least initially.

His main achievement after Sadat's assassination was to navigate Egypt back into the Arab fold without compromising the Peace Treaty. This reopened access to foreign investment. But in 1986 a slump in oil prices hit the economy hard. Egypt experienced a severe balance of payments crisis which necessitated a drastic devaluation of the Egyptian pound and another IMF bailout. This time funds were only released when targets were met. It was the final nail in the coffin of Nasser's welfare state.

Mubarak's presidency received another fillip in late 1990 when he took a strong stand against Saddam Hussein's invasion of Kuwait and spearheaded an Arab contingent to evict him. A grateful coalition of Arab oil states and western powers forgave Egypt all its debts which wiped the slate clean and enabled the country to make a fresh start. Thenceforth the economy averaged an annual growth rate of 5 per cent peaking at 7.2 per cent in 2008 – insufficient overall to make substantial inroads into endemic poverty but enough to defuse serious discontent.

In 2004 under the stewardship of a new prime minister, Ahmed Nazif, Egypt embarked on a sustained programme of privatizations. The sale of state assets for a song coupled with an inflow of Gulf money unlocked a Pandora's Box of corruption and sparked a speculative real estate investment boom. When the boom collapsed in late 2008 following the global stock market crash it left a sense of deep economic malaise which the textile workers of Mahalla al-Kubra mined. Their strikes and demonstrations are credited by some with having sown the seeds of the Revolution.

The political reality, however, was that Egypt, having taken Uncle Sam's dollar, was becoming increasingly irrelevant in the broader geopolitics of the region even as there was a sense at home the country was doing little more than mark time.

Inertia, therefore, was Mubarak's undoing. Caution gave way to laziness and then to the sense of entitlement which feeds the endemic corruption that is the hallmark of the one party state. The state of emergency imposed after Sadat's assassination was never lifted; instead the two term limitation on the presidency was waived to allow Mubarak to serve a third and fourth term and was extended to a fifth. The regime paid lip service to US calls for greater democracy and latterly gave up all pretence of conducting fair elections. In short, Mubarak came to think of himself as indispensible. There was no more telling evidence of this than his refusal, until the Revolution forced his hand, to appoint a vice president.

His rationale for this cavalier disregard for constitutional norms was the Islamic threat which he felt uniquely qualified to tackle. In a sense he was right. He was, after all, standing next to Sadat when he was gunned down and was himself the target of several assassination attempts, narrowly missing being killed in Addis Ababa in June 1995. Mubarak had also to contend with sectarian attacks which culminated in the horrific slaughter at the Temple of Hatshepsut in Luxor in November 1997 in which sixty-two people, mainly tourists, were mown down by Islamist militants. The clampdown he instigated after this atrocity led to the Gamaat Islamaya renouncing violence and Jihad moving abroad into the arms of Al Qaeda. Having dealt so successfully with the Islamist threat Mubarak seemed ideally qualified to mentor the Bush Administration through the trauma of 9/11 and to assist it in the 'War on Terror'.

And so the police state established in the mid 1960s by Zakariya Mohieddin, Nasser's hard-line interior minster, to suppress the Brotherhood was resurrected. It had lain dormant under Sadat, at least until after the bread riots. But its re-emergence came at a political and social price; for the security forces answered to no one.

A great deal followed from this arrogance of power, not least the crony capitalism which melded seamlessly the interests of the Mubarak family and the business elite with those of the military and security nexus. The stories of abuses that emerged shocked public opinion. They centred mainly on deals involving the desert lands on Cairo's fringes that suddenly became very valuable for development as well as coastal real estate and land reclamation schemes. The most egregious was an Israeli gas deal which enabled Israeli and Egyptian middlemen to make inflated commissions that lost the state billions of dollars in revenues. The money was on Mubarak, now in his eighties, running for a fifth term in order to pave the way for his son, Gamal, to succeed him. Perhaps this stuck most in the craw: that Egyptians had overthrown one dynasty in 1952 only for Mubarak to attempt to impose another.

The ultimate irony of Mubarak's political demise is that it surely wouldn't have ended any differently for Sadat had he lived. The military run economy established under Nasser and developed by *infitah* into a full-blown rentier economy had long been unfit for purpose. A modern economy, if it is to thrive, has to encourage initiative from below rather than allow vested interests to co-opt or stifle it from above. Whereas Sadat's economic incompetence and inability to provide *aish* (which translates as living as well as bread) would mostly likely have led to his downfall, it was in fact Mubarak's lack of political nous and his obduracy that led to his, coupled with his son Gamal's blatant attempt to build a parallel power centre in opposition to the military – which prompted the generals to abandon their ageing Commander in Chief when the situation became critical. Only Mubarak suffered the ignominy of having his Metro stop renamed – it is now called Al Shahada (The Martyrs) – Sadat, retrospectively rehabilitated in the public's mind, and of course Nasser and Mohammed Naguib, Egypt's first president, retain theirs.

The Revolution marks a profound turning point for Egypt. Most importantly it redeems the promise of 1973 when Egyptians briefly took control of their destiny only to see it snatched from them by force of circumstance and their own lack of readiness to assume, in Sadat's words, responsibility for themselves. This time it is different; Tahrir Square was an epiphany for all who partook in it, an act of national bonding that touched all Egyptians whether they supported the Revolution or not. Unlike 1973 which was an earthquake that in the end entrenched the status quo by leaving the key regional issue, the Israel Palestine conflict, not only unresolved but festering and the existing power structures intact, 2011 introduced an entirely new dynamic, a region wide quickening of political consciousness that has fundamentally changed the rules of the game.

As for my own epiphany in Agami, it informed my life. I took with me from Egypt a sense of belonging, for which I will be eternally grateful, an ability to be still and let things come into me and the verity that the idea absorbed mentally is barely half the story; the important part is what is digested in the experience of daily living. There is an earthy, 'real' quality to this experience, the clay from which our culture, society and identity is fashioned that is common to all humanity – if we can ever de-layer our cultural conditioning to get down to it. For unlike Wittgenstein's lion, human beings do talk a common language at this basic level.

To move forward on Israel/Palestine and to a better understanding between the West and the Middle East perhaps we in the West need first to follow the lead of the Tahrir Square activists and be less fearful. Above all we need a change of heart, an acceptance that though we may not harbour overt colonial prejudices, they lie embedded in some of our attitudes and certainly in the baggage the colonial era bequeathed us.

We have to get beyond the habit of thinking in prevailing cultures or mindsets and rediscover a common humanity. The Palestinian issue is primarily one of human rights. If Palestinians are denied their rights then so are Egyptians because the same forces deployed to deny Palestinians their rights are being deployed to deny Egyptians theirs. Tahrir Square and its sister revolutions are about overthrowing the police states run by autocratic regimes and in many cases the western interests that underpin these regimes, restoring the rule of law and human dignity, and organizing a fairer distribution of the region's wealth. It is actually a struggle in which we in the West are also engaged: coming to terms with the excesses of neoliberal capitalism and making our political systems more responsive to grass roots needs.

The principle of equity runs deep in Islam as does the notion of a common humanity. No place better epitomizes in its humour, arts, literature and life lived in the daily round than Egypt, the idea that we are all the Sons of Adam. As its inner life, for so long driven underground by centuries of occupation and oppression begins to flourish in the light of day, I like to think Egypt might still surprise us in our own quest to rediscover that common humanity.

Glossary

The aim with the transliteration of Arabic terms and names is to stay as close to the written classical notation without being unduly pedantic and losing the word's phonetic signature. Colloquial Arabic sits atop the written language but there are still words in dialect that have no written form and have to be phonetically transcribed. Further, in the Egyptian dialect certain consonants are lost in speech or the sound is changed.

To complicate matters further certain place names have established an English spelling such as Kasr el-Aini and Kasr el-Nil. Here the *qaf* or consonant 'q' in *qasr* or palace is hardened to 'k' (as it is in Koran) while in the Egyptian dialect the *qaf* is unspoken. So Egyptians refer to Asr el-Aini and Asr el-Nil. Luxor is a corruption of *al-u'sour* or palaces. I often include the *qaf* for clarity.

Likewise with *tha* or the letter 'th' which is corrupted in colloquial Egyptian to 's'. Egyptians refer to Tharawat Street as Sharia Sarawat.

The *jeem* or letter 'j' in classical Arabic is hardened to 'g' in Egypt. Thus *jambia* in Yemen, where classical Arabic is spoken, becomes *gambia* in Egyptian dialect.

Another consistency problem arises between common usage and classical Arabic with the elision in speech of the definite article before a hard consonant. I invariably use the phonetic form; thus Zineddin ben Ali rather than Zine el-Abidine ben Ali.

'eid el-kabir, (Kurban Bairam in Turkish) the Great Feast to distinguish it from the *'eid el*-fitr or Little Bairam that marks the end of Ramadan

'eideya, money gift distributed at the feast

abaya, black outer garment worn by Arab women

ahlan wa sahlan hallo

amn al-dawla Security Police

aud Arab lute

baksheesh, cash tip.

baladi from the country

bedu desert nomad

bismillah in the name of God

bowab doorman, concierge

bukra fil mish mish literally 'tomorrow in the apricot' denoting fickleness and notorious unreliability

dishdasha/thobe white muslin robe worn by Arab men

el-hamdu assalamah expression of thanksgiving for a safe return

el-hamdulillah thanks be to God

fedayeen resistance fighters

fellah/fellaheen peasant farmer/s

felucca Nile sailing boat

ful medammis cooked broad beans

galabeya full length gown worn by Egyptian men

ghawazi gypsy dancing girls

ghutra white or red chequered Arab male headdress

iftar the first meal after sunset during Ramadan

imam prayer leader

habibi my love, a common term of endearment between Arab men.

jambia distinctive curved dagger

karkaday hibiscus tea

khalas finished

khamaseen sandstorm usually generated by hot southerly winds

khubz bread

kishk a paste pudding made with chicken stock, corn flour and sour milk *kosheri* a dish of cooked lentils, rice, caramelized onion and macaroni topped with tomato sauce spiced with red pepper

leila al-qadr the night of the revelatory dream in which the Prophet was transported from Mecca to Jerusalem

madrassa school (but in this context a religious school)

makwagi ironing man

malaya black outer garment worn by Egyptian women

malesh never mind

mashrabeya worked wooden lattices used in place of windows

mawlid saint's birthday *mawlid al-nabby* the Prophet's birthday

molokhaya popular national dish with a spinach-like leaf the consistency of egg yolk

muezzin caller to prayer

muhafiza governorate

mukhabarat Intelligence Services, Secret Police

niqab veil worn with the *hijab* head shawl that leaves only a woman's eyes uncovered

qadi judge

qat, mildly narcotic leaf grown throughout Yemen and the Ethiopian Highlands *sa'eedi* from Upper Egypt

sabah al-kheer good morning

salaam, greeting, salutation

salah- el fajr dawn prayer

shabka wedding gift, usually jewellery, provided by the bridegroom

sham el-nessim national holiday held on the Monday after the Coptic Easter

sheikh religious or a community elder

shisha water pipe, hubbly bubbly

suq market

ta'meya ground beans seasoned with onions, garlic and parsley

ta'riffa half-piastre

tawlah backgammon

umma literally people or nation. In an Islamic context it denotes the Muslim community

wadi valley

yehudi Jew, Jewish

zift literally tar but in common usage shit

zikr Dervish dance of Remembrance